Towards Next Generation Grids

Proceedings of the CoreGRID Symposium 2007

T0144989

Towards Next Generation Grids

Proceedings of the CoreGRID Symposium 2007
August 27-28, Rennes, France

edited by

Thierry Priol
IRISA/INRIA
Rennes, France

Marco Vanneschi
University of Pisa
Pisa, Italy

 Springer

Thierry Priol
IRISA/INRIA Rennes
Campus de Beaulieu
35042 RENNES CX
France
Email: thierry.priol@irisa.fr

Marco Vanneschi
Università di Pisa
Dipto. Informatica
Largo Bruno Pontecorvo,3
56127 PISA
Italy
Email: vannesch@di.unipi.it

Towards Next Generation Grids: Proceedings of the CoreGRID Symposium 2007
Edited by Thierry Priol and Marco Vanneschi

ISBN 978-1-4419-4441-2   e-ISBN 978-0-387-72498-0

Printed on acid-free paper.

9 8 7 6 5 4 3 2 1

springer.com

Contents

Foreword

The symposium was organised by the Network of Excellence CoreGRID funded by the European Commission under the sixth Framework Programme IST-2003-2.3.2.8 starting September 1st, 2004 for a duration of four years. CoreGRID aims at strengthening and advancing scientific and technological excellence in the area of Grid and Peer-to-Peer technologies. To achieve this objective, the network brings together a critical mass of well-established researchers (155 permanent researchers and 168 PhD students) from forty one institutions who have constructed an ambitious joint programme of activities.

The final programme has been organized into eight sessions (parallel sessions are denoted by letters A and B):

1.A. Service Level Agreement and Quality of Service
1.B. Trust, Security and Virtual Organization
2.A. Programming with Software Components
2.B. Communication and Networking
3.A. Job, Information and Resource Management
3.B. Programming Methodology
4.A. Workflow Management
4.B. Data Management

The *Service Level Agreement and Quality of Service* session presents the Next-GRID architectural principles and components to support a SLA framework and service construction and composition (Snelling, Anjomshoaa); the NextGRID approach is further developed in (Tserpes, Kyriazis, Menychtas, Varvarigou, Silvestri, Laforenza) through a design pattern for SLA monitoring and evaluating in business applications. Moreover, this session contains a solution to the virtual domain sharing based on usage SLA (Dumitrescu, Iosup, Sonmez, Mohamed, Epema), and an optimal algorithm for the replica-management optimization problem taking into account of QoS and bandwidth constraints (Rehn).

In the *Trust, Security and Virtual Organization* session, two papers are derived from the XtreemOS project: in (Yang) the XtreemOS vision of native VO support and management, as well as a preliminary security architecture, is presented; in (Lakhani) the security support is analyzed and evaluated using the attacker tree methodology. Moreover, (Arenas, Silaghi, Silva) present a reputation model tailored to service-oriented architectures through the exploitation of monitoring supports. The approach based on dedicated hardware virtual machines for service deployment is investigated in (Kuba, Kouril, Prochazka).

Programming issues are discussed in three distinct sections on Components, Methodology, and Workflow, respectively.

- In the *Programming with Software Components* session, the paper by (Malawski, Bubak, Buade, Caromel, Henrio, Morel) deals with the problem of interoperability of component models through a case study centered on CCA and the Fractal-based GCM model. (Schmidt, Benker, Lucka) propose a framework based upon CCA layered in top of Web services and the Vienna Grid Environment. The problem of dynamic adaptability of component-based applications is studied in (André, Bouziane, Buisson, Pazat, Perez) with reference to the master-worker model of computation.

- In the *Programming Methodology* session, three issues are investigated: an approach to the evaluation and refinement of Grid applications through a formal specification in Orc exploting domain knowledge information (Danelutto, Kilpatrick, Aldinucci); a generic framework for the analysis and performance evaluation of legacy application migration (Enaganti, Damodaran, Chakrabarti); and the study of trade-offs between different code tranfer techniques, namely WS-GRAM and a higher order component approach, in a bioinformatics case (Dumitrescu, Duennweber, Luedeking, Gorlatch, Raicu, Foster).

- In the *Workflow Management session*, (Qin, Wieczorek, Fahringer) present a light-weight workflow engine based on just-in-time scheduling, automatically generated performance predictions and task prioritization. The support of specific computation models at the workflow level is studied in (Kacsuk, Farkas, Sipos, Hermann, Kiss) with reference to master-worker applications in the context of the P-GRADE portal, and in (Villazon, Junaid, Siddiqui, Fahringer) with reference to a set of patterns for porting applications on the grid.

In the session *Job, Information and Resource Management*, the paper by (Xing, Corcho, Goble, Dikaiakos) discusses an evaluation framework for information services in the context of EGEE infrastructures. An approach to a Grid architecture based on a set of independent and composable tools for middleware, brokering and submission is presented in (Elmroth, Gardfjäll, Norberg, Tordsson, Ostgerg). Monitoring job status and resource usage, according to a user-oriented and interactive approach, is described in (Mueller, Nuemann,

William). Finally, in (Ziegler, Eickermann, Kirtchakova, Wäldrick, Barz, Pilz) an integrated network and resource management system is presented based on the unifying concept of Bandwidth on Demand.

The session *Data Management* contains two contributions: (Dickens) studies the integration of a real-time classification mechanism into an high-performance data-transfer system, exploiting packet patterns and statistics; (Alonso Lopez, Torres, L. Silva, P.F: Silva) present a software rejuvenation scheme to improve the availability of Grid services and apply it to OGSA-DAI server crashes.

The session *Communication and Networking* contains contributions on the application and specialization of communication techniques to grid architectures. (Steffenel, Jeannot) study a two-phase implementation and performance model of the all-to-all mechanism in a context characterized by high congestion of network resources. (Agapi, Kielmann, Bal) address the scalability problem of routing packets on multiple, router-disjoint paths in the Internet using large-scale overlay networks, proposing and evaluating a synthetic coordinates-based approach. (Moser, Haridi) investigate atomic commitment in a transactional database on top of a DHT, aiming to reduce the number of communication rounds and metadata amount and to achieve dynamic adaptability.

The Programme Committee who made the selection of papers included:

Arenas, A., RAL-CCLRC, UK
Atkinson, M., University of Edinburgh, UK
Badia, R., Technical University of Catalonia, Spain
Banâtre, J-P., University of Rennes 1/INRIA, France
Bal, H., Free University Amsterdam, The Netherlands
Bubak, M., Inst. of Comp. Sci. and Cyfronet, Poland
Buyya, R., University of Melbourne, Australia
Caromel, D., University of Nice/INRIA, France
Cunha, J., New University of Lisbon, Portugal
Danelutto, M., University of Pisa, Italy
Depei, Q., Xi'an Jiaotong University and Beihang University, China
Desprez, F., INRIA, France
Dikaiakos, M., Univ. of Cyprus, Cyprus
Druais, S., Thales, France
Fisher, M., BT, UK
Fahringer, T., University of Innsbruck, Austria
Foster, I., Argonne National Laboratory, University of Chicago, USA
Fragopoulou, V., Forth, Greece
Gagliardi, F., Microsoft, Switzerland
Getov, V., University of Westminster, UK
Gorlatch, S., University of Muenster, Germany

Gannon, D., University of Indiana, USA
Guisset, P., CETIC, Belgium
Kacsuk, P., SZTAKI, Hungary
Kranzlmueller, D., Joh. Kepler University Linz, Austria
Kuonen, P., Univ. Of Applied Sciences of Fribourg, Switzerland
Laforenza, D., ISTI-CNR, Italy
Laure, E., CERN, Switzerland
Lee, C., The Aerospace Corp., USA
Lee, J., KISTI, Korea
Lengauer, C., University of Passau, Germany
Massonet, P., CETIC, Belgium
Matsuoka, S., Tokyo Institute of Technology, Japan
Matyska, L., Masaryk University, Czech Republic
Meyer, N., Poznan Supercomputing Center, Poland
Moreau, L., Univ. of Southampton, UK
Nabrzyski, J., Poznan Supercomputing and Networking Center., Poland
Pasin, M., Universidade Federal de Santa Maria, Brasil
Perez, C., IRISA/INRIA, France
Perrott, R., Queen's University of Belfast, UK
Piquer, J-M, University of Chile, Chile
Reinefeld, A., ZIB Berlin, Germany
Ristol, S., ATOS, Spain
Sekiguchi, S., AIST, Japan
Sloot, P., Univ. of Amsterdam, The Netherlands
Snelling, D., Fujitsu Laboratories of Europe, UK
Schwiegelshohn, U., University of Dortmund, Germany
Talia, D., Università della Calabria, Italy
Varvarigou, T., NTUA, Greece
Xu, Z. ICT, China
Yahyapour, R., University of Dortmund, Germany
Ziegler, W., Fraunhofer-Institute for Algorithms and Scientific Computing, Germany

The Symposium Organising Committee included:

P. Palosaari, IRISA/INRIA, Rennes, France
C. Pérez, IRISA/INRIA, Rennes, France
T. Priol, IRISA/INRIA, Rennes, France

All papers in this volume were additionally reviewed by the following external reviewers whose help we gratefully acknowledge:

Martin Alt
Rachana Ananthakrishnan
Eduardo Argollo
Mark Baker
Alessandro Basso
Nafeesa Bohra
Hinde Bouziane
Eugenio Cesario
Carmela Comito
Rubing Duan
Jan Duennweber
Tim Freeman
Stefan Freitag
Anastasios Gounaris
Christian Grimme
Mikael Hoegqvist
Gracjan Jankowski
Michal Jankowski
Kate Keahey
Miroslaw Kupczyk
Dymosthenis Kyriazis
Tobias Langhammer
Joachim Lepping
Antonios Litke
Jens Mueller
Syed Naqvi
Bartek Palak
Mumtaz Siddiqui
Jim Smith
Giandomenico Spezzano
Jan Stender
Jeyarajan Thiyagalingam
Linh Truong
Kostandinos Tserpes
Philipp Wieder
Erica Yang

Special thanks are due to the authors of all submitted papers, the members of the Programme Committee and the Organising Committee, and to all reviewers, for their contribution to the success of this event.

Rennes, France, August 2007

> Dr. Thierry Priol and Prof. Marco Vanneschi (Symposium Chairs)

Contributing Authors

Andrei Agapi Vrije University Amsterdam, NL

Marco Aldinucci University of Pisa, IT

Javier Alonso Technical University of Catalonia (UPC), ES

Françoise André University of Rennes, FR

Ali Anjomshoaa EPCC, University of Edinburgh, UK

Alvaro Arenas CCLRC Rutherford Appleton Laboratory, UK

Henri Bal Vrije Universiteit, NL

Christoph Barz University of Bonn, DE

Achim Basermann NEC Europe Limited, C&C Research Laboratories, DE

Françoise Baude INRIA Sophia-Antipolis, FR

Siegfried Benkner University of Vienna, AT

Hinde Bouziane INRIA, FR

Marian Bubak AGH University of Science and Technology, PL

Jeremy Buisson IRISA/INSA de Rennes, FR

Denis Caromel Univ. of Nice, CNRS/I3S, INRIA, IUF, FR

Anirban Chakrabarti Infosys Technologies, IN

Massimo Coppola ISTI/CNR, IT

Oscar Corcho University of Manchester, UK

Anish Damodaran Infosys Technologies Limited, IN

Marco Danelutto Univesity of Pisa, IT

Phillip Dickens University of Maine, US

Marios Dikaiakos University of Cyprus, CY

Cătălin Dumitrescu The University of Münster, DE

Jan Dünnweber University of Münster, DE

Thomas Eickermann Central Institute for Applied Mathematics, Research Centre Jülich, DE

Erik Elmroth Umeå University, SE

Srujan Kumar Enaganti Infosys Technologies Limited, IN

Dick Epema Delft University of Technology, NL

Thomas Fahringer University of Innsbruck, AT

Zoltan Farkas Mta Sztaki, HU

Mike Fisher BT Group Chief Technology Office, UK

Erich Focht NEC HPC Europe, DE

Ian Foster University of Chicago, US

Carsten Franke SAP UK, UK

Peter Gardfjäll Umeå University, SE

Carole Goble University of Manchester, UK

Sergei Gorlatch University of Münster, DE

Seif Haridi KTH, SE

Ludovic Henrio INRIA Sophia-Antipolis, FR

Gabor Hermann Mta Sztaki, HU

Adolf Hohl SAP AG, DE

Alexandru Iosup Delft University of Technology, NL

Emmanuel Jeannot INRIA - Lorraine, FR

Yvon Jégou INRIA, FR

Ian Johnson STFC (Formerly CCLRC), UK

Malik Junaid University of Innsbruck, AT

Peter Kacsuk MTA SZTAKI Research Institute, HU

Thilo Kielmann Vrije Universiteit, NL

Peter Kilpatrick Queen's University of Belfast, UK

Tamas Kiss University of Westminster, UK

Daniel Kouřil Masaryk University, CZ

Martin Kuba Masaryk University, CZ

Dimosthenis Kyriazis National Technical University of Athens, GR

Domenico Laforenza Information Science and Technologies Institute (ISTI), IT

Amit Lakhani STFC (Formerly CCLRC), UK

Rubao Lee ICT, CN

Maria Lucka Department of Scientific Computing, AT

Philipp Lüdeking The University of Münster, DE

Maciej Malawski AGH University of Science and Technology, PL

Brian Matthews STFC, UK

Andreas Menychtas National Technical University of Athens, GR

Hashim Mohamed Technical University of Delft, NL

Matthieu Morel INRIA Sophia-Antipolis, FR

Christine Morin IRISA / INRIA, FR

Monika Moser Zuse Institute Berlin, DE

Ralph Müller-Pfefferkorn Technische Universität Dresden, DE

Syed Naqvi STFC (Formerly CCLRC), UK

Reinhard Neumann Technische Universität Dresden, DE

Arvid Norberg Umeå University, SE

Per-Olov Ostberg Umeå University, SE

Jean-Louis Pazat INSA de Rennes, FR

Christian Pérez INRIA, FR

Markus Pilz University of Bonn, DE

Kassian Plankensteiner University of Innsbruck, AT

Michal Procházka Masaryk University, CZ

An Qin ICT, CN

Jun Qin University of Innsbruck, AT

Ioan Raicu The University of Chicago, US

Veronika Rehn-Sonigo LIP laboratory, UMR CNRS-INRIA 5668, ENS Lyon, FR

Philip Robinson SAP UK, UK

Oscar Sánchez INRIA, FR

Bernd Scheuermann SAP AG, DE

Rainer Schmidt University of Vienna, AT

Mumtaz Siddiqui University of Innsbruck, AT

Gheorghe Cosmin Silaghi University of Coimbra, PT

Luis Moura Silva University of Coimbra, PT

Paulo Silva University of Coimbra, PT

Fabrizio Silvestri ISTI-CNR, IT

Gergely Sipos Mta Sztaki, HU

David Snelling Fujitsu Laboratories of Europe, UK

Ozan Sonmez Technical University of Delft, NL

Luiz Angelo Steffenel Université Nancy 2, FR

Mike Surridge IT Innovation Centre, UK

Johan Tordsson Umeå University, SE

Jordi Torres Technical University of Catalonia (UPC), ES

Konstantinos Tserpes National Technical University of Athens, GR

Theodora Varvarigou National Technical University of Athens, Greece, GR

Alex Villazón University of Innsbruck, AT

Daniel Vladusic Xlab, SI

Oliver Wäldrich Fraunhofer Institute SCAI, DE

Lidia Westphal Central Institute for Applied Mathematics, Research Centre Jülich, DE

Marek Wieczorek University of Innsbruck, AT

Philipp Wieder Central Institute for Applied Mathematics, Research Centre Jülich, DE

Thomas William Technische Universität Dresden, DE

Francis Wray EPCC, University of Edinburgh, UK

Wei Xing University of Manchester, UK

Erica Yang STFC (Formerly CCLRC), UK

Haiyan Yu Institute of Computing Technology of Chinese Academy of Sciences, Beijing, China, CN

Wolfgang Ziegler Fraunhofer-Institute for Algorithms and Scientific Computing (SCAI), DE

I

SERVICE LEVEL AGREEMENT AND QUALITY OF SERVICE

NEXTGRID ARCHITECTURAL CONCEPTS

David Snelling
Fujitsu Laboratories of Europe Limited, Hayes, Middlesex, UB4 8FE, United Kingdom
david.snelling@uk.fujitsu.com

Ali Anjomshoaa, Francis Wray
EPCC, University of Edinburgh, Edinburgh, EH9 3JZ, United Kingdom
ali@epcc.ed.ac.uk, f.wray@epcc.ed.ac.uk

Achim Basermann
NEC Europe Limited, C&C Research Laboratories, D-53757 Sankt Augustin, Germany
basermann@ccrl-nece.de

Mike Fisher
BT Group Chief Technology Office, London, EC1A 7AJ, United Kingdom
mike.fisher@bt.com

Mike Surridge
IT Innovation Centre, Southampton, SO16 7NP, United Kingdom
ms@it-innovation.soton.ac.uk

Philipp Wieder
Central Institute for Applied Mathematics, Research Centre Jülich, 52425 Jülich, Germany
ph.wieder@fz-juelich.de

Abstract   This paper outlines the conceptual model of the NextGRID architecture. This conceptual model consists of a set of architectural principles and a simple decomposition of the architecture in order to facilitate common understanding of the architecture and its development.

Keywords: Grid Architecture, Service Level Agreement, Service Grid.

1.   Introduction

The NextGRID project vision is of future Grids, which are economically viable; in which new and existing business models are possible; in which development, deployment and maintenance are easy; and in which the provisions for security and privacy give confidence to businesses, consumers and the public.

The goal and primary output of NextGRID is to define the architecture of the Next Generation Grid. This will prepare the way for the mainstream use of Grid technologies and their widespread adoption by organisations and individuals from across the business and public domains. In addition to the design of architectural Grid concepts, the NextGRID architecture will facilitate the development of key middleware components, application support mechanisms, know-how and standards that underpin the Next Generation Grid.

2.   NextGRID Architectural Principles

The NextGRID architectural principles define the overall characteristics of the NextGRID architecture and outline its key components. These principles define the *personality* of the NextGRID architecture.

The primary architectural principles of the NextGRID project are:

Service Level Agreement Driven Dynamics: All interactions in NextGRID are predicated by a Service Level Agreement (SLA) that is dynamically created and aims to ensure that the relationship between a provider and a consumer is well defined and understood. This SLA based approach applies to all service interactions, thereby providing a uniform framework for the management and operation of all Quality of Service (QoS) aspects.

Service Construction and Composition: As a dynamic Grid infrastructure, NextGRID provides extensive capabilities for service construction and composition. This includes traditional interface composition, various forms of workflow-enabled orchestration, and support for the dynamic extension of service capabilities.

Minimal Service Infrastructure: All services operating in a Next-GRID environment can expect to find a minimal service infrastructure. This infrastructure is manifested as a set of capabilities, such as service lifetime management or service registries, which are either available in the environment or exhibited by peer services.

2.1   Service Level Agreement Driven Dynamics

A successful NextGRID architecture will have a number of stakeholders, ranging from the large multi-national enterprise organisations, down through the large nationally based enterprises, service providers, small and medium sized enterprises, academic institutions and individual end users. Interactions will most likely involve a combination of these parties.

A SLA covers the entire lifecycle of the interaction with a service provider, from the negotiation of the QoS that the consumer can expect, through to the deployment, execution and monitoring of the service to decommissioning.

2.1.1 Overview of Service Level Agreements.

NextGRID believes that SLAs should be used to build relationships between service providers and consumers. Neither the service provider nor the consumer will gain a significant advantage by violating a SLA. The customer will not get the service they require, and the provider's reputation will be damaged. It is proposed, therefore, to have a framework that is less focused on monitoring of every element of every transaction in isolation, but is rather more focused on providing an overall level of service in terms of the business being carried out.

We believe that a SLA is a key component to be considered at all stages in the lifecycle of a service provision. The policies for managing the service, the mechanisms for monitoring it, and the acceptable quality of service terms to offer to a consumer should be produced at the same time as the service is designed and developed. This ensures that the required information is available to be able to guarantee the QoS levels necessary, such that a consumer will consider entering into an agreement with a provider to use a service.

2.1.2 SLA Structure and Contents.

A SLA exists between two parties, the service provider and the consumer. By building a robust and non-ambiguous SLA framework, the need for trusted third parties, who provide independent verification of monitoring information to give confidence to the consumer, can be reduced and replaced with the provider and consumer performing their own monitoring in a mutually trusting way.

Therefore, a considerable amount of work in NextGRID has been focusing on the structure of the SLA, so it can provide all the information that other components require, in a standard, structured way that allows for automated and more economic processing. We see the SLA as containing not only information relating to the specific guarantees offered on the performance of the service, what we categorise as *dynamic terms*, but also relating to the commercial due diligence terms, which we categorise as *static terms*.

Static terms describe the policies in place in the environment in which the service will be deployed and executed. They are less likely to change between many SLAs between two parties. In dynamic terms, we identify higher level terms, which are closer to those understood by consumers or applications. Guarantees are offered on these terms.

Service levels must be defined in terms of the value delivered to the customer. It would be a bad idea to reveal what computational resources would be used to deliver a service, as these suggest a much lower value to the customer. Of course, the service provider has to know how to manage their resources to deliver the specified results, and what the business-level consequences will be if they experience a resource shortfall.

To make this work, mapping mechanisms are needed as shown in Figure 1: to translate business-level objectives defined in a SLA into resource management policies that can be applied at the technical level within the service provider's environment, and to translate technical-level monitoring information into business level consequences that can be compared with a SLA, and used to provide meaningful feedback to the consumer.

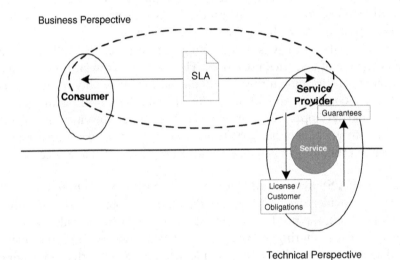

Figure 1.   Business level SLAs and technical resource management are related, but logically separated into a business perspective and a technical perspective, respectively.

2.1.3   Protocol.   Negotiation of a SLA should be as flexible as possible, but at the same time aligned with the negotiated service's lifetime. It is counterproductive to use a protocol needing a longer time span to negotiate than is expected for performing the requested service.

To keep the negotiation effort as low as possible, NextGRID employs a discrete offer protocol: the service provider offers the service customer some services (e.g. Services A, B and C), from which the service customer has to choose one. There is no scope for negotiation as the parameters of the offered services are fixed. In a symmetric fashion, the customer may also make the offer and have it accepted or rejected by the provider.

2.2   Service Construction and Composition

The NextGRID architecture is intended to support rapid and dynamic federation of resources to support user communities. Architecturally, we assume that applications may be constructed by composing NextGRID services, each of which has a set of common properties and behaviours. When executing applications, we can assume that certain core infrastructure services or properties are available in the environment of the application. A key requirement is that such federation mechanisms should result in architecturally self-similar structures that are themselves amenable to NextGRID composition rules, leading to an environment that enables recursive service composition.

The basic modes of service composition are:

> **Resource sharing:** arises when the consumer of a service shares it with another consumer. Resource sharing is strictly a federation between consumers. It makes the consumers part of a related set of interactions as seen by the service provider. Resource sharing is very important for business Grids.

> **Resource orchestration:** arises when a consumer of two services asks them to interact in some fashion. This process effectively combines resources from two service providers to meet the needs of the common consumer.

> **Resource encapsulation:** arises when a service provider delivers a service to a customer through a third party service provider, with no direct interactions between the third party service provider and the consumer.

2.2.1   Implications for SLAs.   Resource sharing and orchestration both involve the creation of new bilateral relationships with a service, which are initiated by an existing consumer. Every bilateral relationship should be governed by a SLA. Our investigations suggest that it should be possible to automatically infer the terms of a new SLA from the terms of original SLAs in place with the consumer. Resource encapsulation does not impose requirements on individual SLAs, but has implications for the overall SLA architecture.

Figure 1 shows that there should always be a mapping between the terms of a SLA related to a service, and the technical management policies and actions needed to deliver that service. The view of encapsulation as a resource pattern then becomes useful in the design of SLAs and for SLA management mechanisms. Instead of using a single mapping mechanism directly from the business level to the resource level, one can introduce intermediate level services and simplify the mappings at each stage.

Figure 2 shows an example of this approach, in which 4 distinct levels are identified. Here the communication (and agreement) between a service consumer and a service provider is on the business level. Instead of mapping

8

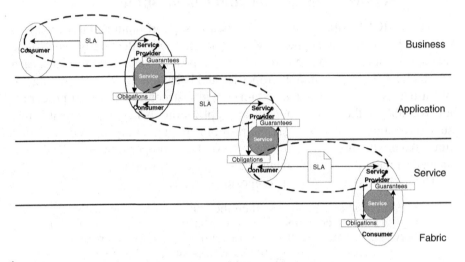

Figure 2.   SLAs and different service levels.

directly to the fabric (computational resource, disk space, networks, etc), this service is provided by encapsulating other services, each encapsulation being governed by its own SLA. The management policies specify the requirements to be met by SLAs from the layer below and the monitoring and corrective action to be used to detect and recover from any breaches of those SLAs.

2.3   Minimal Service Infrastructure

The key aspects of a minimal Grid infrastructure lead to a minimal set of expected Grid service behaviours. These aspects are:

Communication – *protocols* and *languages* through which NextGRID components communicate;

Behaviour – *interfaces* which dictate service behaviour are implemented (actually inherited) by all NextGRID components;

Management systems – those service management systems, e.g. for Naming and Addressing for service discovery, which are always available to Grid users and services; and

Schemas – schemas that underpin NextGRID concepts.

With respect to behavioural interfaces, it is a design requirement for NextGRID services to expose a minimal behavioural interface. The minimal Grid behaviour implemented by all NextGRID entities is largely driven by the degree of basic management functionality required by all services. Information discovery and service introspection provide the requirements for some of this basic management functionality. These behaviours are now being described in a document as a NextGRID Basic Profile.

3. NextGRID Architectural Decomposition

In order to help understand and build the architectural vision of the NextGRID project, some form of system decomposition is necessary. Frequently, systems can be decomposed into a *layered* architecture, where each layer communicates only with its adjacent layers. However, increasing complexity of Grid systems has resulted in the erosion of this simple approach, with some aspects of the system (e.g. security and messaging) spanning all layers of the architecture.

The NextGRID architecture is decomposed into four concepts, as follows:

> **Schemas:** Components of a system need a set of common schemas to communicate. The primary schema categories are: **Message schemas:** describing the contents of messages; **Naming and Addressing schemas:** providing data structures (based on WS-Addressing [1]) to address and access services; **Security schemas:** defining the format for policy and token contents and the basis for token and policy languages; **SLA schemas:** defining the negotiation and agreement languages for QoS agreements; **Service Description schemas:** defining the service discovery framework; **Activity schema:** providing the language to describe activities (e.g. programme executions and Web Service invocations); and **Query schemas:** providing the infrastructure for searching service and information registries.

These schemas are the glue that ties the various systems, which constitute the other three concepts of the NextGRID architecture, as follows:

> **Management Systems:** These components provide the minimal support for the NextGRID architecture to operate, but do not define any operational functions. They are approximately parallel to the basic schema categories discussed above. The bulk of the NextGRID architecture is concerned with these systems.

> **Functional Systems:** These components provide the conceptual framework for any functional activities that can be carried out. Their detailed definition is not part of the NextGRID architecture. They can be roughly categorised in terms of their relationship to data, and their functions exhibit some commonality in terms of cost-per-performance prediction. They are served by NextGRID Management Systems.

> **Orchestration Systems:** These components manage the dynamic composition of services, facilitated by orchestration systems ranging from simple service invocators, through to complex workflow processing engines.

Figure 3 depicts this decomposition and some of the interactions expected between the components.

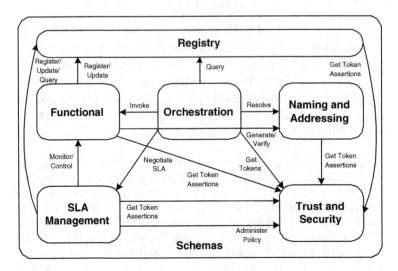

Figure 3.   Overview of NextGRID Component Model and basic interactions.

3.1   Management Systems

3.1.1   Naming and Addressing.   A naming service should be autono-
mous, scalable, distributed, secure, reliable, trusted, and have global scope.
Desirably, the naming scheme (and a name resolution service) should also
be fast, efficient, extensible and support internationalisation. The NextGRID
Naming Service will be a combination of the Handle.net [2] system and a Web
Services front end based on the WS-Naming [3] profile.

The operational capabilities of the naming service include: (1) creation of
a contextual and unique name; (2) verification of a user selected name for
uniqueness; and (3) access to the registry of addresses and aliases for a given
name.

Use-cases for naming and addressing reveal several actors. Firstly, a name
creator, who either requests or validates a name for an entity and then registers
that name with some information (e.g. address or alias) pertaining to that name.
The other primary actor is the address (or information) finder, who uses the name
as input to query a registry for information about (e.g. address of) the named
entity.

3.1.2   Security Facility.   NextGRID provides dynamic authorisation and
claims based security. The Security Tokens and Dynamic Authorisation services are simple services that are easy to create and operate, but their combination enable services to decide dynamically, on a request by request basis,
whether a certain action or request is permitted.

There are two services that are central to the security facility. These are: **The Token Manager:** a Policy Decision Point that provides security access tokens based on policy information pertaining to the entities to be accessed and the claims made by a requestor; and **The Policy Manager:** provides interfaces for administrating the policy that governs access to a service.

The fundamental characteristic that makes these services unique to NextGRID is the emphasis placed on dynamic decision-making and policy management. NextGRID security and access policy can change dynamically throughout the lifecycle of a SLA based interaction between two entities.

3.1.3   SLA Management.

The NextGRID SLA management system is autonomous. Once instantiated the system needs to include capabilities for negotiation of new SLAs, and for providing support for SLAs currently in effect. The latter includes monitoring running SLAs for QoS; accounting for SLA execution during and on completion; and enforcement of post-execution requirements, e.g. penalties and bonuses. These need to take place autonomously from the service provider's perspective or, if desired, by using trusted third parties. It is hoped that using trusted third parties for SLA management can be avoided in the NextGRID architecture through employing sufficient trust anchors.

3.1.4   Registry.

In dynamic Grid environments, service endpoints cannot be hard-coded into applications. Rather, the location of available services, which meet the immediate needs of a consumer, must be found dynamically at application run-time. Service registries in NextGRID allow clients to search for required services among a set of available services. Multiple registries are used to support different environments and can exist in hierarchies for scalability.

3.2   Functional Systems

The NextGRID functional systems consists of a set of components that provide the conceptual framework for any functional activities that can be carried out using the NextGRID architecture. These functional systems can be described in terms of their relation to data.

3.2.1   Data Access.

Access to data will be made available through data services. Data in all forms including, streams, sequences, files, images, traces, databases and archives provide input to analyses and models used by businesses, researchers, designers and decision makers. Abstractly, data access can be described as data where it is now.

3.2.2   Data Transfer.

Like for data access, data transfer to and from data resources will be made available through data services. Additionally, the long-term goal will be to support a multitude of data transport protocols which provide both file transfer and remote movement of data as part of another operation. Such operations include database query or update processing, reading individual elements within a file, or consuming streams of data from live sources, e.g. scientific instruments, online market tickers, etc. Abstractly, data transfer can be thought of as the movement of data in space.

3.2.3   Data Processing.   All computation in a NextGRID architecture can be thought of as falling within the conceptual model of data processing. This includes simple data transformations, such as compression or encryption, or more complicated scenarios, such as multi-part queries and in general the transformation of raw data into information or knowledge. A major aspect of this NextGRID functional system is the description of data through various types of metadata. Abstractly, data processing can be described as the movement of data in meaning.

3.2.4   Data Storage.   As data and information are generated on a Grid, the issue of data storage must be addressed. Storage in the context of Grids has a wider remit than in conventional contexts. The need for replica management, distributed coherency, pre-processing to reduce transfer bandwidth requirements, and security and integrity constraints all add up to create a more complex problem. Abstractly, data storage can be described as the movement of data in time.

3.3   Orchestration Systems

Orchestration systems manage the dynamic composition of services in the NextGRID architecture. Dynamic composition of NextGRID services is facilitated by orchestration systems ranging from simple service invocators, through to complex workflow processing engines. The work on this aspect of the decomposition of NextGRID is just beginning to have an impact on the architecture, and few details are available at this stage.

Acknowledgments

The work presented in this paper is the result of the efforts of the NextGRID project consortium. The efforts of all consortium members involved in this work is duly acknowledged.

This work has been supported by the NextGRID project and has been funded by the European Commission's IST activity of the 6th Framework Programme under contract number 511563. This paper expresses the opinions of the authors and not necessarily those of the European Commission. The European Commission is not liable for any use that may be made of the information contained in this paper.

References

[1] W3C, *Web Services Addressing (WS-Addressing)*, August 2004: http://www.w3.org/Submission/ws-addressing/

[2] The Handle System: http://www.handle.net/

[3] Andrew Grimshaw and David Snelling, OGSA-Naming Working Group, *WS-Naming Specification (Draft)*, Open Grid Forum, 4 December 2006.

VIRTUAL DOMAIN SHARING IN E-SCIENCE BASED ON USAGE SERVICE LEVEL AGREEMENTS

Cătălin L. Dumitrescu
CoreGRID Institute on Programming Models
Mathematics and Computer Science Department, The University of Münster, DE
dumitres@uni-muenster.de

Alexandru Iosup, Ozan Sonmez, Hashim Mohamed, and Dick Epema
CoreGRID Institute on Scheduling and Resource Management
Electrical Engineering, Mathematics and Computer Science, Tech. University of Delft, NL
{A.Iosup,O.O.Sonmez,H.H.Mohamed,D.H.J.Epema}@tudelft.nl

Abstract   Today's Grids, Peer-to-Peer infrastructures or any large computing collaborations are managed as individual virtual domains (VDs) that focus on their specific problems. However, the research world is starting to shift towards world-wide collaborations and much bigger problems. For this trend to realize, the already existing collection of many resources and services needs to be shared across owning VDs in secure and efficient ways, and at the least administrative costs. In this paper we identify the requirements for and propose a specific solution based on usage service level agreements (uSLAs) for this problem of VD sharing. Further, we propose an integrated architecture that provides uSLA-based access to resources, supports the recurrent delegation of usage rights, and provides fault-tolerant resource co-allocation.

Keywords: Resource Management, Virtual Domains, Usage Service Level Agreements

1.   Introduction

E-Science, defined as large-scale, grand-challenge science carried out through distributed global collaborations enabled by the Internet and requiring access to very large scale computing resources [17], is starting to become a common research paradigm [11, 14]. For this vision to materialize, the already existing infrastructures and services need to be shared across existing virtual domains (VDs) in secure and efficient ways, and to be operated at the smallest costs.

Resource owners from multiple VDs, i.e., multi-clusters [6] or computational Grids [7, 10, 15], pool together more and more resources. VD providers may be virtual organizations (VOs [9]- if they also own resources), simple collaborations of companies providing outsourcing services, national Grid infrastructures, groups of scientific laboratories, or universities that provide access to their resources.

In this paper we address the problem of VD sharing. We first describe the characteristics of this problem, and the principles of our usage service level agreement (or uSLA) based approach. Secondly, we analyze the requirements of any Grid scheduling service to provide uSLAs-based support for intra- and inter-VD sharing. Further, we propose an integrated architecture that addresses the identified requirements, starting from an already existing Grid scheduling architecture, KOALA [13]. To make the architecture viable in real environments, we finally propose specific algorithms for resource brokering and scheduling, which we compare by means of simulations in several possible scenarios. We end the paper with our conclusions.

2.   Virtual Domain Sharing

In this section we describe our envisaged VD sharing problem, the generic requirements and a uSLA-based solution for it. We start with a real scenario stemming from the european Grid community, which will serve as a guide to the reader's intuition throughout the rest of the paper.

2.1   Motivating Scenario

Consider the following scenario, in which two large-scale computing infrastructures, namely Grid'5000 [2] and the Distributed ASCI Supercomputer (DAS) [6], are combined into a 3, 000 CPU-strong Grid system:

→ **Infrastructure:** DAS is a wide-area computer system in the Netherlands that is used for research on parallel, distributed, and Grid computing. DAS has been built in three successive waves in the past 10 years, resulting in three independent sets of resources: the new DAS-3, the production-level DAS-2, and the somewhat outdated DAS-1. Grid'5000 is the counterpart of DAS in France, and is currently at its first building wave.

→ **Operation:** The resources composing DAS have been provided over time by more than seven different organizations, and are currently clustered into twelve sites. However, as one building wave occurs, the previous infrastructure is declared obsolete, and only the few users with very high computational demands continue accessing it. Within DAS, resources are shared equally among all the participating organizations, except for a few agreements: *Any application cannot run for more than 15 minutes from 08:00 to 20:00*, and *larger projects can reserve at most 50% of the resources in advance, and use them for periods not exceeding two weeks.* Similarly to DAS, Grid'5000 comprises over ten clusters, shared equally amongst more than ten organizations.

→ **VD Sharing:** DAS wants to share its newest component, DAS-3, with Grid'5000. The sharing mechanism will ensure that the Grid'5000 users do not get too many resources. In case of usage imbalances, automated actions specified as penalties, will be enforced until the penalty period expires, or the administrators cancel it. The Grid'5000 is made available to the DAS users, under similar restrictions.

Similar situations occur for other large-scale Grid communities that target collaboration, e.g., the LHC Computing Grid [7] (over 200 sites, over 40,000 CPUs, over 25,000 storage elements with 3 PB storage), NorduGrid [15] (over 20 sites, over 4,000 resources), and OSG/Grid3 [10] (over 3,000 resources). Also, due to the administrative constraints by allowing a resource allocation mechanism (i.e., including co-allocation) to operate unrestricted, the system is exposed to overload from the exterior. A particular problem is that of a large VD's load fraction overloading a small VD. Therefore, this work complements our previous work by introducing a needed mechanism to prevent such events. Without this extension, co-allocation would not be implementable in practice.

2.2   Problem Overview

The VD sharing problem is expressed as follows: *resource providers* (universities, national laboratories or VOs) give *resource consumers* (specific groups of interests, e.g., scientists from different domains) access to *resources of heterogeneous nature* (e.g., processors, disk space, but also software licenses, services, etc.) under specific *agreements.* We categorize the resource providers as domains, VDs and VOs. We further categorize the resource consumers as VOs, groups, and users. A *VD* (e.g., a Grid system or a Peer-to-Peer infrastructure) consists of several domains (e.g., institutions or universities). Each domain clusters resources of a heterogeneous nature; to avoid confusion with the VD, and to punctuate the single physical location of resources, from hereon we will use the term *site* to denote a domain. Within a VD, a multi-level hierarchy of *groups* and *VOs* exists. *Users* are members of a group within a certain VO, and may submit jobs to their own site or others.

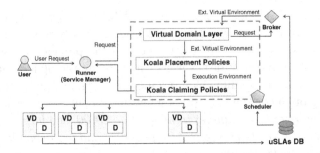

Figure 1.   The uSLA-based Scheduling Architecture based on the KOALA Scheduler.

2.3   Requirements for Virtual Domain Sharing

In order to foster collaborations among VDs, specific mechanisms must be designed to allow the provisioning of resources based on pre-negotiated agreements and local preferences. Important challenges for inter-VD resource management can arise in practice from the lack of automated mechanisms for uSLA discovery, publication, from the complexity of the uSLA operations to be performed (to satisfy the transitive resource delegations), or from the sheer number of resource providers and consumers involved. To support controlled VD sharing by means of uSLAs, we identify as mandatory the following key requirements: (a) uSLA support for situations with and without contention and a semantic to ensure that both consumers and providers can establish well defined agreements upon which resources are used; (b) support for uSLA management: storage, location, enforcement, and translation of transitive uSLAs as needed by resource management; (c) support for enhanced scheduling algorithms to take advantage of the uSLAs made available through various means; and (d) tools to help the consumer make an informed resource selection through uSLA-aware brokering algorithms.

3.   uSLA-based Scheduling and VD Sharing

In this section we present our uSLA-based architecture for inter-VD sharing. KOALA is implemented as a two layer co-allocation scheduler, and consumer requests are handled by means of a specialized component, the *service manager* or *Runner*, a controller that ensures the completion of the user's request.

3.1   Scheduling Architecture and Algorithms

The enhanced architecture is depicted in Figure 1. A runner sends a request to the KOALA's *engine* to instantiate on the consumer behalf an *execution environment*, in which the user's request can be run unto completion. The KOALA engine calls the *scheduling service*, which creates an *extended virtual environment*, where the user is allowed to run, according to the associated uSLAs and previous accounting records. The scheduling service can sometimes rely on a specialized uSLA brokering services for building this extended virtual environment, like GRUBER [5]. Then, the scheduling service calls the *brokering service*, and the brokering service verifies the uSLAs, and recommends an *extended virtual environment*. After creating this environment, the scheduling service applies the scheduling policies, filtering the extended virtual environment until the final *execution environment* is identified (see Algorithm 1).

Algorithm 1 uSLA-BRKG-A: Brokering algorithm using decayed usage.

Input:
    Request ← user request;
    Threshold ← acceptable penalty threshold;
    Virtual Domains ← list of virtual domains, their parameters, and uSLAs;
Output:
    Result ← the list of the top-n resources (initially $\oslash$)
1: **for** each VD_i in Virtual Domains **do**
2:     sort uSLAs by applicability range, into uSLAs-Srt
3:     isVDEligible ← TRUE
4:     **for** window w in 1..n **do**
5:         compute consumer utilization on VD_i
6:         **while** first rule from uSLAs-Srt ∩ window **do**
7:             pop first rule from uSLAs-Srt, as Rule
8:             **if** Request breaks Rule **and** Rule.Penalty > Threshold **then**
9:                 isVDEligible ← FALSE
10:     **if** isVDEligible is TRUE **then**
11:         Score ← BrokerPolicy (VD_i , Request)
12:         Result ← Result ∪ (VD_i , Score)

3.2   The uDecay uSLA

The way udecay is defined is crucial for the behavior of KOALA [12]. In practice, the most encountered decay function is $F_j = k$, where k is a constant factor, e.g., 50%. For a busy system with interactive and batch jobs, a constant factor close to 1 will enforce lower usage shares for heavy users, effectively permitting the interactive job users to work. For a lightly loaded system, setting the decay factor close to 0 will help decrease the decayed utilization rapidly, which allows the users a new complete allocation of resources. Clearly, a constant decay factor cannot accommodate systems with high variations in demand, and various types of users [8].

$$DU = U_0 + U_1 \cdot F_1(S_1) + ... + U_n \cdot \prod_{j=1}^{n} F_j(S_j) \qquad (1)$$

Our operator set is a set of per-window decay functions which map from the system state to a decay factor for the given window, $O = \{F_i\}$, with F_i the decay function for the ith window. We assume that system utilizations (S_i for the ith window), and consumer utilizations (U_i for the ith window) are available, as well as the maximum number n of historic usages (windows). With these notations, the decayed usage is given by Equation 1.

4. Validation Approach, Results and Recommendations

Because the integration work for DAS – Grid'5000 environment is still in progress, we perform our analysis by means of simulations using GangSim [4].

4.1 Scenarios and uSLAs

The experimental setup follows a common workload in e-Science settings: the execution of many instances of BLAST, a bio-informatics application. We consider a slighlty larger environment than the one exemplified in Section 2. Three consumers each submit a workload to five VDs. The four uSLAs considered for comparison are [3, 8]:

→ **no-limit uSLA (no-limit)** is a statement that specifies no limit. Resources are acquired on a first come first executed basis [3];

→**commitment-limit uSLA (commitment)**: specifies two upper limits, an epoch limit R_{epoch} and a burst limit R_{burst}, and requires intervals, T_{epoch} and T_{burst}. A job is admitted if (a) the average resource utilization for its VO is less than the corresponding R_{epoch} over T_{epoch}, and (b) there are idle nodes and the average resource utilization for the VO is less than R_{burst} over T_{burst} [3];

→ **time-decay uSLA (decay)** is a statement that specifies a single limit instead and a decay function for each time interval in the past [12].

→ **usage-decay uSLA (udecay)** is the uSLA introduced in Section 3.1.

4.2 Workloads

The employed workloads arrive at the external schedulers under a Poisson distribution; the job lengths are sampled from a Gaussian distribution with an average of 300s; the input files have size between 1kb and 5kb. In each scenario, we use two types of aggregated workloads. The first type is *synchronous*: all consumers submit their jobs in the same time. For the second type, *unsynchronous*, consumers submit their jobs at different time moments. The simulation interval is 1h in all cases, while the scheduling strategies at both the VO and site levels are FCFS. The VO workloads and allocations are:

→ **Balanced Workloads and Equal Allocations Scenario:** workloads are composed of 400, 600 and 500 jobs. The rules under which domains share their resources are 30%, 30%, and 30%, with burst limits of 60%, 60%, and 50% in the commitment uSLA case. The udecay parameters are 1, 0.5, 0.2, 0.1, and 0.0 for 100%, 50%, 20%, 10%, and 0% utilizations, while the time decay parameters are set to 1, 0.5, 0.2, and 0.1;

→ **Un-Balanced Workloads and Equal Allocations Scenario:** For the second scenario, we use three workloads composed of 160, 800, and 400 jobs; the uSLAs and decay parameters are similar to the previous scenario;

→ **Balanced Workloads and Un-Equal Allocations Scenario:** For the last scenario, workloads and decay parameters are as for the first scenario, with 400, 600, and 500 jobs per workload, but resources are shared under different allocations, namely, 20%, 40%, and 30% and burst allocations of 30%, 60%, and 50% for the commitment uSLA.

4.3   Performance Metrics

The performance metrics considered for analysis are [3–4]:

→ **Aggregated resource utilization** (*Util*): represents the ratio of the CPU time actually consumed by the N jobs executed during the period considered to the total CPU time available.

→ **Total job completion per site, VO or overall** (*Comp*): measures the total number of jobs from a given set that are completed.

→ **Average Grid response time** (*Response*): is computed as the average time per job that elapses from job submission to an external queue until startup;

→ **Average starvation factor** (*Starv*): represents the ratio of the resources requested and available, but not provided to a user, to the resources consumed by the user (ET_i), where i represents a site index. Its equation is:

$$Starv = \sum_{i=1}^{N} min(ST_i, RT_i) / \sum_{i=1}^{N} ET_i \qquad (2)$$

→ **uSLA violation ratio** (*Violation*): represents the ratio of CPU consumed by users (BET_i) to the total CPU power. The formula for this quantity is:

$$Violation = \sum_{i=1}^{N} BET_i / (\#\_of\_cpus * \Delta t) \qquad (3)$$

4.4   Simulation Results

In this section we present our simulation results for four uSLA, two workload types, and three parameter variations.

Balanced Workloads and Equal Allocations Scenario: Tables 1 and 2 capture the five performance metric values for the four uSLAs. The udecay uSLA offers the best overall performance. It is the second best in terms of total system utilization, but the difference between *no-limit* and *udecay* is minimal. This difference is explained by the balancing introduced by *udecay* compared

uSLA / Metric	Util (%)	Comp (%)	Response	Starv (%)	Violation (%)
no-limit	90.16	93.57	252.49	13.14	–
commitment	88.22	91.71	233.89	11.83	24.00
decay	79.62	84.28	263.81	15.15	26.63
udecay	89.55	92.07	218.16	10.65	22.60

Table 1.   Results for Equal Allocations and Balanced Synchronized Workloads

uSLA / Metric	Util (%)	Comp (%)	Response	Starv (%)	Violation (%)
no-limit	87.62	90.71	226.91	13.08	–
commitment	83.75	87.78	248.33	12.17	24.27
decay	79.56	82.14	256.94	14.18	25.79
udecay	85.61	88.21	238.94	11.09	22.70

Table 2.   Results for Equal Allocations and Balanced Un-Synchronized Workloads

uSLA / Metric	Util (%)	Comp (%)	Response	Starv (%)	Violation (%)
no-limit	86.26	93.14	225.10	11.03	–
commitment	70.65	76.5	244.54	17.66	27.33
decay	73.06	80.34	246.17	14.34	25.09
udecay	79.64	89.35	226.03	9.66	20.97

Table 3.   Results for Equal Allocations and Un-Balanced Synchronized Workloads

to the *no-limit* one. We must also note in the *udecay* case the low value for the *Starv* factor, which indicates that jobs entitled to run acquire fast enough allocated resources.

Un-Balanced Workloads and Equal Allocations Scenario: For this scenario, Tables 3 and 4 capture the five metric values for the four uSLAs. The *udecay* outperforms the *commitment* and *decay* uSLAs in terms of all metrics. It is the second best in terms of the total system utilization, while the difference with the *no-limit* uSLA is again minimal.

Balanced Workloads and Un-Equal Allocations Scenario: Tables 5 and 6 capture the five metric values. The *udecay* does not perform as well as before,

uSLA / Metric	Util (%)	Comp (%)	Response	Starv (%)	Violation (%)
no-limit	81.90	92.5	196.35	10.83	–
commitment	66.47	82.07	314.08	19.28	28.57
decay	79.90	89.92	215.60	9.44	20.28
udecay	78.95	91.42	226.37	8.74	19.74

Table 4.   Results for Equal Allocations and Un-Balanced Un-Synchronized Workloads

uSLA / Metric	Util (%)	Comp (%)	Response	Starv (%)	Violation (%)
no-limit	90.16	93.57	252.49	13.14	–
commitment	79.58	79.04	298.56	18.50	29.00
decay	72.98	74.16	241.14	16.87	27.96
udecay	84.82	86.21	239.06	10.97	22.39

Table 5.   Results for Un-Equal Allocations and Balanced Synchronized Workloads

uSLA / Metric	Util (%)	Comp (%)	Response	Starv (%)	Violation (%)
no-limit	87.62	90.71	226.91	13.08	–
commitment	74.84	78.28	300.56	19.61	29.91
decay	73.62	74.25	239.18	15.39	11.17
udecay	84.32	89.12	235.49	11.17	22.73

Table 6.   Results for Un-Equal Allocations and Balanced Un-Synchronized Workloads

Param. / Metric	Util (%)	Comp (%)	Response	Starv (%)	Violation (%)
Slow (.8, .5, .2, .1)	82.51	85.78	285.12	5.09	15.79
Medium (.5, .2, .1)	85.61	88.21	238.94	11.09	22.70
Fast (.2,.1)	87.67	89.5	193.99	12.05	23.51

Table 7.   Results for Different Decay Parameters

but still offers the best performance in terms of *Starv* and *Violation* metrics. The *udecay* performs better in terms of *Response* metric and the motivation is the un-balance of workloads which makes the historical share to be forgotten before a new wave of jobs start.

The Influence of Decay Parameters: The last set of simulations compares the performance of different decay functions for the udecay uSLA. Our results are captured in Table 7. As can be observed, for the set of high decay values fewer resources are obtained by all consumers, thus the lowest values (first columns). However, the *Starv* and *Violation* metrics are lower due to the free resources always available for the slow starters.

4.5   Lessons and Recommendations

Controlled resource sharing within very large environments is difficult in practice, due to the number and the complexity of participants, their local preferences and software. We believe that uSLA-based resource sharing provides a strong starting point for building environments in which resources are shared under owner preferences. While the uSLAs proposed in this paper are comprehensive, we expect that in the near future new semantics will be required for other integration efforst. Economy-based sharing models represent an alternative to be considered for augmenting or replacing uSLA-based sharing.

5.   Related Work

Current solutions for controlling resource access in large scale distributed systems focus extensively on enabling resource sharing among a virtual environment participants [3, 16].

Scheduling in Parallel for Heterogeneous Independent NetworXs (SPHINX) [16] is our first example of a framework for policy-based scheduling of Grid-enabled only resources. The framework has three main features. First, the scheduling strategy can control the request assignment to Grid resources by adjusting resource usage accounts or request priorities. Second, resource usage management is achieved by assigning usage quotas to intended users. Third, the scheduling method supports reservation based resource allocation and QoS.

Grid Service Broker [1], a part of GridBus project, mediates instead access to distributed resources by (a) discovering suitable data sources for a given analysis scenario, (b) suitable computational resources, (c) optimally mapping analysis jobs to resources, (d) deploying and monitoring job execution on selected resources, and (e) accessing data from remote source during execution.

The last work we mention here is GRUBER [5], a uSLA-based broker, aimed at addressing the challenging issues that can arise within VDs that integrate participants and resources spanning multiple administrative domains. GRUBER represents the closest work to our proposed architecture.

6.   Summary and Conclusions

Our intra- and inter-domain sharing mechanisms are based on uSLAs that permit consumers to use resources up to specified levels, for specified periods of time. Based on resource usage patterns encountered in real large-scale environments, we employ a generic, load-dependent mechanism for accounting resource consumption, i.e., the decay-based mechanism. Our proposed uSLA-based architecture manages the definition, storage, location, and enforcement of uSLAs, and offers support for the recurrent delegation of resource usage rights amongst parties. Being based on a proved Grid scheduling infrastructure, the KOALA Grid scheduler, our architecture provides fault-tolerant resource co-allocation. The architecture includes two uSLA-based components for resource management and for user decision support, which also employ the udecay-based mechanism: a scheduler and a broker.

References

[1] R. Buyya and S. Venugopal. The GridBus Toolkit for Service Oriented Grid and Utility Computing: An Overview and Status Report. In *Proceedings of the 1st IEEE International*

Workshop on Grid Economics and Business Models (GECON'04), 2004.

[2] F. Cappello et al. Grid'5000: A Large Scale, Reconfigurable, Controlable and Monitorable Grid Platform. In *Proceedings of the 6th IEEE/ACM International Workshop on Grid Computing (GRID'05)*, 2005.

[3] C. Dumitrescu and I. Foster. Usage Policy based Scheduling in Virtual Organizations. In *GRID '04: Proceedings of the 5th IEEE/ACM International Workshop on Grid Computing (GRID'04)*, pages 289–296, Pittsburgh, PA, USA, 2004. IEEE Computer Society.

[4] C. Dumitrescu and I. Foster. GangSim: A Simulator for Grid Scheduling Studies. In *Cluster Computing and Grid (CCGrid'05)*, Cardiff, UK, 2005.

[5] C. Dumitrescu and I. Foster. GRUBER: A Grid Resource Usage SLA BrokER. In *Proc. of 11th International Euro-Par Conference (Euro-Par'05), Portugal*, 2005.

[6] Dutch University Backbone. The distributed ASCI supercomputer (DAS-2), http://www.cs.vu.nl/das2, 2006.

[7] EGEE Team. LCG (URL: http://lcg.web.cern.ch/LCG/), 2004.

[8] D. H. J. Epema. Decay-usage scheduling in multiprocessors. *ACM Transactions on Computing Systems*, 16(4):367–415, 1998.

[9] I. Foster, C. Kesselman, and S. Tuecke. The Anatomy of the Grid: Enabling Scalable Virtual Organizations. *Lecture Notes in Computer Science*, 2150:200–222, 2001.

[10] I. Foster et al. The Grid2003 Production Grid: Principles and Practice. In *Proceedings of the 13th IEEE International Symposium on High Performance Distributed Computing (HPDC-13 '04)*, Hawai, 2004.

[11] A. J. G. Hey and G. Fox. Special Issue: Grids and Web Services for e-Science. *Concurrency - Practice and Experience*, 17(2-4):317–322, 2005.

[12] MAUI Scheduler, http://www.clusterresources.com/pages/products, Last accessed: 2006.

[13] H. Mohamed and D. Epema. The Design and Implementation of the KOALA Co-Allocating Grid Scheduler. In *Proceedings of the European Grid Conference, Amsterdam*, volume 3470 of *LNCS*, pages 640–650, 2005.

[14] H. Newman, M. H. Ellisman, and J. A. Orcutt. Data-intensive e-Science Frontier Research. *Commun. ACM*, 46(11):68–77, 2003.

[15] NorduGrid Collaboration. Solution for Wide Area Computing and Data Handling, 2006.

[16] J. uk In, P. Avery, R. Cavanaugh, L. Chitnis, M. Kulkarni, and S. Ranka. SPHINX: A Fault-Tolerant System for Scheduling in Dynamic Grid Environments. *International Parallel and Distributed Processing Symposium (IPDPS)*, 01:12b, 2005.

[17] United Kingdom Research Councils. (URL: http://www.rcuk.ac.uk/escience/), 2007.

OPTIMAL CLOSEST POLICY WITH QOS AND BANDWIDTH CONSTRAINTS FOR PLACING REPLICAS IN TREE NETWORKS

Veronika Rehn-Sonigo
École Normale Supérieure de Lyon
LIP, UMR CNRS-INRIA-UCBL 5668
Lyon, France
vrehn@ens-lyon.fr

Abstract   This paper deals with the replica placement problem on fully homogeneous tree networks known as the REPLICA PLACEMENT optimization problem. The client requests are known beforehand, while the number and location of the servers are to be determined. We investigate the latter problem using the *Closest* access policy when adding QoS and bandwidth constraints.

In this paper, we state that the extension of *Closest*/Homogeneous with QoS to bandwidth keeps polynomial. This is an important cognition, as the postulated constraints are of different nature. QoS is a constraint that belongs to a node locally, whereas bandwidth constraints have a global influence on the resources. We propose an optimal algorithm in two passes using dynamic programming.

Keywords: Replica placement, tree networks, *Closest* policy, quality of service, bandwidth constraints.

1.   Introduction

This paper deals with the problem of replica placement in tree networks with Quality of Service (QoS) guarantees and bandwidth constraints. Informally, there are clients issuing several requests per time-unit, to be satisfied by servers with a given QoS and respecting the bandwidth limits of the interconnection links. The clients are known (both their position in the tree and their number of requests), while the number and location of the servers are to be determined. A client is a leaf node of the tree, and its requests can be served by one or several internal nodes. Initially, there are no replicas; when a node is equipped with a replica, it can process a number of requests, up to its capacity limit (number of requests served by time-unit). Nodes equipped with a replica, also called servers, can only serve clients located in their subtree (so that the root, if equipped with a replica, can serve any client); this restriction is usually adopted to enforce the hierarchical nature of the target application platforms, where a node has knowledge only of its parent and children in the tree. Every client has some QoS constraints: its requests must be served within a limited time, and thus the servers handling these requests must not be too far from the client.

The rule of the game is to assign replicas to internal nodes so that some optimization function is minimized and QoS as well as bandwidth constraints are respected. Typically, this optimization function is the total utilization cost of the servers. We restrict the problem to the most popular access policy called *Closest*, where each client is allowed to be served only by the closest replica in the path from itself up to the root.

In this paper we study this optimization problem, called REPLICA PLACE-MENT, and we restrict the QoS in terms of number of hops. This means for instance that the requests of a client who has a QoS range of 5 must be treated by one of the first five internal nodes on the path from the client up to the tree root.

We point out that the distribution tree (clients and internal nodes) is fixed in our approach. This key assumption is quite natural for a broad spectrum of applications, such as electronic, ISP, or VOD service delivery. The root server has the original copy of the database but cannot serve all clients directly, so a distribution tree is deployed to provide a hierarchical and distributed access to replicas of the original data.

In this paper we propose an efficient algorithm called **Optimal Replica Placement** (*ORP*) to determine optimal locations for placing replicas in the REPLICA PLACEMENT problem including QoS and bandwidth. Our work provides an extension of the algorithm of Lin et al [6], which was already mentioned above. Lin et al [6]proposed an algorithm **Place-replica** to find an optimal set of replicas on homogeneous data grid trees including QoS constraints in terms of distance but without bandwidth constraints. Our approach leads to two extensions. First of all, we separate the set of clients from the set of servers. Lin et al also suppose clients to be leaf nodes, but with the double functionality of a server and client. Our separation allows that client nodes do not have to offer the possibility to place replicas on them, which demands less assumptions on leaf nodes. However our model can simulate the latter model while the converse is not true. Indeed, we can model client-server nodes by inserting a fictive node before the client which can take the role of a server. The approach of Lin et al in contrast does not offer the possibility to model clients without server functionality. Our second contribution is the introduction of bandwidth constraints. This is an important modification of the requirements as QoS and bandwidth are of a completely different nature. QoS is a constraint that belongs to a node locally, hence each client has to cope with its own limitation. Bandwidth constraints in contrast have a global influence on the resources as a link may be shared by multiple clients and consequently all of them are concerned. Therefore it is not obvious whether the problem with these completely different constraint types would remain polynomial or would become NP-hard.

The rest of the paper is organized as follows. Section 2 introduces our main notations used in REPLICA PLACEMENT problems. Section 3 is dedicated to the presentation of our polynomial algorithm: the proper terminology of the algorithm is introduced in Section 3.1. The subsections 3.2 and 3.3 treat the different phases. Some related work can be found in Section 4. Complexity and optimality are subject of Section 3.4. Section 5 finally summarizes our work.

2. Notations

This section familiarizes with our basic notations. We consider a distribution tree $\mathcal{T}$ whose nodes are partitioned into a set of clients $\mathcal{C}$ and a set of internal nodes $\mathcal{N}$ ($\mathcal{N} \cap \mathcal{C} = \emptyset$). The clients are leaf nodes of the tree, while $\mathcal{N}$ is the set of internal nodes. Let r be the root of the tree. The set of tree edges (links) is denoted as $\mathcal{L}$. Each link l owns a bandwidth limit $\mathsf{BW}(l)$ that can not be exceeded. A client $v \in \mathcal{C}$ is making $w(v)$ requests per time unit to a database. Each client has to respect its personal *Quality of Service* constraints (QoS), where $\mathsf{q}(v)$ indicates the range limit in hops for v upwards to the root until a database replica has to be reached. A node $j \in \mathcal{N}$ may or may not have been provided with a replica of the database. Nodes equipped with a replica (*i.e.* servers) can process up to W requests per time unit from clients in their subtree. In other words, there is a unique path from a client v to the root of the tree, and each node in this path is eligible to process all the requests issued by v when provided with a replica. We denote by $R \subseteq \mathcal{N}$ the entire set of nodes equipped with a replica.

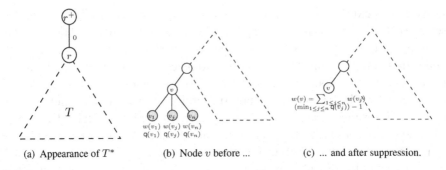

(a) Appearance of T^* (b) Node v before ...   (c) ... and after suppression.

Figure 1.   Transformations.

3.   Optimal Replica Placement Algorithm (*ORP*)

In this section we present *ORP*, an algorithm to solve the REPLICA PLACE-MENT problem using the *Closest* policy with QoS and bandwidth constraints. For this purpose, we modify an algorithm of Lin, Liu and Wu [6]. Their algorithm **Place-replica** is used on homogeneous conditions with QoS constraints but without bandwidth restrictions. Hence to be able to use the algorithm, we have to modify the original platform. We transform the tree T in a tree T^* by adding a new root r^+ as father of the original root r (see Figure 1(a)). r^+ is connected to r via a link l_0, where $\mathsf{BW}(l_0) = 0$. As the bandwidth is limited to 0, no requests can pass above r, so that this artificial transformation for computation purposes can be adapted to any tree-network. We make this changing to be able to model whether the original root r is equipped with a replica or not.

A further, only formal transformation, consists in the suppression of clients from the tree and hence the consideration of their parents as leaves in the following way: for every parent p who has only leaf-children $v_1, .., v_n$, we assign the sum of the requests of the v_j as its requests $w(p)$, i.e., $w(p) = \sum_{1 \le j \le n} w(v_j)$. The associated QoS is set to $(\min_{1 \le j \le n} \mathsf{q}(v_j)) - 1$. (Figures 1(b) and 1(c) give an illustration). This transformation is possible, as we use the *Closest* policy and hence all children have to be treated by the same server. From those parents who have some leaf-children $v_1, .., v_n$, but also non-leaf children $v_{n+1}, .., v_m$, the clients can not be suppressed completely. In this case the leaf-children $v_1, .., v_n$ are compressed to one single client c with requests $w(c) = \sum_{1 \le j \le n} w(v_j)$ and QoS $\mathsf{q}(c) = \min_{1 \le j \le n} \mathsf{q}(v_j)$. Once again this compression is possible due to the restriction on the *Closest* access policy.

ORP works in two phases. In the first phase so called Contribution Functions are computed which will serve in the second phase to determine the optimal replica placements. In the following some new terms are introduced and then the two phases are described in detail.

3.1   Terminology

Working with a tree T^* with root r^+, we note $t(v)$ the subtree rooted by node v, and $t'(v) = t(v) - v$, i.e. the forest of trees rooted at v's children. The i'th ancestor of node v, traversing the tree up to the root, is denoted by $a(v, i)$.

Using these notations, we denote $m(T^*)$ the minimum cardinality set of replicas that has to be placed in tree T such that all requests can be treated by a maximum processing capacity of W (respecting QoS and bandwidth constraints). In the same manner $m(t(v))$ denotes the minimum number of replicas that has to be placed in $t'(v)$, such that the remaining requests on node v are within W. For this purpose we define a contribution function C. $C(v, i)$ denotes the minimum number of requests on node $a(v, i)$ contributed by $t(v)$ by placing $m(t(v))$ replicas in $t'(v)$ and none on $a(v, j)$ for $0 \le j < i$. The computation is presented below (Cf. Section 3.2). But before we need a last notation. The set $e(v, i)$ denotes the children of node v that have to be equipped with a replica such that the remaining requests on node $a(v, i)$ are within W, there are exactly $m(t(v))$ replicas in $t'(v)$ and none on $a(v, j)$ for $0 \le j < i$ and the contribution $t(v)$ on $a(v, i)$ is minimized. The computation formula is also given below.

3.2   Phase 1: Bottom up computation of set e, amount m and contribution function C

The computation of e, m and C is a bottom up process, distinguishing two cases.

1. v is a leaf.   In this case we do not need e and m and we can directly compute the contribution function. $C(v, i)$ is $w(v)$ when $(i \le \mathsf{q}(v) \wedge w(v) \le \min_{\mathsf{BW}} \mathsf{path}[v \to a(v, i)])$, and infinity otherwise.

We point out that there is no solution if any of the leaves has more requests than W or if the bandwidth of any of the clients to its parent is not sufficiently high.

2. v is an internal node with children $v_1, \ldots, v_n$.
$i = 0$: If the contribution on v of its children, i.e. the incoming requests on v is bigger than the processing capacity of inner nodes W, we know we have to place some replicas on the children to bound the incoming requests on W. To find out which children have to be equipped with a replica, we take a look at the $C(v_j, 1)$-values of the children. The set $e(v, 0)$ is used to store the v_j's that are determined to be equipped with a replica. Hence the procedure is the following:

$e(v, 0) = \emptyset$
while $\sum_{v_j \notin e(v, 0)} C(v_j, 1) > W$ **do**

add $v_j \in \mathcal{N}$ with biggest $C(v_j, 1)$ to $e(v, 0)$

Note that the set $\mathcal{N}$ used in the procedure still corresponds to the set of internal nodes of the original tree T. So we can add leaf nodes of T^* that are inner nodes in T, but we can not add compressed client nodes. Note furthermore that there is no client that is added to $e(v, 0)$. Besides we remark that there is no valid solution within W and the present QoS and bandwidth constraints, when all children $v_j \in \mathcal{N}$ of v are equipped with a replica and the incoming requests do not fit in W. Of course this holds also true in the case $i > 0$. Subsequently, the value of $m(t(v))$ is determined easily: $m(t(v)) = \sum_{1 \le j \le n} m(t(v_j)) + |e(v, 0)|$. We remind that $m(t(v))$ indicates the minimum number of replicas that have to be placed in $t'(v)$ to keep the number of contributed requests inferior to W. Finally, the computation of the contribution function: $C(v, 0) = \sum_{v_j \notin e(v,0)} C(v_j, 1)$.

$i > 0$: Treating node v, we want to compute the contribution on $a(v, i)$. As for $i = 0$, we start computing the set $e(v, i)$:

$e(v, i) = \emptyset$
while $\sum_{v_j \notin e(v,i)} C(v_j, i+1) > W$ **do**
add $v_j \in \mathcal{N}$ with biggest $C(v_j, i+1)$ to $e(v, i)$

The computation of the contribution function follows a similar principle:

$$C(v, i) = \begin{cases} \sum_{v_j \notin e(v,i)} C(v_j, i+1), & \text{if } |e(v, i)| = |e(v, 0)| \\ \infty, & \text{otherwise} \end{cases} \qquad (1)$$

$C(v, i)$ is set to ∞, when the number of $|e(v, 0)|$ replicas placed among the children of v is not sufficient to keep the contributed requests on $a(v, i)$ within W.

Example of Phase 1. Consider the tree in Figure 2 and a processing capacity of inner nodes fixed to $W = 15$. The tree has already been transformed. So nodes x and y are compressed client-leaves (grey scaled in the figure), whereas all other leaves correspond to servers (former inner nodes, hence nodes that are within $\mathcal{N}$). We start with the computation of all $C(v, i)$-values of all leaves. Leaf l for example has $C(l, 0) = 3$ as it holds 3 requests. As the link from l to e has a bandwidth of 4, and the QoS is 2, the requests of l can ascent to node e and hence the contribution of l's requests on node e, $C(l, 1)$, is 3. In the same manner, $C(l, 2)$, i.e. the contribution of l's requests on node b is 3 as well. But then the QoS range is exceeded and hence the requests of l can not be treated higher in the tree. Consequently the contributions on nodes a and a^+ ($C(l, 3)$ and $C(l, 4)$) are set to infinity.

Table 2 is used for the computation of e, m and C values of inner nodes. During the computation process it is filled by main columns, where one main column consists of all inner nodes of the same level in the tree. So we start

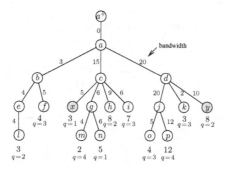

Figure 2. Example

Table 1. Computation of $C(v, i)$-values of leaves.

	l	f	x	m	n	h	i	o	p	k	y
$C(v,0)$	3	4	3	2	5	8	7	4	12	3	8
$C(v,1)$	3	4	3	2	5	8	∞	4	12	∞	8
$C(v,2)$	3	∞	∞	2	∞	8	∞	4	12	∞	8
$C(v,3)$	∞	∞	∞	2	∞	∞	∞	4	12	∞	∞
$C(v,4)$	∞			∞	∞			∞	∞		

with node e. The contribution of its child l, $C(l, 1)$, is 3. As it is the only
child, we have that the contributed requests on e are less than the processing
capacity $W = 15$ and hence we do not need to place a replica on its child l.
Corresponding we get $m(t(e)) = 0$ and a contribution $C(e, 0) = 3$. $e(e, 1)$
and $C(e, 1)$ are computed in the same manner, taking into account $C(l, 2)$.
Computing $e(e, 2)$, i.e. the nodes that have to be equipped with a replica if we
want to minimize the contribution on node $a(e, 2) = a$ by placing replicas on
the children of e but none on e up to a. For this purpose we use $C(l, 3)$, the
contribution of l on a and remark that it is infinity. Hence we have to equip l
with a replica, and as now the set $e(e, 2)$ has a higher cardinality than $e(e, 0)$,
we know that this solution is not optimal anymore and we set the contribution of
$C(e, 2)$ to infinity (Eq. 1). Taking a look at node j: In the computation of $e(j, 0)$,
we have a total contribution of its children of 16, which exceeds the processing
power of $W = 15$ (bandwidth and QoS are not restricting here). Indeed we
have to equip one of the children with a replica, and we choose the one with
the highest contribution on j: node p. Consequently, we get $m(t(j)) = 1$ as
we have to place one replica on the children. The contribution $C(j, 0)$ consists
in the 4 remaining contributed requests of node o. Once we have finished all
computations for this level, we start with the computations of the next level,
which can be found in the next main column of the table.

Table 2. Computation of e, m and C for internal nodes.

	e	g	j	b	c	d	a	a^+
$e(v,0)$	$\emptyset$	$\emptyset$	$\{p\}$	$\emptyset$	$\{g,i\}$	$\{k\}$	$\{b,c\}$	$\{a\}$
$m(t(v))$	0	0	1	0	2	2	6	7
$C(v,0)$	3	7	4	9	11	12	12	∞
$e(v,1)$	$\emptyset$	$\{n\}$	$\{p\}$	$\{e\}$	$\{g,i\}$	$\{k\}$	$\{b,c,d\}$	
$C(v,1)$	3	∞	4	∞	∞	12	∞	
$e(v,2)$	$\{l\}$	$\{n\}$	$\{p\}$	$\{e,f\}$	$\{g,i\}$	$\{j,k\}$		
$C(v,1)$	∞	∞	4	∞	∞	∞		
$e(v,3)$	$\{l\}$	$\{m,n\}$	$\{o,p\}$					
$C(v,1)$	∞	∞	∞					

3.3 Phase 2: Top down replica placement

The second phase uses the precomputed results of the first phase to decide about the nodes on which to place a replica. The goal is to place $m(T^*) = m(t(r^+))$ replicas in $t'(r^+)$. Note that this means that there is no replica on r^+ and hence only the original tree T will be equipped with replicas. If the number of contributed requests on node r is within W, we have a feasible solution.

Phase 2 is a recursive approach. Starting with $i = 0$ on node $v = r^+$, all nodes that are within $e(v,i)$ are equipped with a replica. In this top down approach, i indicates the distance of node v to its first ancestor up in the tree that is equipped with a replica and hence the set $e(v,i)$ denotes the set of children of v that have to be equipped with a replica in order to minimize the contribution of v on $a(v,i)$. Next the procedure is called recursively with the appropriate index i. Algorithm 2 gives the pseudo-code for the top down placement phase, which is the same as the one in [6].

Algorithm 2 Top down replica placement

procedure **Place-replica** (v, i)
if $v \in \mathcal{C}$ **then**
    return
place a replica at each node of $e(v,i)$
for all $c \in$ children(v) **do**
  if $c \in e(v,i)$ **then**
    Place-replica(c,0)
  else
    Place-replica(c, i+1)

3.4 Complexity and Optimality

Due to lack of space, we discuss only sketchy complexity and optimality. A detailed disquisition with proofs can be found in our research report [7]. We state a total complexity of $LN \log N$, where N is the number of nodes in the tree and L the maximum range limit among all nodes. Optimality is subject of the following theorem:

Theorem 1. *Algorithm ORP returns an optimal solution to the* REPLICA PLACEMENT *problem with fixed* W, *QoS and bandwidth constraints, if there exists a solution.*

To prove optimality we perform an induction over levels, where we transform an optimal solution R_0 in the solution found by Algorithm *ORP*. We consider any tree T^* of hight $n + 1$ and start at level 0, which consists in the artificial root r^+. At each step i of the induction we change the placement of the replicas in the i-th level of the solution R_i such that the new placement corresponds to the solution of *ORP*. We prove then that this new solution R_{i+1} is still optimal.

4. Related work

Many authors deal with the REPLICA PLACEMENT optimization problem. Most of the papers neither deal with QoS nor with bandwidth constraints. Instead they consider average system performance as total communication cost or total accessing cost. Please refer to [2]for a detailed description of related work with no QoS constraints.

Cidon et al [3]studied an instance of REPLICA PLACEMENT with multiple objects, where all requests of a client are served by the closest replica (*Closest* policy). In this work, the objective function integrates a communication cost, which can be seen as a substitute for QoS. Thus, they minimize the average communication cost for all the clients rather than ensuring a given QoS for each client. They target fully homogeneous platforms since there are no server capacity constraints in their approach. A similar instance of the problem has been studied by Lin et al [6], adding a QoS in terms of a range limit, and whose objective is to minimize the number of replicas. In this latter approach, the servers are homogeneous, and their capacity is bounded. Both [3],[6]use a dynamic programming algorithm to find the optimal solution.

Some of the first authors to introduce actual QoS constraints in the problem were Tang and Xu [8]. In their approach, the QoS corresponds to the latency requirements of each client. Different access policies are considered. First, a replica-aware policy in a general graph with heterogeneous nodes is proven to be NP-complete. When the clients do not know where the replicas are (replica-blind policy), the graph is simplified to a tree (fixed routing scheme) with the

Closest policy, and in this case again it is possible to find an optimal dynamic programming algorithm.

Bandwidth limitations are taken into account when Karlsson et al [5],[4] compare different objective functions and several heuristics to solve NP-complete problem instances. They do not take QoS constraints into account, but instead integrate a communication cost in the objective function as was done in [3]. Integrating the communication cost into the objective function can be viewed as a Lagrangian relaxation of QoS constraints. Please refer to [1] for more related work dealing with QoS constraints.

5.   Conclusion

In this paper we dealt with the REPLICA PLACEMENT optimization problem with QoS and bandwidth constraints. We restricted our research on *Closest*/Homogeneous instances. We were able to prove polynomiality and proposed the optimal algorithm *ORP*. This algorithm extends an existing algorithm in two important areas. First the set of clients and the set of servers can be distinct now and does not require exclusively double-functionality nodes anymore. The other contribution is the expansion to the interplay of different nature constraints. QoS, which is a proper constraint for each client, and bandwidth, a global resource limitation, subordinate to a common optimization function. This accomplishment completes furthermore the study on complexity of *Closest*/Homogeneous in tree networks.

References

[1] A. Benoit, V. Rehn, and Y. Robert. Impact of QoS on Replica Placement in Tree Networks. Research Report 2006-48, LIP, ENS Lyon, France, Dec. 2006. To appear in ICCS'2007.

[2] A. Benoit, V. Rehn, and Y. Robert. Strategies for Replica Placement in Tree Networks. In *HCW'2007*. IEEE Computer Society Press, 2007.

[3] I. Cidon, S. Kutten, and R. Soffer. Optimal allocation of electronic content. *Computer Networks*, 40(2):205–218, 2002.

[4] M. Karlsson and C. Karamanolis. Choosing Replica Placement Heuristics for Wide-Area Systems. In *ICDCS'04*, pages 350–359, Washington, DC, USA, 2004. IEEE Computer Society.

[5] M. Karlsson, C. Karamanolis, and M. Mahalingam. A Framework for Evaluating Replica Placement Algorithms. Research Report HPL-2002-219, HP Laboratories, Palo Alto, CA, 2002.

[6] P. Liu, Y.-F. Lin, and J.-J. Wu. Optimal placement of replicas in data grid environments with locality assurance. In *ICPADS*. IEEE Computer Society Press, 2006.

[7] V. Rehn. Optimal Closest Policy with QoS and Bandwidth Constraints for Placing Replicas in Tree Networks. Research Report 2007-10, LIP, ENS Lyon, France, Mar. 2007.

[8] X. Tang and J. Xu. QoS-Aware Replica Placement for Content Distribution. *IEEE Transactions on Parallel and Distributed Systems*, 16(10):921–932, 2005.

AN OPEN ARCHITECTURE FOR QOS INFORMATION IN BUSINESS GRIDS

Konstantinos Tserpes, Dimosthenis Kyriazis,
Andreas Menychtas and Theodora Varvarigou
Dept. of Electrical and Computer Engineering,
National Technical University of Athens
9, Heroon Polytechniou Str, 15773
Athens, Greece
tserpes@telecom.ntua.gr
dkyr@telecom.ntua.gr
a_menychtas@telecom.ntua.gr
dora@telecom.ntua.gr

Fabrizio Silvestri and Domenico Laforenza
Institute of Information Science and Technologies,
Italian National Research Council, via G. Moruzzi 1, 56124
PISA, Italy
fabrizio.silvestri@isti.cnr.it
domenico.laforenza@isti.cnr.it

Abstract   Grid Computing is now in the state of development that can offer dynamic management of various parameters that affect the applications' properties such as performance and reliability capabilities. The importance of that achievement is great, given the trend of migrating traditional service markets to inter-enterprise infrastructures and the resulting demand in more or different guarantees on the level of the Quality of Service. In that frame, we present a design pattern for monitoring and evaluating SLA terms on service-oriented architectures. This mechanism takes into account the actual capabilities of the service provider infrastructure and maps them to customer-centric Quality of Service terms, thus ensuring that agreements will not be validated. In this way it enables the estimation of the actual capability of the service to provide Quality of Service at a certain degree.

Keywords: Quality of Service, Service Level Agreement, Business Grids, Service Oriented Architecture

1.   Introduction

Business environments are heavily relied on Quality of Service (QoS) due to their commercial nature and the resulting interaction with clients. What makes a service attractable to customers -if not the nature of the service itself- is its quality. However, when it comes to IT services, the technology has provided us the tools for not only provisioning and managing the quality but also for negotiating upon it. Moreover, in heterogeneous and distributed systems which are now largely based on Service Oriented Computing (SOC) principles, such as Open Grid Service Architectures (OGSA [1]), these functionalities make even more sense, since the quality provisioning capabilities of the services are so diverse that one could assume that the offered QoS levels are non-discreet.

Eventhough business and in turn, enterprise Grids -which nowadays are deployed upon service infrastructures by default-, have some prototype mechanisms to utilize the offered QoS as information, they lack a coherent and ubiquitous way to quantify and manage this kind of information and in turn, make use of it. The most important reason for that is the weakness to identify the source of QoS information and to devise a single way to extract it. It is unclear of whether it is the service provider or consumer that must define the QoS level that is going to be provided or consumed. This is largely due to the confusion that the different representation of quality causes when addressed in different architecture layers or organizational boundaries. However, the need for tools to dynamically express QoS requests and provision capabilities, has already been stated clearly in lots of Grid areas such as Service Level Agreement (SLA) negotiation.

In this study we attempt to record the approaches taken so far with regard to the QoS as information in Grid computing (§2), while in §3, we present our approach. Specifically, we explain the differentiation among quality types depending on the perspective and we take a first approach to analyze the requirements of the customers that are to be included in SLAs in terms of QoS. In §4 we present the architectural pattern of a service-oriented module and we advocate that it is capable to provide QoS information to the service provider in order to avoid SLA violations and maintain his quality provisioning level. Finally in §5 we present our conclusions and the open issues that are following this study.

2.   Related Work for QoS in Grids

Extending the Grid infrastructure in a way that can be used in commercial applications (i.e., to provide guarantees of the negotiated QoS requirements) necessitates the awareness of QoS information for each of the various layers of a Grid Middleware in order to determine the overall quality level. Various assurances are made by Grid environments by the virtue of their establishment.

These include cases where the consumer is interested for Grid services which are hosted on "high-end" resources including expensive equipment and data storage systems, and which are connected via reliable and high-speed networks. More strong QoS information such as deadline guarantees or advanced reservation of resources/bandwidth imply also a set of assurances whose information are of vital importance for the overall provision of quality to the consumer.

There are various approaches that handle QoS in the most known Grid implementations. The Globus Architecture for Reservation and Allocation (GARA) [2] addresses QoS at the level of facilitating and providing basic mechanisms for QoS support, namely resource configuration, discovery, selection, and allocation. This architecture is particularly aimed at using Globus services to support allocation of resources, and utilises specialised resource managers (such as a Diffserv manager) to support admission control and application adaptation at network edges. Current emphasis has been on supporting request authentication and authorisation [3]. Condor-G [4] has been extensively used in the Globus context and provides a substantial instantiation of Globus/GRAM. However, Condor-G supports only coarse-grained and concrete resource types, is statically configured and non-extensible, and has serious limitations in terms of adaptation: all it can do is migrate or restart jobs in the case of failures [5]. Nimrod-G [6] allows the users to lease and aggregate services of resources depending on their availability, capability, performance, cost, and users' QoS requirements. The resource price may vary from time to time and from one user to another. At runtime, the user can even enter into bidding and negotiate for the best possible cost-effective resources from computational service providers. The objective of the Libra project is to expand what had been for Grid computing by Nimrod-G via implementing the Libra scheduler for cluster computing [7].

3.   QoS Provisioning

Next Generation Grid architectures are bound to tackle issues such as the integration of various business processes in the Grid business logic, the effective inclusion of SLA negotiations and the service selection process given specific criteria. All these imply the interference -either in a direct or an indirect way- of the consumer that must now express his QoS requirements according to his own quality experience (QoE).

On the other hand, the provider must somehow be aware of details regarding his quality provisioning capability and in what level he is able to offer them, in order to utilize and negotiate upon them. These details may include statistical information about the operation of services and resources, about the capabilities of the resources, about the billing policy of the service provider and finally about the quality of the service throughout time.

The above statements bring about the distinction between the quality as perceived by the customer and the provider. The customer assesses quality using his own experience as a guide, whereas the provider using metrics and low level information related basically to the infrastructure. These low-level metrics are deriving from the agreed SLA terms and reflect the way that the provider wants to monitor, evaluate and in general assess the issue of quality provisioning. Taking this one step further, one may observe that there are two conceptual entities that govern this process. The one is the concept of low-level, infrastructure-oriented parameters which reflect the service provider's performance capability which we will call QoS parameters. The other concept is the one of higher-level parameters that are closer to the customer's understanding of the QoS and the application. We will refer to the latter as QoS Indices.

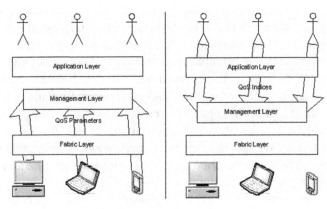

Figure 1. QoS Parameters are crossing Grid Environments from the resources, through the fabric layer, up to the management layer. QoS Indices derive from end-users, across the application layer and end down to the management layer.

The term QoS parameters is broadly used for these parameters referring both to the resource and the service instance properties and which are usually products of benchmarking and performance monitoring tools. On the other hand, QoS indices are commonly used as terms in the SLA contracts and the service consumer is expected to express his/her demands by assigning respective values. The reason is that they can be understood by both parties and therefore an agreement upon specific values can be achieved.

Following that rationale, it is instinctively obvious that there is a correlation scheme between QoS parameters and indices that help the provider do the deduction. Furthermore, one can safely assume that this correlation is a one-to-many relation, in the sense that one QoS index can be mapped to at least one parameter. This kind of mapping is the result of the mixed influence of the application type and the business model of the provider.

On a side note, it is a fact that much of the low-level information contained in QoS parameters can be extracted easily at real time by various Grid components such as monitoring components or even components that model the resources based on specific attributes (like performance). This kind of components are usually using low level modelling specifications and standards such as the Common Information Model (CIM) [8] in order to provide a generic modelling method that will be able to be applied to all the resources.

However, there is still more information to be collected and more methods to be employed in order to reach the point were the QoS will be simply represented in SLAs as a set of indices. In the examples that the authors studied, SLAs are static, referring to simple usage metrics that are QoS parameters. The need for dynamicity and means to describe indices upon which both the customer and the provider are willing to negotiate is the motivating concept for this research effort. This work attempts to take this concept closer to the implementation level and for that reason we studied the case of Business Grids. The goal is to conclude to an acceptable, desired set of QoS indices. In other words we looked into the operation of the Business Grid and tried to define what the customer would require from the Grid and what the service providers could possibly provide. This information is vital for an SLA document which, as stated in [9], it should address the following key aspects:

- What the provider is promising.

- How the provider will deliver on those promises.

- Who will measure delivery, and how.

- What happens if the provider fails to deliver as promised.

- How the SLA will change over time.

According to the above, aspects 1 and 2 are essential to this study. The 1st point implies the information regarding the QoS provisioning capabilities of a provider, usually expressed through an SLA template and QoS indices. The 2nd point is related to the QoS parameters and how their values affect the SLA.

Based on the described study, there are 6 major categories of QoS information that characterize the quality provisioning capabilities of a provider and are expected to be found in a SLA addressing point 1. These are the following QoS indices:

- Availability information. This is an index deriving from low level information related to a service instance. It provides a mean to measure the availability of the service instance throughout time, like if the required service is up and running, or if the libraries or binaries exist.

- Reliability information. Similarly, an index can be created out of these data. It is an index deriving mostly by the statistical analysis of the Availability information, since (in simple terms) a service instance is reliable as long as it is available for a specific time period.

- Performance-related details. This is a very complex issue. Several attempts to measure performance have taken place ([10],[11],[12]), however, they are all based on specific assumptions and are not generic enough. In that frame, the intention is to provide some abstract performance parameters that will contribute in calculating some QoS temporal parameters, such as usage data, etc. Clearly, these details are affected by QoS parameters addressing the lower layers of Grid infrastructure, for example CPU and memory usage.

- Cost-related details. This is more related to pricing information regarding the specific service instance like the billing rate per time periods, etc.

- Statistical information on the Quality of the Result. This can be summarized in an index showing the satisfaction level of the user when he/she received various results through time. This index aims to do be calculated by the feedback provided back to the service providers by the customer, if there is any. This is better known as Quality of the customer experience (QoE) and it is restricted to quality as he perceives it,

- Statistical information about SLA violations. A rather interesting piece of information would include an index showing the rate that which a service instance is violating the agreed SLA.

In the following section we are presenting the requirements that an architectural design must meet in order to enable the provisioning of QoS indices associated to the abovementioned categories.

4.   QoS Provision Module

We designed a component in order to describe the functionalities of a monitoring and evaluation system. The principle of this mechanism is to collect, estimate and provide QoS information to any part of the overall architecture requires it, as long as there is a trusted relationship established amongst them. The prototypes followed are for an open architecture consistent with the NextGRID IST [13] components where we defined the minimum set of interactions by determining the interfaces. This kind of mechanisms are essential to the operation of service providers in order to maintain operation efforts according to the signed SLA and in order to be able to trigger policies whenever a violation is predicted. In simple words, the service provider must monitor QoS parameters and then correlate them with the SLA QoS indices, in order to avoid violations and compensations and also to maintain the desired level of reputation.

The quality of an offered service is spread out to each service instance of a Grid environment rather than in a service or resource level, as the instance comprises the actual implementation. Thus, the QoS information must be extracted by each one of the instances of a service and therefore the design of the mechanism has to take into account various implementations of the same service, in different platforms and with different properties. In order to tackle this problem we proceeded with designing two components, that must be deployed in the provider's domain, as they will handle information belonging to the provider and will produce outputs for the provider. We will hereafter call this mechanism "QoS Information Provisioning Mechanism". The high level design of this mechanism is the following:

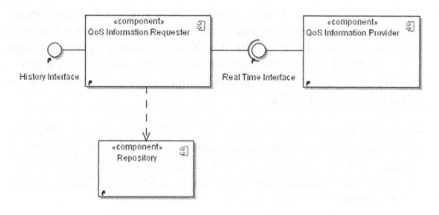

Figure 2.   QoS Information Provision Component Model

As it is depicted in the figure, the mechanism is comprised of two major components: the "QoS Information Requester" and the "QoS information Provider". The Provider is collecting low level information (QoS parameters) directly from the service instances by running scripts and benchmarks, in order to monitor some system metrics, usage or enquire for its current status. It then sends the extracted and calculated parameters back to the Requester.

The Requester's job is fourfold:

- Trigger the Provider in order to "activate" it for the information gathering process in real time. This operation must be initiated by sending a message indicating the parameters that must be returned upon the completion of the operation of the Provider,

- Performing calculations and storing the QoS information in a repository. All the parameters delivered to the Requester are then processed and a set of indices are accruing. These indices are forming the QoS information that will be later delivered to each one who requests it. As mentioned before these indices include but are not restrained on the availability, reliability, performance and pricing properties of the service instance. Once these indices are computed, are then stored in the repository. The repository can be a single database for efficiency purposes but its operation can be extended to encompass other functionalities of other modules as well, or vice versa. In that frame, the QoS information provision module can share the same instances of a repository with a service discovery component, even using the same naming and addressing schemes.

- Handle queries from third parties so as to provide the information back from the repository. Since, Service Oriented Architectures must remain open and flexible, the QoS information provision mechanism must permit other components to access the data if they have the proper access rights or a certain degree of trust s established in their communication link. A "history interface" should allow the submission of queries which in turn the Requester is handling.

- Collect information from other SOA components or third parties. Some parameters required for the calculation of the QoS information indices can be already found in other components. For instance, information about SLA violations can be provided by the potential SLA monitoring mechanisms.

The QoS Information Requester is placed within the provider's organizational boundaries in terms of trust, that is, it can be part of or a trusted third party to the provider. This can maintain the privacy properties for data that the service provider would like to keep within the VO that it is part of and leave the task of disseminating this kind of information entirely up to the provider's policy. In a similar rationale, the repository must be also part of the service provider. Of course, from a different perspective both the Repository and the Requester services can be provided by a trusted third party as services to the service provider. However, there seems to be no alternatives for the QoS Information Provider (in terms of architecture design), which must be deployed in each service provider, operating for each service instance, otherwise its existence is unnecessary (if, for instance the provider is offering the low level details with owned mechanisms).

The implementation and operation of the QoS-Information Provision Component is regulated by the WSRF specifications, that is, the whole environment is based on Web Services. Thus, starting from the service provider's side, the services are deployed as WS-Resources with their lifetime defined by a WS-ResourceLifetime [14] whereas the QoS parameters are exposed as resource properties through WS-ResourceProperties [15]. The QoS History is a registry employing WS-Addressing [16] to store the service details and WS-BaseNotification [17] to propagate the information related to an SLA violation. The WS-Security [18] context is used for handling the security tokens. Finally, WSLA [19] can be used for the SLA representation, monitoring and creation, keeping at the same time in mind that it has not been adopted by any formal, international Grid forum or Organization.

In detail, the Repository is implemented using an XML database (Oracle Berkeley DB), whereas its container is based on a custom XML schema that fits the particular needs. Its operations are exposed through a web service which provides four interfaces, one for each operation:

- Insert, whenever a new QoS index is to be inserted. Along with the value itself, the requester sends a series of other details in the form of an SOAP message, such as the URI of the service (which acts as a unique identifier) and the lifetime of the parameter.

- Update, whenever new values need to be added or old to be altered. This is demanded whenever the requester's outcome dictates such a change (e.g. when the lifetime of a value has expired), or the other components (such as SLA repositories) contribute by sending extra information (e.g. SLA Violations). A specific placeholder for this has been created, however, we have left the XML schema for the container open to changes, as new needs might emerge in the future.

- Query, which is used whenever the Requester or a third party uses the database for retrieving information.

- Delete, for deleting records, for instance, whenever a service is removed from the Virtual Organisation. At this point of time, this process is not automated, however effort is pulled in order to retrieve information from a NextGRID Registry [20] as to whether a service is available or not.

The database operations are accessed through other web services using XQueries. Similarly, the Requester is implemented and exposed as a web service over Apache AXIS. It provides interfaces for retrieving the values depicted in the table below:

For the values above, the respective web service for the QoS Information Provider, runs simple benchmarking tools. It then sends the values to the Requester whenever it is invoked for a particular parameter. This is again achieved through the exchange of SOAP messages. This closes the flow of actions (in reverse order) that need to be done in order to store and use a QoS index, starting from low level QoS parameters, extracted by the service itself.

Table 1. Categorized QoS parameters that the QoS information provisioning mechanism monitors.

Category	QoS Parameters
CPU Capability	Flops Count/simple BM (linpack)
	Kernel Version
	Architecture Type
CPU Load	System Load
	User Load
	I/O Load
Queue info	Policy (how many jobs at a time, max time)
	Length (residency times?)
	Number of running jobs
Inter-processor connections	BW Between processors in a cluster
	Latency between processors in a cluster
	MPI messaging
Memory/Cache	Capacity
Disk	Disk bandwidth (bonnie)
Installation	Software and versions
	Environment, variables

5. Conclusions

In this work, we provide the architecture which addresses the requirements of mechanisms that collect and provide in a ubiquitous manner the information which is related to the capability of a service to provide Quality at a certain level in a Service Oriented Grid Architecture. Apart from the type of information that this mechanism is offering to a Grid environment, the differentiation to other works is mainly concentrated to the fact that components following this pattern should be able to operate within a competitive business environment, optionally offering its knowledge to the customers or the providers, depending on whether the two negotiating parties agree or not.

The QoS Information Provisioning component, was implemented and used in the frame of a series of experiments in NextGRID IST and in particular to the Digital Media application scenario, delivering very good performance. According to this scenario, an animation designer executes a workflow that leads to the 3D-rendering of his job. One of the main requirements for this application is to provide information which is understood to the designer that will enable him to select the appropriate service that will deliver a result maintaining the QoS guarantees. This was made feasible by the component, since he could retrieve information about QoS indices which are customer-centric and that reflect the actual capability of the provider to deliver QoS and in turn to hold on his promise. The results were encouraging in terms of usability, as the designer could retrieve the information he wanted and that could assist his selection process, however, there is no clear indication that the violations were reduced, as the reliability of the system is so high even without our component, that it would require a more pragmatic approach to lead to safe conclusions (e.g. have a designer use the system for a year or so).

At this point it is important to state, that for the abovementioned experiment we assumed that the service provider has agreed on providing the customer with details about its infrastructure. However, this is not the actual case, as even if these details are mapped to high level parameters, the provider will be reluctant to expose this kind of information. A metric for the success of the component is -for example- the reduction of SLA violations in terms expressed as QoS indices. The service provider can use this information and through reverse mapping of the QoS indices to QoS parameters to conclude as to whether he must change the initial offer and thus, the SLA templates.

The main concern for future work is to enable dynamicity in SLA negotiation by identifying the main categories of high level QoS indices. Current solutions include SLAs with static terms, usually referring to the usage, which comprise the QoS parameters. Even this seems to be an efficient way to build a system, it is problematic because these parameters are hardly understood by a simple customer and even more, hardly interesting to them. What is needed is mechanisms that will be able to easily deployed in every system and to facilitate the matching between QoS indices and parameters making the negotiating terms comprehendible to the provider too. The requirements of such a mechanism are described in this document.

Acknowledgments

The work presented in this paper is the result of the efforts of the NextGRID project consortium. The effort of all consortium members involved in this work is duly acknowledged.

48

This work has been supported by the NextGRID project and has been funded by the European Commission's IST activity of the 6th Framework Programme under contract number 511563. This paper expresses the opinions of the authors and not necessarily those of the European Commission. The European Commission is not liable for any use that may be made of the information contained in this paper.

References

[1] Open Grid Services Architecture (OGSA), www.ggf.org/documents/GFD.30.pdf

[2] Foster, C. Kesselman, C. Lee, B Lindell, K. Nahrstedt, A. Roy , "A Distributed Resource Management Architecture that Supports Advance Reservation and Co-Allocation", Proceedings of the International Workshop on QoS, pp.27-36, 1999

[3] Al-Ali, R.; Rana, O.; Walker, D.; Jha, S.; Sohail, S. "G-QoSM: Grid Service Discovery Using QoS Properties." Computing and Informatics Journal, 21 (4), 2002. 363-82.

[4] Frey, J., Tanenbaum, T., Livny, M., Foster, I., Tuecke,S., "Condor-G: A Computation Management Agent for Multi-Instructional Grids", Cluster Computing, Vol 5, pp237-246, 2001

[5] Wei Cai, Geoff Coulson, Paul Grace, Gordon Blair, Laurent Mathy, Wai Kit Yeung, "The Gridkit Distributed Resource Management Framework", Proceeding of European Grid Conference, Science Park Amsterdam, The Netherlands, February 14 -16 2005.

[6] Buyya R, Abramson D, Giddy J. "Nimrod-G: An architecture for a resource management and scheduling system in a global computational grid." Proceedings 4th International Conference and Exhibition on High Performance Computing in Asia-Pacific Region (HPC ASIA 2000), Beijing, China, 14–17 May 2000. IEEE Computer Society Press: Los Alamitos, CA, 2000.

[7] Jahanzeb Sherwani, Nosheen Ali, Nausheen Lotia, Zahra Hayat, and Rajkumar Buyya, "Libra: A Computational Economy based Job Scheduling System for Clusters", International Journal of Software: Practice and Experience, Volume 34, Issue 6, Pages: 573-590, Wiley Press, USA, May 2004

[8] Distributed Management Task Force, Inc., "Common Information Model (CIM) Infrastructure Specification", DSP0004, Version 2.3, Final, October 4, 2005

[9] Edward Wustenhoff, Service Level Agreement in the Data Center, Sun Professional Services Sun BluePrints™ OnLine - April 200

[10] Ioan Raicu. "A Performance Study of the Globus Toolkit® and Grid Services via DiPerF, an automated DIstributed PERformance testing Framework", University of Chicago, Computer Science Department, MS Thesis, May 2005, Chicago, Illinois.

[11] D. Gunter, B. Tierney, C. E. Tull, V. Virmani, "On-Demand Grid Application Tuning and Debugging with the NetLogger Activation Service", 4th International Workshop on Grid Computing, Grid2003, Phoenix, Arizona, November 17th, 2003.

[12] G. Tsouloupas, M. Dikaiakos. "GridBench: A Tool for Benchmarking Grids", 4th International Workshop on Grid Computing, Grid2003, Phoenix, Arizona, November 17th, 2003.

[13] The Next Generation Grid (NEXTGRID), www.nextgrid.org

[14] Web Service Resource Lifetime (WS-ResourceLifetime) v1.2 Specification, http://docs.oasis-open.org/wsrf/wsrf-ws_resource_lifetime-1.2-spec-os.pdf

[15] Web Service Resource Properties (WS-ResourceProperties) v1.2 Specification http://docs.oasis-open.org/wsrf/wsrf-ws_resource_properties-1.2-spec-os.pdf

[16] Web Services Addressing (WS-Addressing), http://www.w3.org/Submission/ws-addressing/

[17] Web Service Base Notification (WS-BaseNotification) v1.2 Specification, http://docs.oasis-open.org/wsn/2004/06/wsn-WS-BaseNotification-1.2-draft-03.pdf

[18] Web Service Security (WS-Security) Core Specification v1.1, http://www.oasis-open.org/committees/download.php/16790/wss-v1.1-spec-os-SOAPMessageSecurity.pdf

[19] H. Ludwig, A. Keller, A. Dan, R. P. King, R. Franck, "Service Level Agreement Language Specification", http://www.research.ibm.com/wsla/WSLASpecV1-20030128.pdf

[20] Peer Hasselmeyer, "Performance Evaluation of a WS Service Group based Registry", 7th IEEE/ACM International Conference on Grid Computing (Grid 2006), Barcelona, September 28th-29th, 2006.

II

TRUST, SECURITY AND VIRTUAL ORGANIZATION

THREAT ANALYSIS AND ATTACKS ON XTREEMOS: A GRID–ENABLED OPERATING SYSTEM[*]

Amit D. Lakhani, Erica Y. Yang, Brian Matthews, Ian Johnson, Syed Naqvi, Gheorghe C. Silaghi
Rutherford Appleton Laboratory,
Science and Technology Facilities Council, Didcot,
Oxon, UK
OX11 0QX
a.lakhani, y.yang, b.m.matthews, i.j.johnson, s.naqvi, g.c.silaghi@rl.ac.uk

Abstract   We perform a preliminary threat analysis on a grid–enabled operating system, namely XtreemOS, in this paper. While currently under development, XtreemOS aims to provide native Virtual Organisation support in a secure and dependable manner. We investigate security within the XtreemOS architecture by identifying the security requirements and objectives. Further, we list assets within the system that need protection and detail attacks using the attacker tree methodology. At the end, we describe a specific attack on the overall XtreemOS–supported architecture using an attacker tree. Analysis of this nature will help in generating a number of test cases for testing an early prototype of XtreemOS and provide assurance to the security of the XtreemOS system.

Keywords: XtreemOS, Threats, Attacks, Grid, Threat Analysis, Attacker Tree

[*]This work is supported by the European Commission under the IST program #FP6–033576.

1. Introduction

Grid Middleware security has been researched extensively in literature [1, 7, 8, 9]. While various middleware security services have been developed, the unification and use of such services is left at the discretion of the implementers. We propose to develop a Grid–enabled Operating System, called XtreemOS [2], which has native support for Virtual Organisations (VOs). In the context of Grid and Web services, a VO is a static or dynamic group of entities (organisations, individuals, institutes etc.) that pool resources and use services to achieve common objectives. Security in XtreemOS is a major concern, and administrators and users require a high level of assurance in this area. To this end, we are in the process of developing a secure VO management strategy and also plan to use evaluation criteria, such as Common Criteria, to inspect the claimed security provided by XtreemOS.

In this paper, we describe our threat analysis and attacks identified in XtreemOS by understanding the basic threat model in Grid and Web Services architecture. We analyse various attacks possible in such a setting and build attacker trees to inspect various attacker tools. The benefits of our threat analysis are manifold. Such attacker trees will generate a number of test cases to test a working prototype of XtreemOS once developed. Our analysis will also identify threats, in addition to common threats in Grids and Web services which are created by XtreemOS. Included in the analysis is the study of risks in designing such underlying services and a consideration of mechanisms that can be used to mitigate such risks. While various other research proposals address Grid Operating Systems [3–4]; to our knowledge, there does not exist any threat analysis for a Grid-enabled Operating System.

2. Threat Analysis

To carry out a proper threat analysis we first need to define the security requirements, identify assets and consequently determine threats in the system. In the next subsection we start our analysis with security requirements of XtreemOS.

2.1 Security Requirements and Objectives for XtreemOS

While the exact XtreemOS architecture is still under development, a detailed description of the overall system and XtreemOS is given in [2].

The basic security objectives of XtreemOS are similar to those applicable to traditional operating systems, namely confidentiality, integrity and availability. In addition in the Grid, authentication and authorisation become a prime concern. However, the fulfillment of such objectives become more difficult due to the distributed nature of the Grid. Of greater importance are synchronisation issues, inconsistencies within which can particularly lead to non–fulfillment of security objectives. We consider both stored data and data in–transit. The most important security requirements we consider for our system model are:

- Confidentiality of stored data
- Confidentiality of communicated data
- Integrity of stored data
- Integrity of communicated data
- Identification and authentication of users
- Authorized access to application services
- Guaranteed access to services by authorization parties
- Accountability of data access and service execution
- Isolation of data within a VO
- Isolation of services within a VO

In order for the secure running of the XtreemOS–supported system, these requirements should be fulfilled **at every point of time** and not just during VO formation or dissolution. Such emphasis becomes absolutely necessary due to distributed nature of the system.

2.2   Assets

Having defined the security objectives and requirements we list the identified assets in our system. We consider both stored and communication assets for our analysis. Our assets for an XtreemOS–supported system are as follows:

- user and administrator authentication credentials for the Grid;
- user and administrator authorization credentials for the Grid;
- VO–membership credentials;
- filesystems – both local and filesystems shared on the Grid;
- user and process data transmitted between nodes by XtreemOS;
- VO–specific data on a resource (there will be data of different VOs on a resource, so isolation of these data from each other is important);
- services within a VO and their identifiers;
- infrastructure–specific information (such as keys for Public–Key Infrastructure);
- user and service attributes;
- reputation data of services and resources (we envisage use of reputation for selecting services and resources at a later stage of XtreemOS development);
- OS–specific information (e.g. synchronization data);
- logging information.

All these assets require a level of protection to be specified and mechanisms to be put in place to provide such protection.

2.3   Threats

Threat modelling for the Grid systems has been done in many other research studies [5–6]. While various common threats are identified for the overall Grid architecture, threats in Grid middleware and the underlying operating systems have not been studied in–depth. In the context of XtreemOS, we classify below some common threats and some XtreemOS–specific threats.

Threats to availability   Denial–of–service attacks are the most common attacks in Grid systems. Although not specific only to Grids, these threats are easier to realise than any other threats in Grid systems. Denial of service to nodes, denial of service to services, denial of service to a VO, denial of service to filesystems are all examples of these threats. Recently, a new kind of threat has been derived from these threats; distributed denial of service (DDoS) on the Internet using Grid nodes (e.g. DDoS attack on Sun Grid in 2006). The realisation of such threats is drastic and defeats the purpose of collaboration in Grid systems, thereby making these threats significant to mitigate in any Grid system including XtreemOS.

Threats to authentication   Threats in this category range from injecting false authentication credentials, to test misconfigurations in management of authentication mechanisms, to masquerading as genuine users of the Grid. Theft of authentication credentials, exploiting revocation policy within the system by re-playing invalid credentials and brute–forcing user private keys are examples of threats in this category. These threats probably form the second largest category that Grid systems are exposed to.

Threats to authorization   Authorization restricts access to resources and services only to users who provide respective credentials. Threats to authorization include false injection of authorization credentials, masquerading as authorization providing entity (e.g. masquerading as KTC in Kerberos) etc. Although realisation of these threats require skilful attack strategies, authorization threats if realised can be highly damaging to the normal functioning of Grid systems.

Threats to confidentiality of data   The realisation of such threats will lead to unauthorised disclosure of data. Eavesdropping (both active and passive) and masquerading to reveal data are examples of such threats. Confidentiality is required while passing job results, inter–VO communications and during authentication in Grid systems.

Threats to integrity of data   It is one of the fundamental requirements for XtreemOS to preserve the integrity of data. Threats to integrity will address unauthorised modification of data in–transit and stored data to achieve the goals of the attacker(s). It becomes difficult to detect such threats if the consequent state of the system remains unchanged. Active eavesdropping and man–in–the–middle attacks are realisation of such threats.

Threats to isolation of data   Isolation of VO–specific data is of great concern in Grid systems due to possible conflict–of–interests between VOs. These threats are specific to Grid systems and to XtreemOS in particular. VO–session hijacks, compromising node security, worms, trojans etc are examples of threats in this category. To mitigate such threats, we are currently looking at virtualisation and Trusted Computing (TCPA) as possible solutions.

3.   Attacks

Having identified various threats in XtreemOS, we move on to focus on attacks on XtreemOS system. At a later stage we visualise a few of these attacks by using attacker trees.

The overall XtreemOS architecture framework is given in Figure 1.

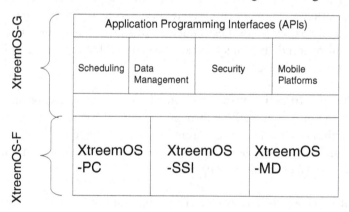

Figure 1.   XtreemOS Architecture

For the attack analysis, in the XtreemOS architecture only the two layers, namely XtreemOS–F and XtreemOS–G layer are important to us. XtreemOS–F layer is concerned with kernel–level extensions to the native Linux operating system. As we envisage developing XtreemOS for a variety of platforms, various flavours of XtreemOS will exist to support mobile platforms (XtreemOS–MD), for PCs (XtreemOS–PC) and for clusters (XtreemOS–SSI). The XtreemOS–G layer implements the grid–oriented extensions and services for security, scheduling, data management (XtreemFS) and support for mobile platforms.

Considering this architecture and the overall system, the following are the types of attacks the attacker may execute.

User and Admin Credential Attacks: Attacks on user identity credentials and VO–membership credentials fall into this category. A Grid user credentials are normally proxy certificates given to the user on successful registration. These proxy certificates have a validity period (e.g. for VOMS it is normally 12 hours), which makes the attack harder to execute. These attacks can be carried out either by brute–forcing user passwords, compromising user system to reveal private keys, replaying revoked credentials to inspect cycling or even masquerading as Certificate Authority.

Communication Attacks: These types of attacks focus on gaining credentials and assertions in communications between nodes, VO administrators and VO members. Eavesdropping, packet–filtering of unencrypted communications, brute–forcing encrypted communications etc are examples of these types of attacks.

Site Management attacks: Detecting vulnerabilities in site management and exploiting those vulnerabilities are part of these types of attacks. XML Poisoning, insufficient authentication credential verification (AuthN/Z), insecure logging etc are examples of these attacks. Attacks of this nature should be detected by intrusion detection systems (IDS) and by having strong policies and mechanisms to implement them.

Perimeter and Injection attacks: Attackers may try to compromise a site's perimeter security by tunnelling through firewalls (SSH tunnelling), malicious inputs, dictionary attacks, brute–forcing, SOAP message poisoning etc. Once attackers gain access to site resources, they can try to disrupt communications by denying services or eavesdropping.

Denial of service (DoS) attacks: The attacks of this kind try to disrupt communications and deny services to resources to users. These are probably the best identified and prevalent attacks in current Grid systems. Examples include denying service for registration, job submission, results delivery etc.

In case of XtreemOS, if we consider the architecture in Figure. 1, in the XtreemOS–F layer we need to consider User Credential attacks, Site Management Attacks and DoS attacks.

User Credentials are stored in native Linux as passwords in /etc/passwd and /etc/shadow files. Security of these files is of prior importance to prevent User Credential Attacks. Proxy Certificates and proxy agents used should be secured and unauthorised tampering should be prevented. Site Management attacks could be realised by improper management, for e.g. by insecure auditing or logging. For example, we plan to extend the Pluggable Authentication Modules (PAM) to authenticate users. Testing of modules should be done prior to using them in XtreemOS–F and any conflicts with other modules which arise need to be inspected. In addition, in every administrative domain a strong password policy should be implemented in order to mitigate brute–forcing password threats.

Site Management Attacks include a wide range of attacks. If logging is enabled for accountability, logs should be secured and if possible backups stored in a location separate from production nodes. For detecting abnormalities in usage, Intrusion Detection Systems (IDS) and firewalls should be used.

Defence against DoS attacks is difficult. However, proper policy management and implementation can lead to lessening of such attacks. Detection of unauthorised use and proper authentication procedures will make it difficult for attackers to compromise security controls. In XtreemOS–F layer, authorised access control, proper authentication and secure logging and log inspection will lead to a considerable decrease in such attacks.

In the XtreemOS–G layer, the opportunity of attacks becomes wider. From the above classification it is obvious that all the types of attacks can be realised at this layer. A short description is given below.

In the XtreemOS–G layer, we include security services provided to achieve security objectives. In respect to User Credential attacks, security services for authentication become prominent. Communications between users, VO administrators, Certification Authorities (CAs) and other authorities (for e.g. if Kerberos is used than between KTC and user) need to be encrypted. This is not only a requirement in XtreemOS–G, but also a building block for leveraging other services like authorization. Revocation of user credentials is another important aspect at this layer. The revocation mechanism, window of acceptance and updates to Certificate Revocation Lists (CRLs) must be correctly implemented at this layer.

Site Management is a major security issue in this layer. As we are using VOs, VO Management (VOM) needs to be robust against various attacks. VOM should not have conflicting policies and policies should be implemented as designed. In case of node failures, job controllers and users should be notified and before restarting jobs policies should be consulted. Authorization to use resources depends heavily on site management. User roles, capabilities and other attributes need to be verified before granting access to resource. Misconfigurations in any of these critical decisions will lead to vulnerabilities and attack realisation.

DoS attacks at this layer can be realised by denying access to resources and services. For resources, replicas of files can be a considerable defence against these attacks. In addition, regular backups and replicated systems can help in providing near–constant availability. For services, proper timeout features and suitable error handling can prove to be a defence.

For perimeter attacks, detection of unauthorised use is probably the best method. Site perimeters are often deployed with application and packet–filtering firewalls. Strong firewall rules based on access policies, accompanied by IDS and constant log inspections can help to disregard such attacks. Port scans, unsuccessful login attempts and XML poisoning detection through XML firewalls will help in securing sites against perimeter attacks.

4. Visualising Attacks

In this section, we use a common approach to visualise attacks in networks, namely attacker trees. Having identified a set of attacks in XtreemOS and overall system we here create attacker trees to identify what tools attacker(s) may use to realize these attacks. Due to space restrictions, we only present a single attacker tree here, but currently we are developing a number of attacker trees covering the range of threats to Xtreemos as part of our threat analysis.

Case Study: Unauthorised Access to Resources attack

A specific attack was identified while considering the below attacker tree. The attack is a Site Management Attack whereby the attacker observes the conflict between VO and local site policy and exploits such a vulnerability to mount an attack.

Setting: A realistic setting is assumed in the attack. A set of users are members of the VO and are administered by their local site policy. The VO itself has its VO policies in respect to access, membership etc. A VO manager grants users access to resources. On the resource side, local site administrators govern access to resources. Local site policy for access to resources exists for VO/Grid users. For the current attack, we consider one particular case. Access to resources is granted based on *union* of site and VO policy (for other case studies we also consider other approaches to combine local and VO policies).

Assets: Assets in this case are user credentials, VO attributes, roles (Grid User, VO Admin, Local Admin), filesystems and authentication, authorization, discovery, VO registration services.

Threats: Since we only consider stored data in this case study, we identify the following threats:

- Unauthorised disclosure of information and stored data.
- Unauthorised modification of stored data.
- Unauthorised disclosure of job results.

Attacker Tree: The Attacker tree is shown below with the attack marked.

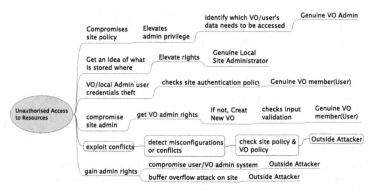

Figure 2.   Attacker Tree

Attack: The attack was identified on recursively expanding the attacker tree. In this particular case, as the access is granted based on union of VO and site policies, either a user or VO admin will get more than required access. For example, if VO policy grants only `read` access to a user and the local policy grants only `write` access, the user will have `read/write` access on the resource rather than just a `read` access. Merging VO and site policies is a difficult problem, but we are required to provide a service within XtreemOS that can detect such conflicts if they occur.

5.   Conclusions

We have presented here a preliminary threat analysis on XtreemOS, a Grid–enabled operating system. We have identified various threats and attacks in accordance with our set security requirements and visualised attacks in attacker trees. This work is ongoing and we will continue to expand on our threat analysis as our system develops and document a variety of threats throughout the process. A rigorous threat analysis will help in making XtreemOS robust against a wide range of attacks. We will then use this analysis to provide a set of test cases and, thus, provide a level of assurance to the user community. This analysis will also be used for formal security modelling of the XtreemOS system and consequently help in derivation of the system's security policy.

Acknowledgments

We would like to thank all the members of XtreemOS consortium for their constant support and hard–work.

References

[1] Grid Security Infrastructure http://www.globus.org/security/overview.html.

[2] C. Morin. *XtreemOS: a Grid Operating System Making your Computer Ready for Participating in Virtual Organizations.* 10th IEEE Intl. Symposium on Object–oriented Real–time distributed Computing (ISORC 2007) – to appear.

[3] P. Padala, GridOS, http://www.eecs.umich.edu/ ppadala/research/gridos/

[4] Legion Project, http://legion.virginia.edu/index.html

[5] S. Naqvi and M. Riguidel. *Threat model for grid security services.* LNCS. Volume 3470 pp. 1048–1055, 2005.

[6] Demchenko Y., *Web Services and Grid Security Vulnerabilities and Threats Analysis,* EGEE JRA3 Technical document.

[7] V. Welch, F. Siebenlist, I. Foster, J. Bresnahan, K. Czajkowski, J. Gawor, C. Kesselman, S. Meder, L. Pearlman, S. Tuecke. *Security for Grid Services.* Proceedings of HPDC–12, pp. 48–57, IEEE Press, 2003.

[8] I. Foster, C. Kesselman, G. Tsudik, S. Tuecke. *A Security Architecture for Computational Grids.* Proceedings of the 5th ACM Conference on Computer and Communications Security Conference, pp. 83–92, 1998.

[9] R. Alfieri, R. Cecchini, V. Ciaschini, L. dell'Agnello, A. Frohner, K. Lrentey, and F. Spataro. *From gridmap–file to VOMS: managing authorization in a Grid environment.* Future Generation Computing Systems. Volume 21(4), pp. 549–558, ACM Press, 2005.

A UTILITY-BASED REPUTATION MODEL
FOR SERVICE-ORIENTED COMPUTING[*]

Gheorghe Cosmin Silaghi
STFC Rutherford Appleton Laboratory and University of Coimbra, DEI
Chilton, Didcot, OX11 0QX, UK   *Polo II, 3030-290, Coimbra, Portugal*
g.c.silaghi@rl.ac.uk   gsilaghi@dei.uc.pt

Alvaro E. Arenas
STFC Rutherford Appleton Laboratory
Chilton, Didcot, OX11 0QX, UK
a.e.arenas@rl.ac.uk

Luis Moura Silva
University of Coimbra, DEI
Polo II, 3030-290, Coimbra, Portugal
luis@dei.uc.pt

Abstract   Reputation systems have emerged as a method for fostering trust amongst strangers in electronic transactions. In this paper we propose a utility-based model for reputation tailored for service-oriented computing. In contrast to most other reputation models that require direct feedback from users, our model build the reputation from information provided by monitoring systems, making it suitable for service-oriented settings such as Grids. Usefulness of the model is described by showing how the efficiency of resource brokering in Grids can be improved by using a reputation-based scheduler scheme.

Keywords: Reputation; Service-Oriented Computing; Utility Computing; Grids.

[*]This work is funded by the European Commission under the IST FP6 projects CoreGRID –project No.004265– and GridTrust –project No. 033827–.

1. Introduction

Reputation systems have emerged as a method for fostering trust amongst strangers in electronic transactions. A reputation system gathers, distributes, and aggregates feedbacks about participants' behaviour. The feedback is usually provided as a-posteriori operation requiring human intervention. One major drawback is that users will try to misrepresent the obtained quality of services in order to make more profit, or to lie or provide misleading ratings in order to achieve some specific goals [5].

This way of building reputation is useful in semi-automatic contexts, such as electronic marketplaces where users rate sellers, but it becomes a limitation in fully automatic contexts. For instance, Grid computing focuses on the development of a distributed service environment that integrates a variety of resources with various quality of service capabilities in order to support scientific and business problem solving environments. In a typical Grid scenario, middleware services like brokers select resources by obtaining basic information about them from directory services; the type of information usually includes functional and quality of service properties of the resource. The selection process can be enriched by providing reputation information about resources. However, in several Grid applications, resource usage is transparent to the end user, making difficult to obtain a qualification.

This paper proposes a reputation model that overcomes above limitations by using some basic assumptions considered valid in service-oriented architectures, and Grids in particular, such as the existence of trustworthy monitoring systems. A monitoring system provides information about services and the actual service delivery. Instead of asking the user to provide the feedback after having a transaction, we use monitoring information as a substitute to build the direct reputation.

Our reputation model is based on ideas of utility computing. User feedback is represented as a utility function which reflects the satisfaction a user perceives from consuming a service. The user provides such a utility function *before* committing to use a service either by building the utility function herself or by selecting the function from a library of utility functions. The user's utility function will be then applied on the monitoring information in order to calculate the reputation of the service.

Section 2 describes our proposed reputation model. Next, in section 3 we show how the metrics of the model work by experimenting with various types of service delivery, and describe a potential application of our reputation model for improving resource brokering in Grids. Then, section 4 compares related work. Finally, we conclude the paper in section 5 by summarising main results and highlighting future work.

2. A Utility-Based Reputation Model

This section describes a utility-based reputation model that aims at registering the reputation of service providers based on the satisfaction of users.

DEFINITION 1 *(Services, Issues and Expectations)*
Let $X = \{x_1, x_2, \ldots, x_n\}$ denote the set of services, with x ranging on X. Let SP denote the set of services providers, with b ranging on SP, and function $S : SP \rightarrow \mathscr{P}(X)$ denoting the services provided by a service provider, where $\mathscr{P}$ represents the power set operator. Let SC denote the set of users (service consumers) of the system, with c ranging on SC.

Each service has associated issues of interest, denoted by set I, which users are interested in monitoring; variable i ranges on I. Function IS represents the set of issues of interest for a service: $IS : X \rightarrow \mathscr{P}(I)$. Function $O^c : X \times SP \times I \rightarrow \mathscr{R}$ denotes the expectation of user c on the services he uses, where $\mathscr{R}$ denotes the real numbers. Notation $v_{x,i}^{b,c}$ represent the expectation of user c on issue i of service x supplied by provider b.

For instance, in classical service-oriented architectures, a potential issue of interest could be the *quality of service*. In this case, the user expectation would be the *service level agreement*, the formal negotiated agreement between a user and his service providers.

Based on his expectation, a user can develop a utility function which reflects the satisfaction he perceives from consuming the service.

DEFINITION 2 *(Utility Function)*
Let $U_{x,i}^{c,b}(v)$ denote the utility that user c gets by obtaining the actual value $v \in \mathscr{R}$ on issue i from service x of provider b. Utilities will be normalized and scaled to $[0, 1]$, getting the user a utility of 1 if provider b actually supplies with the expected value $v_{x,i}^{b,c}$ for issue i from service x. If the provider supplies a better quality, the user gets the utility of 1. Therefore, we have $U_{x,i}^{c,b} : \mathscr{R} \rightarrow [0, 1]$.

If the service has a direct valuation scale (i.e. bigger supplied value, better the satisfaction the user gets), equation (1) can be an example of a utility function.

$$U_{x,i}^{c,b}(v) = \begin{cases} 1 & v \geq v_{x,i}^{b,c} \\ \frac{v}{v_{x,i}^{b,c}} & v < v_{x,i}^{b,c} \end{cases} \tag{1}$$

We assume that the IT infrastructure provides a trustable monitoring service that delivers regularly events indicating the current value of the issues of interest for those services in execution. Events are captured by the reputation engine in order to generate the reputation values at different levels - issue, service or service provider.

DEFINITION 3 *(Events)*
An event $e = (\,(c,b,x,i),\ t,\ v\,)$ indicates that at time t the issue of interest i for service x provided by b for user c has value v. The set of events E consists of triples $(\,(SC \times SP \times X \times I) \times \mathcal{N} \times \mathcal{R}\,)$, where $\mathcal{N}$ and $\mathcal{R}$ stand for the natural and real numbers respectively.

For each event reported by the monitoring service, having the utility function of a consumer c, one can compute the instant utility $U_{x,i}^{c,b}(v)$, indicating the actual satisfaction the consumer is getting at that moment. This allows us to calculate the reputation of a service provider.

DEFINITION 4 *(Reputation Function for Issues of Interest)*
The reputation of a service provider b in relation to issue i of service x at time t can be defined as follows:

$$R_{x,i}^{b}(t) = \frac{\sum_{c \in SC} \sum_{((c,b,x,i),t_e,v_e) \in E \wedge t_e \leq t} \varphi(t,t_e) * U_{x,i}^{c,b}(v_e)}{\sum_{c \in SC} \sum_{((c,b,x,i),t_e,v_e) \in E \wedge t_e \leq t} \varphi(t,t_e)} \qquad (2)$$

where $\varphi(t,t_e)$ is a time discount function which puts more importance on events closer to present.

It is worth noticing that the reputation measure incorporates information supplied by various users who consumed the service in the past. Reputation equation (2) is inspired by the aggregation presented in [9].

As in [9], we developed the reputation deviation to provide a fitness measure for the reputation value. The reputation deviation shows how much the reputation varies in time. In contrast to [9], in our model, the lower the reputation deviation, the better the confidence one can put on the reputation value $R_{x,i}^{b}$.

DEFINITION 5 *(Reputation Deviation for Issues of Interest)*
The reputation deviation of a service provider b in relation to issue i of service x at time t can be defined as follows:

$$DR_{x,i}^{b}(t) = \frac{\sum_{c \in SC} \sum_{((c,b,x,i),t_e,v_e) \in E \wedge t_e \leq t} \varphi(t,t_e) * \left| U_{x,i}^{c,b}(v_e) - R_{x,i}^{b}(t) \right|}{\sum_{c \in SC} \sum_{((c,b,x,i),t_e,v_e) \in E \wedge t_e \leq t} \varphi(t,t_e)} \qquad (3)$$

Based on above definitions, we can derive the reputation of a service as the aggregation of the reputations on the issues of interest of such service.

DEFINITION 6 *(Reputation and Reputation Deviation for a Service)*
The reputation and reputation deviation for a service provider b in relation to

service x at time t can be defined as follows:

$$R_x^b(t) = \frac{\sum_{i \in IS(x)} R_{x,i}^b(t)}{\#IS(x)} \qquad DR_x^b(t) = \frac{\sum_{i \in IS(x)} \left| R_{x,i}^b(t) - R_x^b(t) \right|}{\#IS(x)} \quad (4)$$

where # corresponds to the cardinality of a set.

Likewise, the reputation of a service provider can be defined as the aggregation of the reputation of the services it provides.

DEFINITION 7 *(**Reputation and Reputation Deviation for a Service Provider**)*
The reputation and reputation deviation for a provider b in relation with all services it delivers at time t can be defined as follows:

$$R^b(t) = \frac{\sum_{x \in S(b)} R_x^b(t)}{\#S(b)} \qquad DR^b(t) = \frac{\sum_{x \in S(b)} \left| R_x^b(t) - R^b(t) \right|}{\#S(b)} \quad (5)$$

In our model we require a user to deliver the utility function for their tasks. Can the user indeed formulate the utility function for his tasks? In [2], it is acknowledged that finding the utility function of all grid actors is a difficult task. In economic market approaches to the grid ([2, 1]), the emphasis is put on producers and consumers which take decisions according with their internal utility functions and the outcome of these decisions is the pricing assessment for the grid services. Therefore, one can learn the internal utility functions of the grid agents by observing how they price the grid services. As our goal is to keep our reputation model simple, we do not intend to enter the scope of accountability in grids. Therefore, if the user is not able to define his utility functions, the reputation manager will simply ask the user to characterize how important is the realization of the expected values for a given task. Based on this response (which can be a discrete one, i.e. very important, don't know, not so important), the reputation manager can assign a utility function selected from a template library.

3. Evaluation of the Reputation Model

Some simulations were performed in order to validate the intended properties of our reputation model.

3.1 Initial Experiments

Initially, we consider the simplistic approach in which a resource provider supplies one service –storage– and the service has one issue of interest –storage capacity–. The user expectation for storage capacity is 100Gb, and uses the same utility function (equation (1)) for all his tasks during the time of the experiment.

68

Further, we assume that the provider delivers the service according with some pre-established patterns. The reputation function for a issue of interest (equation 2) requires a time discount function; following [3], the time discount function is defined as $\varphi(t, t_j) = e^{-\frac{t-t_e}{\lambda}}$. We took a time frame of 1000 time units (tu) for our experiments, using $\lambda = 200$. The reputation engine is set up to compute the reputation values according with the formulas presented in section 2 at every 20 time units.

The provider supplies a storage capacity uniformly distributed around the expected value of 100Gb. We took a variation band of 20Gb, from 85-105. Figure 1 shows how the reputation measure reflects this pattern of delivery for the service and the issue. We can notice that after a short learning time frame, the reputation stabilizes itself around some value. Next, we generated a harder drop down in the delivery of the capacity issue at a provider site. Between time units 200 and 300 the provider drops the supplied capacity with 20Gb. Figure 2 shows the results. We can notice that the reputation value immediately drops after the the fall in delivery and it does not recover at the initially existing level even at the end of the time frame.

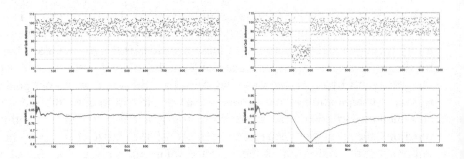

Figure 1. Reputation when the issue is delivered normally distributed around the expected value

Figure 2. Reputation when there is a decay in delivery

The next experiment emphasizes the usage of reputation deviation. We consider two providers: first provider supplying uniformly distributed values in a variation band (line dotted with circles in Figure 3), and second provider supplying normally distributed values with the same mean and a deviation being half of the bandwidth selected for the first provider (line dotted with squares in Figure 3). Let the variation band to be between 85 and 105. Analyzing the upper diagram of figure 3, we can notice that reputation itself is not enough to characterize which provider is more reputable. However, the reputation deviation, as expected, is smaller (i.e. better) for the second provider, which makes the difference between the providers. Based on the reputation deviation, one

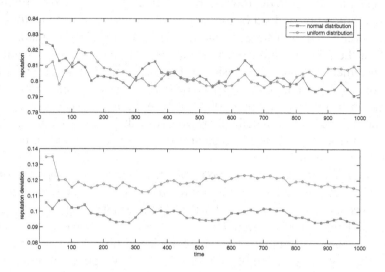

Figure 3. Reputation and reputation deviation in the case of different QoS deliveries

can decide which reputation value is more reliable and distinguish between the above patterns of delivery.

3.2   Enhancing Resource Brokering with Reputation

Resource brokering is defined as the task of selecting and allocating the most appropriate resource for a given job. Resource brokering is a wide research area in grids and is not the scope of this paper to enter the full details of this problem. Instead, we want only to point out that using reputation can be beneficial for the effectiveness of the brokering process, compared with simplistic approaches that use no intelligent technique to tackle this problem.

We performed our experiments using the SimGrid simulator [8], on which we implemented the following reputation-based scheduling scheme: when scheduling a job to a resource, the resource broker considers all available nodes that fulfill all service requirements for that job; it then schedules the job to the most reputable node. We implemented also a monitoring service that observes the quality of the service delivery during the execution and reports events to a reputation manager, following our reputation model.

In our experiments, we compared a simple brokering algorithm like round-robin scheduling with our reputation-based scheme. Round-robin scheduling has also been used as a base comparison in [2]. In the round-robin approach, the broker immediately schedules a task that arrives in its queue to the next grid node that comes in the round-robin scheme. To measure the difficulty of the brokering problem, load factor parameter was used [2]: load factor is light if in a certain period of time the number of jobs submitted is small, and the length of the jobs are short; otherwise the system load is heavy. We use the same parameter for the x dimension of Figures 4 and 5. For our experiment, we allow 20% of the nodes to produce random values uniformly distributed in a variation band between $85 - 105\%$ of the expected service value. We use the time discount function defined previously, with λ tuned to 200. In order to keep low the memory of events related with an issue of a service provider, we discard all events for which $\varphi(t, t_e) < 0.01$

In the experiment we record two parameters: the *total completion time* for the entire batch of jobs and the *total welfare* produced in the system by counting all utilities acquired by the users for the submitted jobs. Figure 4 depicts the total completion time for different loads of the system. We can notice that with reputation-based scheduling, the total completion time is better with around 25%. This 25% gain in completion time can be very significant in the case of high load factors.

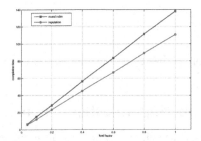 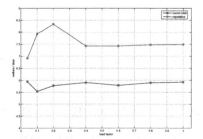

Figure 4.   Completion time comparison   *Figure 5.*   Total welfare produced per unit of time comparison

Figure 5 compares the total welfare produced on the time unit. In the case of the reputation-based scheduling, the efficiency of the system, measured as the amount of welfare produced on a time unit, is higher. Regardless the load of the system, the user feels more satisfied from consuming the services in the utility-based scheduling. A good outcome is the fact that the amount of welfare produced per unit of time stabilizes for high load of the system. Again, about 25% gain of welfare is recorded. For both cases, only 20% of nodes in the grid violated the expectations with only maximum 15%, leading to an average of only 3% violation of the expectations for the overall grid.

4. Related Work

There are some previous models of reputation for Grids system. The Grid-EigenTrust model [7] integrates trust management as part of the QoS management system. They consider both direct and indirect trust, acquired at the level of grid entities and contexts (i.e. service delivery), after transaction execution. PathTrust [6] proposed a reputation system for member selection in the formation phase of a virtual organization. When inviting members to join a VO, the initiator selects only those members whose reputation is above a certain threshold and probabilistically selects a member to be in the VO, as we did for selecting node where to schedule some task. The reputation is built by aggregating positive and negative feedback the user submits after transaction execution. These two approaches have the limitation on depending on the direct feedback from users.

Reputation can be built based on the internal beliefs of the agents, as in the subjective logic of [4]. In multi-agent research, techniques based on aggregating over several sources of trust have been considered [3, 9]. REGRET model [9] aggregates over the individual, social and ontological dimension in order to obtain a reputation to be used on an electronic marketplace. They inspired us with the aggregation metric for the reputation and with the reputation deviation. But their model is based on impressions collected after the transaction, which limits the applicability of the model to the grid. We distinguish from them overcoming this limitation by asking the utility function of the user before the transaction and by the usage of the trusted monitoring information. More, in our approach, the reputation is aggregated considering the view of several users.

5. Conclusion

In this paper we have presented a reputation model based on ideas of utility computing, tailored for service-oriented contexts. For each service, the user defines issues of interest and expected values on such issues. The satisfaction of the user on a service is measured by a utility function. Reputation of a service issue is then built by comparing its expected value with the actual value, delivered by a monitoring system. Reputation of a service is built as the aggregation of the reputations of its issues. Likewise, reputation of a service provider is built as the aggregation of the reputation of all services it delivers. This robust and scalable way of calculating reputation does not depend on direct feedback collected after the transaction. We have shown the usefulness of the model in improving the efficacy of resource brokering in Grids when using a reputation-based scheduling scheme.

References

[1] R. Buyya, D. Abramson, and J. Giddy. A case for economy grid architecture for service oriented grid computing. In *IPDPS '01: Proceedings of the 10th Heterogeneous Computing Workshop - HCW 2001 (Workshop 1)*, page 20083.1, IEEE Computer Society, 2001.

[2] Li Chunlin and Li Layuan. Multi economic agent interaction for optimizing the aggregate utility of grid users in computational grid. *Applied Intelligence*, 25(2):147–158, 2006.

[3] T.D. Huynh, N.R. Jennings, and N.R. Shadbolt. An integrated trust and reputation model for open multi-agent systems. *Autonomous Agents and Multi-Agent Systems*, 13(2):119–154, 2006.

[4] A. Jøsang and S.J. Knapskog. A metric for trusted systems. In *Proceedings of the 21st National Information Systems Security Conference, (NIST-NCSC 1998)*, 1998.

[5] A. Jøsang, R. Ismail, and C. Boyd A Survey of Trust and Reputation Systems for Online Service Provision *Decision Support Systems*, 43(2):618–644, 2007.

[6] F. Kerschbaum, J. Haller, Y. Karabulut, and P. Robinson. Pathtrust: A trust-based reputation service for virtual organization formation. In *iTrust2006: Proceedings of the 4th International Conference on Trust Management*, volume 3986 of *Lecture Notes in Computer Science*, pages 193–205. Springer, 2006.

[7] G. von Laszewski, B.E. Alunkal, and I. Veljkovic. Towards reputable grids. *Scalable Computing: Practice and Experience*, 6(3):95–106, 2005.

[8] A. Legrand, L. Marchal, and H. Casanova. Scheduling distributed applications: the SimGrid simulation framework. In *CCGRID '03: Proceedings of the 3st International Symposium on Cluster Computing and the Grid*, page 138, IEEE Computer Society, 2003.

[9] J. Sabater and C. Sierra. Regret: a reputation model for gregarious societies. In *4th Workshop on Deception, Fraud and Trust in Agent Societies*. ACM Press, 2001.

VIRTUAL ORGANIZATION MANAGEMENT IN XTREEMOS: AN OVERVIEW*

Erica Y. Yang, Brian Matthews, Amit Lakhani
RAL, STFC, U.K.

y.yang@rl.ac.uk

Yvon Jégou, Christine Morin, Oscar David Sánchez
IRISA/INRIA, France

Carsten Franke, Philip Robinson
SAP Research, CEC Belfast, U.K.

Adolf Hohl, Bernd Scheuermann
SAP Research, CEC Karlsruhe, Germany

Daniel Vladusic
XLab d.o.o., Slovenia

Haiyan Yu, An Qin, Rubao Lee
ICT/CAS, China

Erich Focht
NEC HPC Europe, Germany

Massimo Coppola
ISTI/CNR, Italy

Abstract   XtreemOS aims to build and promote a Linux based operating system to provide native Virtual Organization (VO) support in the next generation Grids. XtreemOS takes a different approach from many existing Grid middleware by: first, recognizing the fundamental role of VO in Grid computing and hence taking VO support into account from the very beginning of our design; and, second, getting around the overheads brought by layers of existing Grid middleware by enabling native VO support in the Linux operating system. This paper presents our vision of VOs in a Grid operating system and describes various aspects of VO management in our system architecture, ranging from lifecycle management, application execution management, security, to node-level enforcement mechanisms in operating system.

Keywords: XtreemOS, Virtual Organization (VO), VO Management, Grid

*We would like to thank the support from the European Commission under IST program #FP6-033576.

1. Introduction

XtreemOS is an European project with the objective to design, implement, evaluate and distribute an open source Grid OS, named XtreemOS, which supports Grid applications, and capable of running on a wide range of underlying platforms, from clusters to mobiles. The goal is to provide an abstract interface to its underlying local physical resources, as a traditional OS does for a single computer. While much work has been done to build Grid middleware on top of existent OS, little has been done to extend the underlying OS to support Grid computing, for example, by embedding important basic services directly into the OS kernel. The approach being investigated is to base XtreemOS on existing Linux. A set of system services, extending those found in the traditional Linux, will provide users with all the Grid capabilities associated with current Grid middleware, but fully integrated into the OS.

A key feature of XtreemOS is native support for Virtual Organizations. The term Virtual Organization (VO) is well-established within the context of economics. The typical goals of a VO include the temporal collaboration of several entities from different departments and their respective organizations towards achieving a common business objective. In Grid computing, synergies can be achieved by grouping users (provided by an identity infrastructure) which share OS- and application-specific resources and interfaces of computing nodes in a Grid [1].

The exact realisation of a VO differs from project to project. Some approaches concentrate on the legal or contractual arrangements between the participating entities. Other task-oriented approaches emphasize the workflow to achieve a goal. VOs can range from long-lived collaborations with many users (typically found in large-scale scientific applications) to short-lived, dynamic ventures to achieve one task between a small number of participants (typically commercial scenarios). A general purpose Grid OS should take a flexible approach to satisfy as wide a range of applications as possible; the use cases in XtreemOS reflect this diversity.

Thus, XtreemOS defines a minimal definition of the features of VOs and provides a toolbox which can be configured to the needs of the application. Key components of a VO are: VO administrators; a set of users and resources in different domains; a set of roles which users and resources can play in the VO; a set of policies on resource availability and access control; an expiry time of the VO. VO goals or workflows are not modeled, though XtreemOS tools allows these to be supported at application level. This will typically require enforcement of policies, event notification of the completion of processes, and monitoring of exceptional events, such as jobs still executing at VO expiration.

2. Requirements

The requirements for XtreemOS have been derived from a range of 14 applications [3]. In the following, we focus on requirements directly related to VO management and security services.

Three different roles are involved in managing VOs: *Domain administrators* maintain a pool of resources that are allowed to be integrated into a VO. They have the ultimate control over what resources will be available to a VO and regulate how a *VO user* uses its resources, and they ensure the reliability and security of resources being provided to VOs. *VO administrators* compose VOs from the resources provided by various domains, and they manage (e.g. create, delete, and modify) user accounts and the permissions VO users have within a VO. The role of the VO administrator can be assigned to one or more persons from the participating institutions.

Users can register with one or more VOs so that they can utilize resources from different VOs concurrently and independently. An individual may have different roles and be assigned with different capabilities in different VOs. To obtain a VO user account it is not necessary to have a pre-existing local user account in one of the domains belonging to the VO. Moreover, it must be possible to transfer data, files and directories between local and VO accounts (e.g. by copy or mount). Overlapping VOs are required, i.e. multiple VOs can be established on the same node. The applications require exchange of information between different VOs by means of messages (also instant messages), shared memory and data transfer.

It is required that VO management actions be highly automated, allowing them to be completed in a specified time threshold, typically to the order of a few seconds. It must be possible to guarantee the lifetime of a VO for a specified or an unspecified amount of time (until a notification e.g. by a user or application). VO management must be supported by an API, a command line interface and a GUI including VO monitoring facilities.

XtreemOS has to allow for dynamically changing the composition of VOs during application runtime, e.g., if certain computing resources fail. In such circumstances, the unavailable resources need to be automatically substituted by alternative resources also including a migration of the affected running application components.

Data stored on resources must only be accessible by users and administrators that are members of a VO with the appropriate access rights. Confidential data communicated must be encrypted. Loss of integrity of stored data must be preventable and detectable. Data should be hashed and digitally signed by a trusted key stored on the OS. The integrity of transferred data must be validated before being committed (need for an OS reference monitor mechanism). The OS must be capable of signing and verifying signatures of data in an end-to-end manner. A transaction framework is necessary, considering the distributed nature of the resources. Users should authenticate via single sign-on to gain authorized access to VO resources. Administrators are capable of recording the usage (by whom and when) of resources without users being able to deny (repudiate) such usage. This includes a secure audit service with the ability to the record timestamps and the VO in which a certain resource was used.

Isolation of VO users: As users may be involved in multiple VOs, it is then necessary to separate their user data and have means of determining which VOs they are currently working in, when accessing data. Isolation of data per-VO: Data stored on the same resource for different VOs must show non-interference. Isolation of services per-VO: Parties in different VOs must not be able to recognize that they are sharing resources nor can they gain knowledge of what other parties are doing with those resources. If one of two virtualized services on the same physical resources fails, this must not interfere with the other. It is proposed to investigate in how far virtual machines or containers (e.g. provided by OpenVZ) can be used for the purpose of isolation.

3. VOs in XtreemOS Architecture

This section first sums up the VO management challenges addressed by XtreemOS and then, describes various aspects of VO management in our system architecture, ranging from lifecycle management, application execution management, security, to node-level enforcement mechanisms.

3.1 Challenges

XtreemOS aims to provide native support for the management of VOs in a secure and scalable way, without compromising on flexibility and performance. Several key challenges are identified from both the requirement analysis and investigation of most state-of-art Grid VO solutions.

Interoperability with diverse VO frameworks and security models. Different VO management frameworks and security models have been developed so far and new ones keep on emerging. The diversity of their implementations is embodied in their adoption of different user identities (e.g. X.509 end user certificates, Shibboleth handles), different message sequences (e.g. push, pull and agent models), different places to convey security attributes (e.g. proxy certificates or SAML tokens) and different policy models (e.g. role-based access control). XtreemOS must be able to interoperate with, rather than replace these existing solutions and even traditional local security mechanisms (e.g. Kerberos). It is a challenge that the operating system-level abstraction of VOs in XtreemOS allows for integration of various existing VO structures.

Flexibility of policy languages. XtreemOS puts emphasis on that both scientific and enterprise business applications are equivalently supported. Users from these two representative application domains have different views of policies in a VO, in terms of subjects (users), objects (resources), access rights, Service Level Agreement (SLA) and QoS constraints. Therefore VO policies in XtreemOS have to be expressive and flexible enough to accommodate various levels of resource access rules.

Scalability of management of dynamic VOs. In order to support large numbers of users in a dynamic environment (dynamicity of resources and of users) while still providing accurate isolation of these users, solutions such as rather static files containing user information must be avoided. For example, when VOs are dynamically changed, it is impractical for the VO manager to update gridmap files on all resources, due to the heavy admin burden caused as well as the difficulty to maintain data consistency.

Strong isolation, access control and auditing. Some applications request for strong isolation of user applications on the Grid: hiding user identities, protecting files and processes, strict division of performance load, and so on. These requirements are typical for most of the industrial applications. In some environments this ability to generate strong isolated execution environment could even be used to isolate individual processes on a single resource. Implementing such requirements is difficult without operating system support. Furthermore, a secure Grid system must provide strict access control from the service level down to the system object level (files, sockets, ...). In all cases, it must be possible to monitor and log operating system service usage as well as system object accesses. The audit log must contain references to user credentials (security ticket) and be securely provided to the resource owner as well as the VO manager.

3.2 VO Management

In this paper, we use the concept, VO Management (VOM), to cover all the infrastructural services that are needed to manage the entities involved in a VO and ensure a consistent and coherent exploitation of the resources, capabilities, and information inside the VO under the governance of the VO policies. A VO policy is defined as an authorization statement that describes what activities a subject (e.g. an entity in a VO) is allowed to perform on an object (e.g. resources) with certain constrains (e.g. time, location), if there is any.

There are several stages of VO lifecycle: VO identification, VO formation, VO operation, VO evolution, and VO dissolution. VOM plays a different role in different stages of this lifecycle. During the identification stage, VOM is mainly responsible for user management (e.g. registration, attribute management) and

VO policy specification (e.g. constrains on resource usages). During the formation stage, VOM involves in the processes of resource matching, negotiation and establishment of Service-Level Agreements (SLAs) by applying VO policies. The operation stage leverages the information made available during the previous stages. In this stage, VOM coordinates logging, accounting, auditing operations on nodes and ensures the availability of such information, if needed. For jobs that require interactive sessions, VOM also provides authorized users with facilities (e.g. credentials) to access the sessions of runtime applications. The evolution stage takes place when the VO is altered during its lifespan, for example, by a change in the participating entities or in their conditions of use. During the last stage, VOM ensures the deletion of non-persistent information (e.g. temporary files and accounts) and the reclamation of credentials.

3.3   VOM and AEM

In XtreemOS, application execution is managed by Application Execution Management (AEM) services [2]. AEM services can be conceptually grouped into two types of services: Job Management Services (JMSs) and Resource Management Services (RMSs). JMSs cover all the job related tasks, such as job scheduling, monitoring, event handling, and execution management. JMSs are mostly operated on an individual job basis, that is, these services do not have a global view of the system. RMSs cover all the resources related tasks, including resource monitoring, selection, matching, negotiation, and allocation. This section focuses on the interactions between VOM and AEM during the job submission stage which is illustrated in Figure 1.

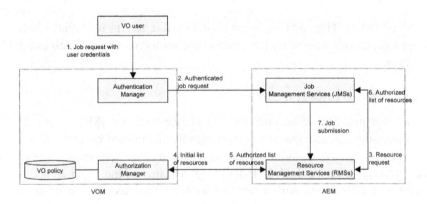

Figure 1.   Interactions between VOM and AEM during the Job Submission Stage

VOM consists of two main components: authentication manager and authorization manager. The job submission process starts from a VO user submitting a job request to the authentication manager. The authentication is performed against the credentials attached to the job request. Once a user is authenticated, the job request is forwarded to JMSs, which in turn contacts RMSs to select an initial list of resources. The selection is based on the job description and resource characteristics. The list is then subject to the scrutinization of the authorization manager to ensure that the job request and selected resources conforms to the overall VO policies in this context. As a result of the policy checking, an authorized list of the resources is then sent back to RMSs which will forward it to JMSs for conducting resource negotiation. Once the resources are successfully negotiated, JMSs will submit the job to RMSs which will then be responsible for launching the job on remote nodes.

In this process, the functionalities of VOM are to ensure that: a) only authenticated VO users can access AEM services; and b) the job execution will conform to VO policies by engaging the authorization manager in the process of resource selection.

3.4 Security

Because VOM involves in different stages of a VO lifespan, the design and implementation decisions on security services will have a significant impact on the efficiency and quality of the final XtreemOS operating system. This section discusses some of the key issues.

In Figure 1, when a user initiates a job request, the request is shown to be bundled with the user's credential for authentication purpose. In practice, this can be implemented in two different ways. The usual approach is to implement the authentication independent from underlying operating system level authentication. This is a popular approach adopted by many existing Grid middleware, e.g. Globus. It has the simplicity of implementation but comes with the complexity of configuration and management. That is, people who provide Grid services have to set up and manage two largely independent layers of services. In reality, it is common that more layers of services (e.g. Web services on top of Grid services) are introduced to establish extra levels of controls.

In XtreemOS we propose an alternative approach by aiming to integrate VOM as part of the OS. More specifically, VOM can be implemented as a service that can be integrated directly with existing authentication infrastructure. The benefits of this approach are described as follows. First, it reduces the management and performance overheads introduced by the layers of controls. Second, the hassle of accessing VO resources can be reduced. XtreemOS targets for both simple applications (i.e. a single request for the entire execution) as well as complex applications that involve interactivity and multiple execution requests, for example, for debugging purpose. Because of this reason, we anticipate that the integration of VOM as an OS level service should streamline the session management required for managing complex application.

3.5   Node-Level Enforcement

The policies specified by a VO, such as security, resource limitations, scheduling priorities and rules on how shared resources could be used by VO members, will be finally checked and ensured at resource nodes.

In order to adapt to different VO models and reduce kernel code changes, XtreemOS will use the PAM (Pluggable Authentication Modules) system [7], which allows a system administrator to add (possibly VO-specific) authentication methods by installing new PAM modules.

Local user accounts in XtreemOS are allocated dynamically on each resource to match the actual global users exploiting that resource. The XtreemOS PAM plugins would be in charge of implementing (or interfacing to) a local service allocating fresh local UID/GID couples upon request, of managing local UID names, of managing user home-directories (either from XtreemFS, the XtreemOS Grid file system [4], or on a scratch directory) and of managing the user credentials for XtreemFS access. The dynamic allocation of user accounts ensures XtreemOS scalability and reduces the complexity of VO management: no need to configure resources when users are added or removed from VOs.

During session initialization, XtreemOS stores the user security ticket in the kernel session keyring: this ticket will be associated to all local processes generated by the user request (fork, execve, etc.), and will be retrieved each time the global user identity or credentials need to be exploited: access to local or external service, auditing, ...

Dynamic management of local UID/GID also provides some level of isolation between Grid users: they do not share access to local files, and it is possible to hide the real identity of a user in the local name space. XtreemOS does not exclude the use of virtual machines, or process containers, to provide stronger isolation properties, like performance isolation (e.g. hiding CPU usage, memory limits).

The policy enforcement points provide access control and auditing on operating system services. Fine grain access control is also possible when the application activity generates requests to external services. This is the case for XtreemFS or NFSv4 filesystems. Fine grain access control and auditing on operating system objects (processes, sockets, ...), requiring the support of the Linux kernel, can be provided through the LSM (Linux Security Module framework).

4.   Related Work

This section briefly discusses two exemplary tools that are relevant to XtreemOS in the area of VO management.

VOMS [5] is an important VO reference implementation to XtreemOS because it is currently a popular approach to integrate VO information (e.g. a user's roles in a VO) into node-level enforcement mechanisms.

However, managing VOMS effectively is an non-trivial task because authorization decisions are often a result of a joint process between the VOMS server (participating in the form of VOMS credentials) and nodes. Because both node policy and configuration will be taken into account, it is difficult to figure out what privileges a user has at a given time for a certain job. This is a practical issue which can be a potential hurdle for the future acceptance of XtreemOS.

In order to make node-level access control and account mapping decisions, nodes need to be knowledgeable of VO properties (e.g. roles and groups). However, managing such knowledge consistently and coherently can be non-trivial. This becomes a potential scalability problem for large VOs with a significant number of properties. It also makes it difficult to create new VOs and introduce new properties dynamically.

CAS takes control over the policy specification by explicitly spelling out the relationship between VO users and resources [6]. CAS represents a push model of enforcing VO policies because its policy enforcement is decoupled from VO information (e.g. user groups/roles). Therefore, it is comparatively easy to create dynamic VOs using the CAS model. However, it is not always easy to figure out what VO resources users need to use in advance.

Overall, VOMS and CAS represent two different ends of the spectrum. VOMS is lean to a pull model where access control is done at nodes by pulling policy information on demand (i.e. from the VOMS credentials) whilst CAS is a push model where authorization decisions are being pushed to nodes. Both are complementary to each other. Because XtreemOS aims to provide generic OS level support for Grids, we are investigating a combined use of both models in our system.

5. Conclusions

In this paper, we have described the outcome of the first stage of the XtreemOS project which has concentrated on developing requirements and initial architectural design of VO support, at both the kernel level and within the Grid support services of XtreemOS. This work is ongoing. The initial prototype of XtreemOS which will provide the basic instantiation of this architecture is under implementation. This will then be tested on a variety of use cases and further refined.

Further extensions to the basic VO support are planned. These would include: mechanisms for federated authentication; trialing of expressive policy languages; the role of virtualisation to support highly secure commercial VOs; the integration of trust domains. Further, we regard it an essential for a practical system that there should be some assurance provided that the systems does meet recognised security criteria. Work is ongoing to derive a systematic analysis of threats to the XtreemOS system, with a view to validating the integrity of XtreemOS.

References

[1] Ian Foster, Carl Kesselman and Steven Tuecke. The Anatomy of the Grid Enabling Scalable Virtual Organizations. http://www.globus.org/alliance/publications/papers/anatomy.pdf

[2] XtreemOS consortium. Requirements and specification of XtreemOS services for Application Execution Management. Deliverable D3.3.1, November 2006. http://www.xtreemos.org/publications/public-deliverables/.

[3] XtreemOS consortium. Requirements Capture and Use Case Scenarios. Deliverable D4.2.1, January 2007. http://www.xtreemos.org/publications/public-deliverables/.

[4] XtreemOS consortium. The XtreemOS File System. Requirements and Reference Architecture. Deliverable D3.4.1, December 2006. http://www.xtreemos.org/publications/public-deliverables/.

[5] DataGrid VOMS (release v0.7.1). http://edg-wp2.web.cern.ch/edg-wp2/security/voms/

[6] CAS in Globus 4.2. http://www.globus.org/toolkit/docs/development/4.2-drafts/security/cas/

[7] Andrew G. Morgan and Thorsten Kukuk. The Linux-PAM guides. http://www.kernel.org/pub/linux/libs/pam/Linux-PAM-html/.

SEALED GRID WITH DOWNLOADABLE SERVICES

Martin Kuba, Daniel Kouřil, Michal Procházka
Masaryk University, Botanická 68a, 602 00 Brno, Czech Republic
{makub,kouril,michalp}@ics.muni.cz

Abstract   In a service-based grid, the data to be processed are usually moved to the service. However this is not always possible for security and data privacy reasons, as in biomedical grids processing patients' data. The other way, moving services to the location of the data, brings challenges in dealing with heterogeneity of deployment environments. A solution for this problem is proposed in this paper, based on services deployed in hardware virtual machines. Such setting allows a user to download all needed grid services into a tightly controlled environment, possibly even disconnected from the network, thus creating a "sealed grid" for processing sensitive data.

Keywords: grid, services, virtual machines, trusted platform module

1.   Introduction

The vision of Grid was originally motivated by High Performance Computing community needs to pool resources in order to have more computing power and to be able to solve computationally intensive problems in less time. However, over time, more diverse communities become interested in the Grid not because they needed more computational power, but because they needed the sharing of resources across organizational boundaries, which Grid enables, and these resources were not only processors and disk storage, but also remotely controlled instruments, information and knowledge.

Our work in the MediGrid project is focused on the type of the grid, intended for sharing knowledge in the biomedical domain, which can be expressed algorithmically and shared among geographically dispersed medical specialists [1, 3, 4]. The biomedical knowledge is encapsulated as data processing grid services, and the grid infrastructure helps its users to discover and apply the services to their data.

This type of grid is not a High Performance Computing (HPC) grid, nor a High Throughput Computing (HTC) grid, as the point here is not to do a large amount of computing or to process a lot of data. The medical applications usually do not need to process large amounts of data, and the processing is not very computation heavy. But one of the three defining features of a grid is that it "coordinates resources that are not subject to a centralised control" [2]. And this is the essence of the MediGrid – it coordinates medical knowledge resources owned by independent organizations, providing non-trivial quality of service by combining them. So it is the sharing of resources across organizational boundaries, that needs the usage of grid technologies, and makes clusters or other centrally administered tools insufficient.

The biomedical domain has particular requirements for dealing with patients' data, as most countries have special laws protecting personal data, and the data about patients cannot effectively leave the institution which collected them. Even when such biomedical data are anonymized, i.e. all identification data like name, address, date of birth, and various identification numbers are removed, it is not possible to completely anonymize all data. For example, there are some diseases so rare that only several patients suffer from them in a whole country and the mere fact that an anonymous patient has the disease is sufficient to identify the patient.

Given such limiting restriction on handling data, it is often not possible to send the data outside the hospital or the other biomedical institution for processing. So if we need to process such data, the only option is the other way round, to move the processing software to the location of the data. Note that this is the opposite of the classic computational grids, where the valuable resource is the computing power. Here computing power is not important, and the valuable resource is the knowledge behind the processing algorithms.

Our biomedical users specifically expressed the desire to be able to "download" all grid services into their personal computer and then disconnect from the network, so that they can be sure that no data would leak. Such a disconnected personal computer running a whole grid is a special case of a more general scenario, in which grid services are downloaded and put into a tightly controlled grid environment separating them from the outside world. The tightly controlled grid environment is administered by a single organization owning the data to be processed, so the organization can be sure that the privacy of the data cannot be compromised. Such a tightly controlled grid environment we can call a "sealed grid", because no data can escape from it. It is discussed in the section 2.

However, moving software to data has its problems too, namely requirements for the execution environment. A promising way how to satisfy the requirements is the use of hardware virtual machines, where images of virtual computers with complete operating system and installed services can be downloaded and deployed, as is detailed in the section 3.

The possibility of moving services to data brings some consequences for responsibility for the quality of data processing, which is discussed in the section 4.

An important issue in biomedicine is the reproducibility of services' results, and that can be solved with the help of hardware Trusted Platform Module chips, now available in many new computers. This issue is discussed in the section 5.

An extension of the idea of a sealed grid is then given in the section 6, where a machine outside the data owning organization can be used with the trade-off that the downloadable images of grid services must be checked before deployment.

2.   Sealed Grid Environment

As was sketched out in the section 1, there are domains where data confidentiality and privacy are paramount. But even these domains may profit from sharing resources on the grid, just it is not the data that may be transfered across organizational boundaries. Then it must be the software for data processing, that must be transfered.

Because the data must not be in any case transfered outside the owning organization, the software must be put into a sealed environment, which will not allow any communication outside its boundaries.

Providing software in the form of services, the so called Service Oriented Architecture, solves many problems with dependencies and interdependencies. Thus wrapping the software as services with interfaces described in machine-understandable format, registered in a service registry, is the current architecture of choice.

There may be more infrastructure services than just the service registry. In the case of our biomedical grid, we added services for ranking of services, for semantically aided building of a workflow and executing the workflow. We can assume that the ranking of services and building of workflow can be done on the "open grid", as it does not involve the sensitive data. However, for the data processing, the infrastructure services for registry and workflow execution need to be available *inside* the sealed environment, as the deployed data processing services would not be able to reach them otherwise. So the sealed environment will need to provide a private copy of a part of the grid infrastructure, at least the service registry, into which the services must register themselves.

3.   Service Deployment in Hardware Virtual Machines

Every software has requirements on its execution environment in terms of specific versions of operating systems, installed libraries or other software on which it depends.

Even programs made for an execution environment specified in terms of application-level virtual machines, like languages compiled into bytecode (Java JVM, .NET CLI) or scripting languages (JavaScript, Shell, Perl, etc.) usually do not run exactly in the same way on all implementations and versions of the target platform. It is an inherent problem, because various implementations of the same platform have different bugs, and an application must work around all of them. A famous example is JavaScript implementations in WWW browsers, where each version of each browser behavior differs slightly from the others. Sometimes even the same version of the same browser behaves differently on different versions of the same operating system. This problem is caused by the simple fact that the execution environment specification provides too large space for errors and depends on the expected behavior of all standard libraries.

On the other hand, *hardware virtual machines* (HVM) [5], like VMware or Xen, provide discrete execution environments on a single computer, each of which runs an operating system, thus providing the illusion of having an entire computer. Software deployed inside a hardware virtual machine can have exactly its required execution environment. All dependencies on a specific operating system and its version, installed libraries or other software, are trivially satisfied.

The touching point between the whole virtual computer and the virtual machine is much smaller than in the case of the application-level virtual machines. It is mostly the CPU instruction set and a few peripherals like the network card that need to be properly emulated, and in the case of the CPU it is often even delegated to the real CPU, so the space for error is much smaller.

An image of a virtual computer, including its file system and state of memory, can be packaged as a single file, and transferred over the Internet. Thus a grid service can be installed inside a virtual computer, which can be than packaged and distributed as a downloadable image.

There are already images available on the Internet with pre-installed Linux and selected applications, like a database server, a web server, or anti-virus email gateway, each packaged in a file just few megabytes large.

When such a HVM image with a grid service inside is deployed and started, it can obtain an IP address using DHCP, and the service can search for a service registry (using network broadcast or multicast) and register itself in the registry. In this way the private service registry inside the sealed environment would be aware of all the available services.

4.   Downloaded Services and Trusted Computing

In the biomedical domain the data processing is a very sensitive issue. Not only the data must be kept confidential, also the responsibility for the quality of data processing needs to be known. Thus digital signatures of data producers attached to all data are highly desirable. However, when a service is run under the control of its provider, the provider can take some responsibility for the quality of processing, but when the service is downloaded from its provider and subsequently run by the data owner, the original provider is unlikely to take full responsibility, as the service is no longer under its control. In that case the data owner should provide the signatures.

Thus every service instance should be able to provide the signature of the subject which currently runs it. In the case of the hardware virtual machines we can leverage the TPM chip (Trusted Platform Module) which becomes routinely available in all modern computers. The TPM chip uniquely identifies each computer and stores private keys. Software can utilize the TPM chip to encrypt data so that when the data is moved to another computer, it becomes unusable.

The chip is accessible from hardware virtual machines [8], so a downloaded image of a HVM can use the credentials of the hosting real hardware computer. Thus a grid service deployed inside a HVM can have the identity of its original provider, when run on its hardware, and it can have the identity of the data owner when downloaded and run by the data owner.

Trusted Platform Module

The Trusted Platform Module (TPM) [7] is one of the building blocks of the Trusted Computing Platform (TCG) [6], which aims to setup controlled secure environment. The TCG covers many parts including network communication, operating systems, client applications and users credentials. It defines specifications in each area, which a secure environment must comply with. TPM is a microcontroller chip which is bound to the motherboard of a PC. TPM is used in this environment for number of purposes. It uniquely identifies the computer, it does basic cryptographic operations and can be used as a secure storage for RSA keys. Till now TPM looks like a typical hardware token but TPM has more functionality. It can be used for providing hashes of states of the system; these hash values can be verified by other parties thus checking the integrity of a remote system. TPM modules can talk to each other and can exchange keys in a secure way.

Main components of the TPM are Attestation Identity Key (AIK), Endorsement key (EK), Platform Configuration Registers (PCRs), Random Number Generator (RNG), and Direct Autonomous Attestation (DAA). The EK is implemented as X.509 certificate with its private key stored in the TPM. The TPM protects the private key and prevents from exporting it elsewhere. The EK is used for establishing that AIK keys were generated in the TPM. AIK is also in the form of a X.509 certificate, it is used for providing identification of the TPM to other parties. PCRs are special registers that can hold hashes, hashes can be changed only by authorized users or with the knowledge of the previous value from which the previous hash was computed. DAA is a protocol which can securely and anonymously transfer data from remote TPM's PCRs.

5.   Service Integrity and Versioning

Using images of hardware virtual machines gives us also another advantage, which is easy checking for software integrity and correct version. The HVM image can be checksummed (with MD5 or other checksum) and that checksum can be compared to a value obtained from a trusted source. This solves the problem with versioning—a service consumer can be sure that a service is identical to a proven and tested version of the service, and was not silently upgraded by its provider, possibly removing some known bugs and introducing new ones.

The ability to check that a service was not modified is crucial for obtaining reproducible results, which is important in biomedicine. It is very hard or maybe intractable to ensure that a remotely accessed service was not modified, because the only thing that a service consumer has is the service's contract, its interface. Its implementation is hidden and can be replaced anytime. The separation of the interface and implementation is a defining feature of services. But without access to the implementation, the service consumer cannot check that the implementation was not modified, and thus reproducibility of the results cannot be ensured.

When using downloadable services in hardware virtual machines, the service consumer has the service implementation wrapped inside the HVM, so a simple checksum can verify that a service was not modified. In the knowledge grid with potentially many highly specialized data processing services, that we are working on, users need to know an exact version of a service, because they select services based on reputation of the services. Also, it is a known practice in computational chemistry, that some bugs in software are never corrected, even when everybody knows that the bugs are present, so that the results of computations are comparable. The reproducibility of results is clearly more important to such users than the correctness of the results. Knowing that a service was not modified is then a natural requirement.

Secure Credential Delegation to Services

In our architecture the images of hardware machines will be available from specialized repositories maintained by skilled administrators and users who have the expertise necessary to install the system and application inside the images. The images and their corresponding description will be cryptographically signed using the private key of the maintainer who produced the image. Such a precaution will make it possible for the end users to verify integrity of the retrieved image and also to identify its producer if necessary. Thus, a user who specified her personal preferences can choose an image produced by a preferred image provider in an easy and trusted manner.

Once the image is downloaded from the repository and verified it can be installed into a virtual machine. After loading into the machine it is necessary to personalize it using the identity of the user. In order to provide a secure yet easy way to personalize multiple virtual machines we will use the key migration mechanism supported by the TPM specification. The migration protocol makes it possible to transfer sensitive data (e.g. private keys) between two TPMs in a secure way without revealing the content to any third-party entity who has access to communication, including administrators of the TPM machines. Using the migration process it is possible for a user to send her private keys to the virtual machines where she prepared the images.

Once started all the services will use the user's identity and thus they will be able to work on the user's behalf. The user has full control over the location where her private key was installed and the migration process ensures the credentials cannot be intercepted during the transition. Such an approach can be viewed as a viable alternative to the wide-spread use of proxy certificates that do not provide the needed control over their use to their owner once they are delegated to a service.

6. Sealing an open environment using TPM

The notion of a sealed grid was motivated by the possibility of having a controlled environment consisting only of trusted machines inside an organization, which are not connected to any outside network. In this case the data are only processed by the internal machines and cannot leak outside the organization. If we relax slightly the strict requirements on private processing and want to allow the data to be handled in more open environment we could benefit from the remote attestation mechanism that is one of the crucial components of the trusted computing. Using this mechanism it is possible to check integrity of any remote machine using the TPM as well as verify applications run by the machine. In our architecture the machines would run an HVM instance and the user deploying images of virtual machines would first verify the HVM is correct and has not been tampered with and only then install the image on the machine.

7.   Conclusion

We have presented a grid solution for domains where data confidentiality, results reproducibility and defined responsibility for data processing are the important requirements, like in the domain of biomedicine. The solution is based on deploying services in hardware virtual machines, whose images can be packaged and downloaded over the Internet. The downloaded images can be put into a sealed environment with a copy of the part of a grid infrastructure that is needed for data processing. No data can escape from such a sealed environment, so the data confidentiality is guaranteed.

The downloaded images of virtual machines with grid services can use user credentials to sign produced data thanks to hardware TPM chips, which store private keys and are even able to delegate user credentials from one computer to another one in a secure way, that even administrators of the machines cannot intercept them.

8.   Acknowledgments

This research is supported by a research intent "Optical Network of National Research and Its New Applications" (MSM6383917201) and research project "MediGrid – methods and tools for GRID application in biomedicine" (Czech Academy of Sciences, grant T202090537)

References

[1] Kuba M., Krajíček O., Lesný P., Vejvalka J. and Holeček Tomáš. "Grid Empowered Sharing of Medical Expertise", Proceedings of HealthGrid 2006, IOS Press, Amsterdam, NL, 2006. ISBN: 1-58603-617-3

[2] Foster I. "What is the Grid? A Three Point Checklist", GRIDToday, July 2002

[3] Bocchi L., Krajíček O., Kuba M.: Infrastructure for Adaptive Workflows in Semantic Grids. Proceedings of the first CoreGRID Integration Workshop. Pisa : University of Pisa, 2005. p. 327-336. 2005, Pisa, Italy

[4] Kuba M., Krajíček O., Lesný P., Holeček T.: Semantic Grid Infrastructure for Applications in Biomedicine. DATAKON 2005 - Proceedings of the Annual Database Conference: 2005, p. 335-344. 2005, Brno, Czech Republic, ISBN 80-210-3813-6

[5] Figueiredo R., Dinda P. and Fortes J. "A case for grid computing on virtual machines", In proceedings of Distributed Computing Systems, 2003, pages 550-559.

[6] Trusted Computing Group,
http://www.trustedcomputinggroup.org.

[7] Trusted Computing Group. "Trusted Platform Module Main Specification, Part 1: Design Principles, Part 2: TPM Structures, Part 3: Commands". October 2003, Version 1.2, Revision 62, http://www.trustedcomputinggroup.org.

[8] Procházka M., "Usage of TPM under the Xen". DESY, Hamburg, Germany : 2007

III

PROGRAMMING WITH SOFTWARE COMPONENTS

INTEROPERABILITY OF GRID COMPONENT MODELS: GCM AND CCA CASE STUDY*

Maciej Malawski[†] and Marian Bubak
Institute of Computer Science and ACC CYFRONET
AGH University of Science and Technology
Al. Mickiewicza 30, 30-059 Krakow, Poland
malawski@agh.edu.pl

Françoise Baude, Denis Caromel, Ludovic Henrio and Matthieu Morel
INRIA Sophia Antipolis – CNRS – Univ. of Nice Sophia Antipolis
2004, Route des Lucioles, BP 93 FR-06902 Sophia Antipolis, France
francoise.baude@inria.fr

Abstract   This paper presents a case study in the generic design of Grid component models. It defines a framework allowing two component systems, one running in a CCA environment, and another running in a Fractal environment, to interact as if they were elements of the same system. This work demonstrates the openness of both Fractal and CCA component models. It also gives a very generic and exhaustive overview of the interaction strategies that can be adopted to allow full integration of these two models, like strategies for reusing in Fractal single components from the CCA world and connecting a Fractal system to an already running CCA assembly. Finally, it presents the implementation and results of investigation of interoperability between two given component frameworks: MOCCA and ProActive. In generall, this paper presents the key concepts useful to make any two component models interoperate.

Keywords: Component model, interoperability, CCA, Fractal, GCM, MOCCA, ProActive

*This work was supported by EU IST CoreGRID project and Polish grant SPUB-M.
[†] Support from the Foundation for Polish Science is kindly acknowledged.

1. Introduction

Component model may be considered as one of the most appropriate paradigm for programming Grid applications [7]. It allows to tackle the problem of complexity originating from an application and an infrastructure by providing such features as composition by interfaces, support for flexible deployment and reconfiguration mechanisms.

There are few component models which address the Grid applications: the most important ones are Common Component Architecture (CCA) [3], Grid extensions of CCM (CORBA Component Model) [10] and Grid Component Model (GCM) [1] developed recently by CoreGRID project. GCM is based on the Fractal [5] and is being developed as a standard component model for programming the Grid. To achieve this goal, the abilities to interoperate with existing applications and to integrate existing "legacy" components are required. The CCA model which has been developed by the HPC community for several years, now has a number of implementations (frameworks) such as CCAFFEINE [3], XCAT [9] and MOCCA [11], and scientific components are expected to be available soon. Therefore, the problem of interoperability between GCM and CCA becomes an interesting and important issue.

In this paper, we address the problem of interoperability between GCM and CCA component models. We focus on the base component model of GCM, namely Fractal, as it defines the fundamental properties of the components and their interactions. We start with an analysis of both models to identify similarities and differences between them. Next, we discuss integration strategies and propose the solutions to the identified problems, such as issues with typing system. We propose a generic and framework independent solution, which is based on the adapter (wrapper) design pattern. In order to validate the approach, we have developed a prototype, which allows ProActive (a GCM prototype) [4] and MOCCA (a CCA implementation) [11] frameworks to interoperate. The extensions to Fractal introduced in GCM, such as collective interfaces and autonomic controllers are left for the future work.

2. Background

Interoperability can be defined as an ability of two or more entities to communicate and cooperate despite differences in the implementation language, the execution environment, or the model abstraction [14]. Today, a popular solution for interoperability between components is Web Services where standardized protocols based on XML provide the common language for applications to communicate [6]. This has been successfully applied also to high-performance modules like ASSIST modules, wrapped as GRID.it components [2].

Interoperability has been outlined as a requisite for the Grid Component Model: a realistic programming model, in the context of heterogeneous systems, component frameworks and legacy software, must be able to interoperate with existing component frameworks and allow applications to be built from a mixture of various kinds of components. Naturally, the GCM proposes to achieve general component interoperability through standardized web services. Besides of it there are alternative interoperability approaches: our idea is to introduce mediators and adapters to build up an ad-hoc interoperability layer between selected component frameworks without superimposing on them another general-purpose interoperability framework (like a CORBA bus, or a meta-component model implemented on top of some selected existing component frameworks [13]). This alternative approach is undertaken in the work described in this paper.

3.   Overview of CCA and GCM

The CCA[3] specification is defined using the Scientific Interface Description Language (SIDL) [8] which specifies the core entities: components, ports and a framework. Ports are the external interfaces of a component and they must extend the `Port` interface. A component declares both its client and server interfaces called *uses* and *provides* ports respectively. The framework is represented to the component by the `Services` interface, which is used by the component to register its ports. This interface also defines a `getPort()` method which allows a component to obtain a reference to the uses port in order to invoke methods on this client interface. The external interface exposed by the framework to the application developers is called `BuilderService`. It provides methods for creating/destroying component instances and connecting/disconnecting their ports. Besides of these core interfaces, CCA also specifies optional ports, such as component repository, connection event service, service registry and parameter ports, intended to facilitate interoperability between different frameworks.

Fractal is a *hierarchical* component model that provides *introspection* and *intercession*; it is easily *extensible* [5]. There are two kinds of components in Fractal: *primitive* components which are black boxes, and *composite* components that are composed of other components and can be used to build up yet other composites. Fractal enforces a clear separation between functional and non-functional aspects; non-functional features are provided by *controllers*, and encapsulated in a *membrane*. This model provides reconfiguration (adding, removing, binding, and unbinding) of the functional content of composites components, in order to support adaptivity of the component systems.

The GCM is a component model targeted at Grid computing, which focuses on the following extensions to the base Fractal model:

- A *deployment* paradigm based on virtual nodes allowing to specify a logical deployment of a system, and a physical deployment separately.

- Support for *several communication patterns*. First, asynchronous method calls is considered as the default semantics, and other semantics as streaming and event-based communication may be supported. A major contribution of the GCM is to standardize multicast and gathercast interfaces that allow 1-to-n and n-to-1 communications.

- Support for *non-functional adaptivity and autonomicity*. The GCM specifies how to design non-functional aspects in a component way, and thus allow the reconfiguration of the non-functional features of a component system. Finally, a set of autonomic controllers is also standardized and they allow component to adapt themselves in a much hierarchical and autonomous way.

4.   Comparison of CCA and Fractal

Both CCA and Fractal component models enforce a separation between interface and their implementation, allow composition of applications by connecting client and server ports of components, and provide some reflective capabilities.

The basic and obvious similarity is that the functional interfaces of components in both models are equivalent, e.g. when considering Java implementation, both Fractal and CCA components are Java classes implementing their functional interfaces and some additional interfaces imposed by the specification. Interaction between components in both models is based on the method invocation on the client interface which is connected to a server counterpart.

The first conceptual difference is the way the components in both models interact with the outside world. In CCA, a component is given an explicit reference to the framework, and the component itself has the "initiative" to actively inform the framework about its internals, i.e. ports (interfaces). On the other hand, the Fractal model assumes that the component has a passive role in the introspection process and can reveal its internals on demand.

The second difference is the way the component interfaces are connected. In CCA the BuilderService is responsible for creating the connections and the framework manages them, while the component is only required to invoke getPort() method to get a valid reference to the port before using its client interface. In Fractal, the connection is managed by the component, by implementing a BindingController interface.

ContentController in Fractal does not have its counterpart in CCA because CCA does not support composite components as explicitly as Fractal. Also, there is no standard life cycle controller mechanism.

Although CCA does not distinguish non-functional interfaces (controllers) there are some standard ports, which are optional. One of them is is a Basic-ParameterPort which can be used to read and modify arbitrary properties of a component, analogously to Fractal Attribute controller.

The mechanism of component creation is also different in both models. The method for creating instances in CCA is included in the BuilderService port, whereas Fractal defines the Factory interface for this purpose. In both cases the creation mechanism may be implementation specific, and depends on the actual framework.

Although there is no standard Application Description Language (ADL) for CCA components, the BuilderService provides all the required functionality to construct such a description. The Application Factory project defined the XML-based ADL for XCAT [9], whereas CCAFFEINE [3] defines its own scripting language for composing applications.

5.   Overcoming Typing and ADL Issues

One of the main issues in this work is to deal with the fact that Fractal (and GCM) components have an immutable type (i.e. a set of exported interfaces cannot evolve dynamically) whereas CCA component can subscribe new ports to be exported at any time. More precisely, in CCA, each component can register a port at any moment, so there is no concept such as a component type. On the contrary, in Fractal, except collection interfaces which can be instantiated several times along the life of the component, the type of a component and the set of its interfaces is fixed upon its instantiation. The "static" typing of Fractal components can be used to verify the correctness of the bindings, according to interface types. We propose the following ways of solving the typing issue:

1 Generate a Fractal component automatically upon instantiation of a CCA component, i.e. to use only the port declared by the setServices method. This allows to build a Fractal component automatically without any additional code (no ADL need to be specified) but prevents adding new ports after component initialization.

2 A programmer should specify the ADL for the CCA component. This means more manual effort, but no set of interfaces has to be automatically inferred. One of the main advantages of this approach is that some ports provided during the component lifetime could be specified as Fractal *optional* interfaces.

3 An improvement of the previous approach consists in generating the ADL specification upon a CCA component instantiation (not necessarily the real one) and then reuse the ADL inferred in the scenario 2 above. The user may then modify the ADL generated (to add some of the ports that will be provided during the component lifetime).

4 One can also generate an ADL from available CCA description (e.g. as SIDL [8]). The CCA script language (used by frameworks, but not

standardized) may be reused to declare which ports of the CCA component/assembly should be exported.

We have chosen the second approach as it seems the most general, it enables a very good understanding of the differences between CCA and Fractal, and it is centered on the interaction between the two frameworks. Moreover, it can be automatized later on with solutions 3 and 4.

In the all aforementioned approaches a mapping between exported CCA ports and GCM interfaces is required. More precisely, CCA ports are identified by the component name and port name, and this must be mapped to Fractal interfaces defined in the ADL. In other words, we need to define a bijection between CCA ports (i.e., component name + port name) and Fractal interfaces as it is defined in the ADL.

6. Integration Strategies

We separate CCA integration inside a GCM component system into two approaches: the encapsulation of a single CCA component (Section 6.1) and of a complete CCA system, consisting of several CCA components (Section 6.2).

Along the life time of a CCA-Fractal composition, the integration framework must support: (a) communication from the Fractal component system to the CCA system; (b) communication from the CCA system to Fractal components; (c) plugging or unplugging of Fractal interfaces to the CCA system (both on the client and on the server side); (d) exportation of new CCA ports if this is supported (see Sec. 5).

Additionally, we are looking for solution that are as general as possible, i.e. independent of CCA framework implementation as much as possible.

6.1   Simple Integration

We first focus on a simple case: how to encapsulate a single CCA component into a Fractal one?

The proposed solution enables the creation (instantiation) of a CCA component as a primitive Fractal component in a single address space. It relies on a wrapper that encapsulates a CCA component, and exposes cca.Services interface to a CCA component (see Fig. 1). Before instantiation we should know the type of a component in order to define the Fractal type of the component; this might be obtained from a provided ADL description.

In practice, the wrapper stores the references to bound interfaces and pass them to getPort() method. All the communication is done by a Fractal framework (no need to have any CCA framework running at all – the wrapper will constitute a mini-framework for that component).

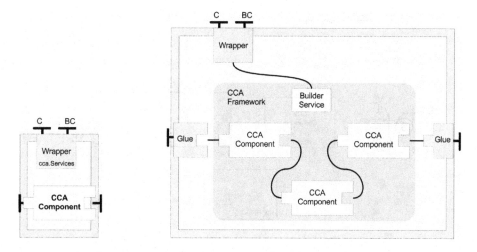

Figure 1. Integration of a single CCA component into a Fractal one

Figure 2. Interoperability between CCA and Fractal components

6.2 Real Interoperability

In this case CCA components are created in their own framework and they are connected to Fractal components running in their framework.

Complete interoperability between two frameworks requires instantiation of a whole CCA assembly, and ability to interact with it from a Fractal framework as if it was a Fractal composite component. In this case, we have a CCA component or a set of CCA components which are created and connected among themselves by a CCA framework (e.g. MOCCA). So, we wrap the component assembly as a Fractal component in such a way that it can be connected to other Fractal components.

The solution we propose is based on a wrapper which adds a Membrane to a CCA assembly. The wrapper should interact with the CCA framework only via `BuilderService` external interface (obtained in framework dependent manner). The wrapper is given the mapping between CCA system ports and external Fractal ports as discussed in Sec. 5 and using this information it creates Glue-Ports as CCA components (using `BuilderService` for each of the exported ports). The implementation of a GluePort is framework specific, and translates the Fractal invocations to CCA invocations and reversely. The GluePorts expose Fractal interfaces to the outside world, and they can be connected (bound) to other Fractal components using `BindingController` and `Component` interfaces of the wrapper. The wrapper uses the `BuilderService` to connect exported CCA ports to corresponding GluePorts using CCA framework,

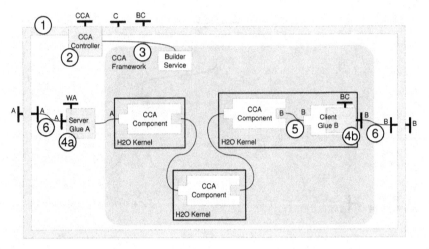

Figure 3. Wrapping an assembly of CCA components running in MOCCA framework as composite Fractal/ProActive component

so the communication between CCA component assembly and GluePorts is handled by the CCA framework.

In other words, the Wrapper component is both a CCA and a Fractal component. Although Fig. 2 shows the CCA system "inside" the wrapper, it is possible also to see the Fractal system from the CCA perspective as "wrapped" one, so the solution is symmetric.

7. Implementation - ProActive and MOCCA

In order to verify the proposed above solution a prototype using Java-based ProActive and MOCCA implementations was developed.

Integration of a single component was realized as planned in Sec. 6.1. A wrapper which encapsulates a CCA component and which exposes Services interface to a CCA component is created by the Fractal framework. The wrapper instantiates the CCA component as a local object and it invokes setServices (this) on a CCA component, passing the reference to itself. The CCA component registers its uses and provides ports, and consequently the wrapper can create direct (local) bindings to exported CCA ports.

In the real interoperability scenario we assume that there are CCA components running in a framework and connected using a mechanism specific to this framework (e.g. a script, or Java API), forming the existing CCA assembly. Fig. 3 shows the example of wrapping an assembly of three CCA components which provides one port of type A and uses one port of type B. The scenario consists of the following steps:

1 The Fractal framework creates a CompositeWrapper Component.

2 The wrapper implements a CCAController which is used to pass the description of the CCA assembly to the wrapper. This description includes all parameters allowing to connect the external ports of the assembly.

3 The reference to BuilderService is returned by a framework-specific bootstrap method. In the case of MOCCA the reference is obtained from the URI to Builder pluglet.

4 The type of Wrapper Component is obtained from an ADL or Fractal API invocations. Provided with the mapping from CCA ports to Fractal interfaces (Sec. 5), the wrapper creates the GluePorts:

   (a) For each Provides port of wrapped CCA assembly one ServerGlue port is created. It is created as a primitive Fractal component with one server interface and it has one attribute controller called WrapperAttributes, which is immediately used to pass the reference to the corresponding CCA provides port (see e.g. ServerGlue A on the Fig. 3). The ServerGlue component has a MOCCA client code which delegates the method invocation to the wrapped component.

   (b) For each Uses port of the wrapped system one ClientGlue is created: it is a primitive one, becoming *at the same time* the Fractal and CCA component. It is instantiated in H2O kernel (a container for MOCCA) and upon creation it launches ProActive runtime to expose the BindingController (BC). Consequently, ClientGlue can be connected to CCA components on its server side and to Fractal interfaces on the client side (see ClientGlue B on the Fig. 3).

5 The wrapper uses the BuilderService to connect the exported CCA uses ports to corresponding GluePorts.

6 CCAController connects all Glue ports to the composite Wrapper using standard Fractal bindings.

7 Fractal BindingController of a composite wrapper may be used to connect exported ports to other interfaces of the Fractal application.

It should be noted that both Client and Server Glue components are conceptually symmetric and their role is to translate invocations from one framework to the other. It was the implementation choice to create a Server Glue as ProActive component which includes the MOCCA code, whereas a Client Glue is created as MOCCA component with an "embedded" ProActive one (Fig. 3).

8.   Conclusions and Future Work

The analysis of CCA and GCM component models, shows that despite some differences, it is feasible to integrate components from one model into another framework, as well as to create the glue code which enables inter-framework interoperability. The prototype functionality has been verified with a number of examples, including a non-trivial application (simulation of gold cluster formation [12]) and integrated with the ProActive library.

We observed that if the properties of two different component models can be well understood, then the generation of wrappers and glue code bridging two different component frameworks can be generic and thus automated.

Our approach resembles the one adopted in SciRun2 [13] with Bridge components acting like our GluePort ones. However, we avoid introducing the notion of a new (meta) component model and we allow components running in their native frameworks to interoperate (i.e. not requiring an additional one).

Future work will focus on automatic ADL building, generation of glue at runtime, investigating advanced features by which GCM extends Fractal model and performance tests to measure the overhead introduced by glue layer.

References

[1] CoreGRID Programming Model Virtual Institute. Basic features of the grid component model (assessed), 2006. Deliverable D.PM.04, CoreGRID, http://www.coregrid.net.

[2] M. Aldinucci et al. Building interoperable grid-aware ASSIST applications via WebServices. In *PARCO 2005: Parallel Computing*, pages 145–152, Malaga, Spain, 2005.

[3] R. Armstrong et al. The CCA component model for high-performance scientific computing. *Concurr. Comput. : Pract. Exper.*, 18(2):215–229, 2006.

[4] F. Baude et al. From distributed objects to hierarchical grid components. volume 2888 of *LNCS*, pages 1226 – 1242. Springer, 2003.

[5] E. Bruneton, T. Coupaye, M. Leclercq, V. Quéma, and J.-B. Stefani. The FRACTAL component model and its support in Java. *Softw., Pract. Exper.*, 36(11-12):1257–1284, 2006.

[6] I. Foster. Service-oriented science. *Science*, 308(5723):814 – 817, 2005.

[7] V. Getov and T. Kielmann, editors. *Component Models and Systems for Grid Applications*. Springer, 2005.

[8] S. R. Kohn et al. Divorcing Language Dependencies from a Scientific Software Library. In *Proc. of the 10th SIAM Conf. on Parallel Processing for Sci. Comp.*, Portsmouth, USA, Mar. 2001. SIAM.

[9] S. Krishnan and D. Gannon. XCAT3: A Framework for CCA Components as OGSA Services. In *Proc. Int. Workshop on High-Level Parallel Progr. Models and Supportive Environments (HIPS)*, pages 90–97, Santa Fe, New Mexico, USA, Apr. 2004. IEEE.

[10] S. Lacour et al. Deploying CORBA components on a computational grid. volume 3083 of *LNCS*, pages 35 – 49. Springer, 2004.

[11] M. Malawski et al. MOCCA – towards a distributed CCA framework for metacomputing. In *Proceedings of the 10th HIPS Workshop in Conjunction with IPDPS*. IEEE, 2005.

[12] M. Malawski et al. Experiments with distributed component computing across grid boundaries. In *Proceedings of the HPC-GECO/CompFrame workshop in conjunction with HPDC 2006*, Paris, France, 2006.

[13] S. Parker et al. Integrating component-based scientific computing software. In M. A. Heroux et al., editors, *Frontiers of Parallel Processing For Scientific Computing*, chapter 15. SIAM, 2005.

[14] A. Vallecillo et al. Component interoperability. Technical Report ITI-2000-37, Departmento de Lenguajes y Ciencias de la Computacion, University of Malaga., 2000.

A COMPONENT PLUGIN MECHANISM AND FRAMEWORK FOR APPLICATION WEB SERVICES

Rainer Schmidt, Siegfried Benkner, and Maria Lucka
Department of Scientific Computing
University of Vienna
Nordbergstrasse 15/C/3
1090 Vienna, Austria
rainer@par.univie.ac.at

Abstract   We present the architecture and application of VGE-CCA, a distributed component framework that is layered atop a Web service based Grid environment. The framework implements the CCA component model and utilizes the Vienna Grid Environment (VGE) as underlying middleware. In this paper, we introduce the concept of application specific component libraries that can be easily plugged into the container. Moreover, we report work on coupling distributed and concurrently running application components that are dynamically assembled and executed as single application composites by clients. For co-scheduling the various application components, the system makes use of advance resource reservation as provided by the VGE QoS module. Furthermore, we discuss the component and composition model as well as its application to a service-oriented architecture.

Keywords: Grid, Web Services, Service-oriented Architecture, Component Architecture

1. Introduction

Grid technology provides tools and infrastructures for the coordinated sharing of computational resources that are physically distributed, spanning multiple administrative domains. The adoption of Web service technology for Grid computing environments has been a major research issue in this area, providing defined access mechanisms for distributed resources based on Web service standards like XML, SOAP, and WSDL. Service-based Grids typically comprise of various collaborating services providing capabilities like security, information, data or resource management as described by the OGSA [8] specification. An important challenge in this area is the development of software engineering methods for Grid applications that are built upon a multitude of services as well as programming models that hide the complexity of the underlying environment.

Component technology provides a powerful way for constructing complex software systems by decoupling software implementation from application assembly. Several successful frameworks for developing distributed scientific application exists (e.g. XCAT3 [13], ProActive [2], ICENI [9], Paco++ [15], MOCCA [14]) implementing and extending a variety of component models including Corba, CCA, Fractal, or Web services. The Common Component Architecture [5] (CCA) specification defined by the CCA Forum [6] is specifically designed for the development of large scale scientific applications. The architecture focuses on the integration of existing scientific software libraries into a framework for component creation, introspection, and composition, which fits well into the Web/Grid services model as described in [11].

In this paper, we present the architecture and application of VGE-CCA, a distributed CCA implementation that allows to develop, deploy, and assemble component-based high performance applications for a Web service based Grid environment. The framework builds upon the Vienna Grid Environment [4] (VGE) - a Grid infrastructure for secure, automatic and QoS aware provision of compute-intensive applications running on parallel hardware over standard Web service technology. We introduce a mechanism allowing to extend VGE components using application specific software libraries that can be easily plugged into the container. Furthermore, we report work on coupling distributed and co-scheduled application components that are dynamically assembled by clients and run as single application composites. The following sections provide an overview of the architecture and implementation of the VGE-CCA framework as well as the underlying Grid middleware. We discuss the component and composition model as well as its application to a service-oriented architecture. Finally, we present conclusions and future work.

2. The VGE Grid Infrastructure

2.1 Architectural Overview and Technologies

The Vienna Grid Environment [4] is a service-oriented Grid infrastructure for the on-demand provision of HPC applications as Grid services and for the construction of client-side applications that access Grid services. The VGE service provision framework is based on a generic application service model and automates the provision of HPC applications as services based on standard Web service technology such as SOAP, WSDL, WS-Addressing, and WS-Security. VGE supports a flexible QoS negotiation model where clients may dynamically negotiate QoS guarantees on execution time and price with potential service providers. A VGE Grid usually comprises multiple services and clients, one or more service registries for maintaining a list of service providers and the services they support, and a certificate authority for providing an operational PKI infrastructure and end-to-end security based on X.509 certificates. VGE is being utilized and evaluated in the context of the EU Project GEMSS [3] and @neurist [1] which develop Grid infrastructures for medical simulation services and data access.

2.2 Services provided by VGE Containers

VGE generic application services are configurable software units that provide common operations for remote job management, data staging, error recovery, and QoS negotiation.

The **file handling service** provides operations for uploading and downloading input/output data based on file transfer via SOAP attachments. Support for direct data exchange between services is provided by corresponding *push* and *pull* operations. The **job execution service** provides operations for launching and managing remote jobs by interfacing with a *compute resource manager*. VGE does not provide means for clients to send job scripts to the server and only allows application providers to control which scripts are to be executed on the respective machines. The **QoS negotiation service** enables clients to dynamically negotiate with VGE services on a case-by-case basis on various QoS guarantees such as execution time and price. Resulting QoS contracts between service providers and clients are formulated as Web Service Level Agreements (WSLA) and go along with advance resource reservations. The **monitoring service** generates XML structured data regarding the application status and information gathered by individual monitoring scripts. The **error recovery service** provides support for checkpointing, restart, and migration, if supported by the application.

110

3. The Component and Composition Model

Scientific component frameworks implement and extend a variety of component models including Corba, CCA, Fractal, or Web services. A distinguishing aspect of existing component frameworks is the way they implement and exploit the various concepts of the component model. Another important design issue is the integration and leverage of a component framework with respect to the capabilities of the underlying system architecture. In the following, we briefly describe the component model and mechanisms implemented by the VGE-CCA framework.

3.1 Service-Oriented Architecture

The VGE-CCA component framework provides an abstraction layer and functionality that resides atop a Service-Oriented Architecture (SOA). This layer allows the construction of distributed Grid applications based on CCA mechanisms and transparently utilizes the underlying Web services layer. A SOA provides essential benefits such as loose coupling, location and implementation transparency. Well defined sequences of service invocations used to control remotely executing applications can be specified and executed using workflow representation and enactment techniques. VGE-CCA implements mechanisms that extend the service-oriented programming model allowing to directly interlink Web service components along accepted and provided interfaces, independently from workflow orchestration. The approach is powerful, enhancing VGE towards dynamic component interaction, data-flow, and the coupling of co-scheduled application components.

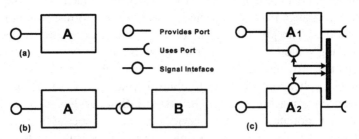

Figure 1. a) Independent Web Service b) RPC-based Component Interaction c) Event-based Application Coordination

3.2 Handling State and Composition

Figure 1 (a) depicts a Web service viewed as an encapsulated piece of software providing service through a typed interface (*provides port*). The software component may expose one or more interfaces, each defining a contract containing a set of operations together with binding information used by clients to invoke the service over a network. VGE-CCA extends this model by applying the concept of port dependencies allowing a Web service to express dependencies on services provided by other components based on defined interfaces called *uses ports*. A connection between two components, drawn by a client application developer, results in placing a handle to the selected service port into the connection table of the component requesting a remote port.

If a service maintains state, it is essential to establish a context between the requestor and the actual resource represented by the component. The way the component framework handles component instantiation is therefore an important aspect. In the context of Grid and Web services, instantiation can be realized by providing an application factory service as pointed out by Gannon et al. [10]. In VGE, we pursue a slightly different approach by maintaining a conversational identifier that is mapped to the respective application instance created and managed by the application service. In our model, stateless components may provide services (e.g. security) to other components but usually do not exhibit dependencies.

3.3 Types of Composition

VGE services encapsulate parallel applications and provide generic interfaces for controlling the execution of a component (scheduling, executing, monitoring) as well as operations for handling the data-flow between components (upload, download, data push). VGE services are stateful and multi-threaded creating a client context by maintaining a conversational identifier stored within the SOAP message header using WS-Addressing. The VGE-CCA framework provides libraries and services that extend the application services with the required mechanisms for component-based composition. Moreover, the framework provides a plugin mechanism that supports the development and deployment of individual *application component libraries* (clibs) (Section 4.1.1) encapsulating application specific logic, ports and dependencies. The current VGE-CCA implementation supports different types of composition which are explained in the following paragraphs:

Sequential Data-Flow: VGE components support data-flow by port connections allowing to directly stage i/o files between services (Figure 1 (b)). In such workflow scenario, the output of a computation typically serves as input for the following ones, for example an image reconstruction that is followed by a visualization. Data connections are explicitly controlled by the user and invoked through a corresponding *push* operation. A component may have data connections to multiple services which can be monitored and executed concurrently.

Coupled Parallel Applications: The *clibs* plugin mechanism provides the required functionality to transform applications running on different HPC computing resources into actively interacting components which can then be launched by clients as one composite application. The application components communicate through typed port-connections and may be coordinated by asynchronous message exchange using the signal interface (Figure 1 (c)). An example using distributed Ant colony optimization is described in section 4.1.1. The event mechanism is currently implemented as a one-to-many CCA port connection. For future versions, we plan to incorporate a notification-based system like WS-Notification. For co-scheduling concurrently running component instances, we utilize scheduling and advance resource reservation as provided by the VGE QoS module.

Stateless Service Dependencies: Within VGE Grids, stateless services are typically "supporting infrastructure elements" providing services like security or information. Infrastructure services are often directly utilized by the computing elements and usually do not require any session or scheduling mechanisms. A dependency on an infrastructure service can be explicitly visible to a client but is usually implicitly handled by the component and configured descriptively at service deployment time (e.g. auditing, security).

4. The VGE-CCA Component Framework

VGE-CCA implements a distributed component framework on top of a Web service based Grid of HPC application services as well as general infrastructure services such as security and information. A key design goal of VGE-CCA was the preservation of the service-oriented architecture and the provision of component extensions, without conflicting the Web services model. VGE-CCA provides a set of libraries that can be used to extend Web/Grid services as well as a set of infrastructure elements providing services to components and client runtimes. The software design allows to optionally install the VGE-CCA distribution without requiring to change code of existing services and thereby preserving the original interfaces and functionality. On the client-side, VGE-CCA provides support for component based application construction as well as workflow steering and execution.

4.1 Coupling Co-Scheduled Application Components

4.1.1 Pluggable Component Libraries (CLIBS). VGE-CCA provides a mechanism that allows to create individual software libraries that are specifically tailored to an underlying application. The component libraries (clips) can be plugged into VGE application services and are automatically deployed with the service. By default, VGE-CCA components provide interfaces for

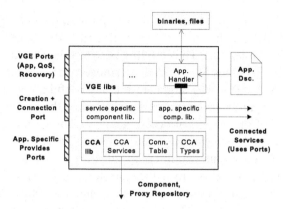

Figure 2. Design of a VGE-CCA component

application, data, and QoS management (cf. VGE) as well as a *Builder Service* for component creation, and connection (cf. CCA). *Clibs* are used to add individual ports, dependencies, or application specific logic to services running VGE-CCA. Moreover, the plugin mechanism allows to extend the behavior of existing services at defined entrance points, for example to trigger an activity right before/after a certain file is uploaded to the service. Application libraries are developed by subclassing a predefined component class that provides the mechanisms and handles required to augment the service and inject the desired behavior. The individual component libraries are descriptively configured and automatically loaded into the container at deployment time. Figure 2 shows a schematic design of a VGE-CCA component including VGE and CCA libraries as well as application and service specific *clibs*. Coordination among co-scheduled VGE components is distributed and currently handled using a simple signaling mechanism. The current implementation therefore extends the port connection mechanism towards supporting connections from one *uses* to n *provides* ports. Message generation and distribution is handled transparently by the framework.

4.1.2   Example: Ant Colony Optimization.   Consider an application using a parallel, savings-based ant colony optimization (ACO) algorithm to solve a vehicle routing problem [7]. The application implements a multi-colony approach where several colonies of ants cooperate in finding good solutions. On the fine-grained level, each colony of ants is partitioned into n (number of processors) subcolonies that share the same pheromone matrix. The goal of parallelizing the ACO algorithm is twofold: to speed up the execution and to improve the solution quality. In order to aggregate multiple computing clusters, the application has been distributed using a custom ant component library. The VGE component was extended in order to start a daemon that keeps track of the current local optimum, written to a file by the application. If a colony calculates a better solution than the global optimum the current solutions and parts of the pheromone information are multicasted to connected components using the *signal()* interface. The coupling between the individual ant colonies is loose allowing colonies to be added or removed during runtime.

The VGE-CCA client API targets to provide useful abstractions that allow component-based application construction by hiding the complexity of the distributed system. Components are co-scheduled using QoS constraints at creation time resulting in an advance resource reservation as provided by the VGE QoS module. Connections within composites are peer-based and interaction driven, which reduces complexity at the workflow level. In the case of ACO, the client developer constructs an application by interconnecting multiple distributed ant colony components. The experiment can then be run based on a single composite entity. The code snippet in LISTING 1 shows how the client API is used to create a (simple) ACO composite. Operations for runtime steering and monitoring provided by VGE application services (e.g. *start()*, *getStatus()*) can be used likewise with the application composite.

```
//Listing 1: Ant client snippet
VgeComponent ant1 = ComponentFactory.create(coid1); //...
VgeComponentGroup antComposite =
  new VgeComponentGroup(ant1, ant2, ant3);
antComposite.upload(vrp_infile);
antComposite.start(); //...
```

4.2   The Software Distribution

In the following, we provide a short description comprising the basic building blocks of the VGE-CCA distribution. For a detailed description of implemented CCA mechanisms the reader is referred to [16].

A library package implementing the **service-side CCA framework** (Figure 2) is used to equip the application service with additional interfaces for remote component registration (component interface), creation, and connection (builder interface). Additionally, the Web service is provided with a local CCA *services* library, a connection table, as well as the component plugin mechanism used to create and insert individual application components. The CCA libraries are in general used by the application component but may also be used by the individual service implementation to locate and directly connect to infrastructure services, e.g. auditing, or certificate revocation list retrieval.

A **component registry** realized as Web service implements the remote portion of the CCA *services* interface. Components register the ports they provide as well as dependencies on other components by descriptors containing the required information for discovering and utilizing the component (e.g. interface descriptors, proxy class, associated properties). Moreover, a *provides* port may also be associated with a proxy implementation that can be uploaded to the proxy registry and dynamically retrieved by components or clients. The registry service allows for dynamic service discovery and delivers the information required for component introspection (e.g. supported ports, underlying application, QoS attributes) and for component interaction (component handle, binding information) back to the requestor.

The programming environment is provided as a versatile Java **client API** that supports the creation and execution of distributed applications. Components may be described and created based on an unique identifier or an abstract component description. Applicable services are located and selected at runtime using the registry service. Client assemblies are created by interconnecting pairs of compliant *uses* and *provides* ports, which results in the establishment of peer connections between the services. The API is extensible and has a layered design supporting messaging and security, general programming constructs such as basic CCA types and mechanisms, as well as specialized application components and composites. A **negotiation broker** service is utilized during the component creation phase to locate and create components that meet a certain Quality of Service level. The broker service utilizes the capabilities provided by the VGE QoS module to negotiate with multiple services on the various QoS guarantees. The VGE-CCA client environment integrates QoS support by providing means for qualitatively describing a VGE component. The negotiation and selection of an appropriate component is transparently delegated to the negotiation broker. A successful QoS negotiation goes along with an advance reservation of the required resource, i.e. the number of nodes on a cluster within a certain time frame, which is an essential mechanism used by the framework to co-schedule coupled application components.

5. Conclusion and Future Work

VGE-CCA serves as a framework for constructing Grid applications from native application components provided by HPC application services. We introduced a plugin mechanism for application specific component libraries allowing to specifically tailor VGE services to the underlying application. Furthermore, we presented mechanisms and an example for coupling co-scheduled application components into single composite entities on the client side. The current VGE-CCA distribution relies on Java and Web services technology. All Web service interfaces and types are described using XML schema which allows bindings to clients and components in other programming languages, such as C++ or Microsoft .Net. For future work, we plan to work on interoperability with other distributed CCA frameworks, such as XCAT-C++ [12] or Legion-CCA.

References

[1] The AneurIST Project. www.aneurist.org/.

[2] F. Baude, D. Caromel, and M. Morel. From Distributed Objects to Hierarchical Grid Components. *International Symposium on Distributed Objects and Applications (DOA)*, Catania, Italy, 2003.

[3] S. Benkner, G. Berti, G. Engelbrecht, J. Fingberg, G. Kohring, S. Middleton, and R. Schmidt. GEMSS: Grid Infrastructure for Medical Service Provision. *Journal of Methods of Information in Medicine*, 44, 2005.

[4] S. Benkner, I. Brandic, G. Engelbrecht, and R. Schmidt. VGE - A Service-Oriented Grid Environment for On-Demand Supercomputing. In *Proceedings of the Fifth IEEE/ACM International Workshop on Grid Computing*, November Pittsburgh, PA, USA, 2004.

[5] D. E. Bernholdt et al. A Component Architecture for High-Performance Scientific Computing. *Intl. J. High-Perf. Computing Appl.*, 2006.

[6] The Common Component Architecture Forum. http://www.cca-forum.org.

[7] K. Doerner, R. Hartl, S. Benkner, M. Lucka. *Cooperative Savings based Ant Colony Optimization - Multiple Search and Decomposition Approaches*, Parallel Processing Letters, 2005.

[8] I. Foster, A. Savva, D. Berry, A. Djaoui, A. Grimshaw, B. Horn, F. Maciel, F. Siebenlist, R. Subramaniam, J. Treadwell, and J. V. Reich. The Open Grid Services Architecture, Version 1.0. GGF OGSA Working Group (OGSA-WG), 2005.

[9] N. Furmento, J. Hau, W. Lee, S. Newhouse, and J. Darlington. Implementations of a Service-Oriented Architecture on Top of Jini, JXTA and OGSI. In *Second Across Grids Conference*, 2004.

[10] D. Gannon, R. Ananthakrishnan, S. Krishnan, M. Govindaraju, L. Ramakrishnan, and A. Slominski. *Grid Computing: Making the Global Infrastructure a Reality*, chapter 9, Grid Web Services and Application Factories. Wiley, 2003.

[11] D. Gannon, R. Bramley, G. Fox, S. Smallen, A. Rossi, R. Ananthakrishnan, F. Bertrand, K. Chiu, M. Farrellee, M. Govindaraju, S. Krishnan, L. Ramakrishnan, Y. Simmhan, A. Slominski, Y. Ma, C. Olariu, and N. Rey-Cenvaz. Programming the Grid: Distributed Software Components, P2P and Grid Web Services for Scientific Applications. *J. Cluster Computing*, 5(3):325–336, 2002.

[12] M. Govindaraju, M. R. Head, and K. Chiu. XCAT-C++: Design and Performance of a Distributed CCA Framework. *The 12th Annual IEEE International Conference on High Performance Computing (HiPC) 2005*, Goa, India, December 18-21.

[13] S. Krishnan and D. Gannon. XCAT3: A Framework for CCA Components as OGSA Services. In *Proceedings of the 9th International Workshop on High-Level Parallel Programming Models and Supportive Environments (HIPS 2004)*. IEEE, 2004.

[14] M. Malawski, D. Kurzyniec, and V. Sunderam. Mocca - Towards a Distributed CCA Framework for Metacomputing. In *IPDPS '05: Proceedings of the 19th IEEE International Parallel and Distributed Processing Symposium (IPDPS'05)*, page 174.1, 2005.

[15] C. Pérez, T. Priol, A. Ribes. Paco++: A Parallel Object Model for High Performance Distributed Systems. *37th Hawaii Intern. Conf. on System Sciences (HICSS-37)*, 2004.

[16] R. Schmidt, M. R. Head, M. Govindaraju, M. J. Lewis, and S. Benkner. Design and Implementation Choices for Implementing Distributed CCA Frameworks. *in GECO-COMPFRAME06: Workshop HPC Grid programming Environments and COmponents and Component and Framework Technology in High-Performance and Scientific Computing (at HPDC-15)*, Paris, France, June 2006.

TOWARDS DYNAMIC ADAPTABILITY SUPPORT FOR THE MASTER-WORKER PARADIGM IN COMPONENT BASED APPLICATIONS

Françoise André
Université de Rennes 1/IRISA, Campus de Beaulieu, 35042 Rennes cedex, France

Hinde Lilia Bouziane
INRIA/IRISA, Campus de Beaulieu, 35042 Rennes cedex, France

Jérémy Buisson, Jean-Louis Pazat
INSA de Rennes/IRISA, Campus de Beaulieu, 35042 Rennes cedex, France

Christian Pérez
INRIA/IRISA, Campus de Beaulieu, 35042 Rennes cedex, France
{Francoise.Andre,Hinde.Bouziane,Jeremy.Buisson,Jean-Louis.Pazat,Christian.Perez}@irisa.fr

Abstract   When executing scientific applications, resources that may be used can vary from multi-core processors to grids. Therefore, abstracting the programming model enables portability on various resource infrastructures. Furthermore, software component technology appears to be a very promising approach to deal with the growing complexity of scientific applications. Hence, we proposed a model to improve the support of *master-worker* paradigm in component models. Capitalizing on our experience of adaptability frameworks, we propose to enhance our model so that *master-worker* applications can adapt at runtime to varying conditions. This paper studies how to transparently introduce adaptability in our model for *master-worker* applications, what impact it has on the model, and what requirements it expects from the adaptability framework.

Keywords: Software components, Grid, Master-worker, Dynamic evolution, Adaptability framework.

1.   Introduction

While computing grids are becoming more and more common, the question of their programmability is raising attention. The underlying motivation not only stems from the high complexity of grids that shall be hidden to programmers but it also comes from the increasing complexity of applications. In order to take advantage of the huge possibilities of grids, more complex applications like code coupling applications are getting popular.

Software component technology appears very promising to handle the complexity of both grids and applications. Code reuse enables to build complex applications based on validated building blocks while component composition provides a mechanism to support complex relationships independently of the architecture of the execution platform.

An example of such a relationship is the *master-worker* paradigm. While it is an algorithmic concept, its implementation varies quite a lot depending on the execution platform. Hence, we defined a high level master-worker relationship between components [5, 4]. While it provides a model close to the abstract concept to the programmers, it can be configured by the execution environment to fit to the actual resources. However, this previous work did not consider dynamic adaptation. For example, the number of workers may change depending on the number of incoming requests or the number of available machines. The goal of this paper is to study how to introduce adaptability support in a master-worker paradigm and to evaluate the impact on adaptation frameworks.

The paper is organized as follows. Section 2 summarizes our model to handle *master-worker* (M-W) relationship between components as well as an analysis of various levels of adaptability. Section 3 presents our adaptability framework. Section 4 discusses different strategies to introduce adaptability within the M-W relationship. An example and its impact on the M-W model are analyzed in Section 5. Section 6 concludes the paper and presents some future works.

2.   A high-level *master-worker* composition model

We proposed in [5] to increase the abstraction level of component models with respect to the *master-worker* (M-W) paradigm. Our motivation is twofold. First, we aim to relieve programmers from dealing with resource dependencies, such as the number of *workers* to instantiate or request transport concerns. Second, we target to reuse existing *master-worker* environments, like DIET [7], as they implement advanced request transport and scheduling algorithms.

The proposal defines a generic model, which we have projected to specific component models like FRACTAL [5], CCM and CCA [4]. In this paper, we present it according to the FRACTAL formalism.

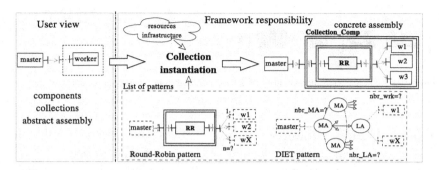

Figure 1. Overview of the *master-worker* model from the user and framework points of view.

2.1   Overview

The model is based on the concept of *collection*, which is defined as a set of *exposed* ports, bound to some internal component type ports. A collection behaves like a component: it can be connected to other components. However, such a composition is done by an *abstract* architecture description, which represents the user's view of the application. Ideally, at deployment time, a collection is turned into a composite by defining an initial number of internal component instances and by selecting a *request transport pattern*. A *pattern* represents a request transport algorithm that may be used between *master* and *worker* components. It is a composite whose implementation should be done by some experts and can or can not be based on software components, such as DIET [7]. Request transport *patterns* are defined independently of a collection. Figure 1 presents an overview of the concepts of the proposed model.

2.2   Need for dynamic behavior

The proposed model dealt with building a static *master-worker* application because the translation of the abstract collection to a concrete composite fixes the number of workers as well as a pattern at deployment time. However, such choices have to be dynamic to take into account modifications of the application behavior and/or of the resources. The application behavior encompasses collection level behaviors like the frequency and the kind of incoming requests, the number of requests waiting for a worker, or the number of connected masters. It also comprises application's level behavior when there are several collections within an application. Resource behaviors are made of standard considerations like availability, end of a resource reservation, etc.

For a collection, there are three elements that may be dynamically modified: *1)* the number of workers, *2)* the used pattern and *3)* the tuning of the pattern.

For example, let consider an increase of the number of waiting requests. If the pattern is not the bottleneck, the solution is to add more workers if there are

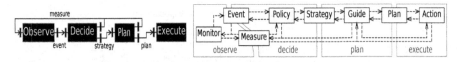

Figure 2. DYNACO as an assembly of FRACTAL components and their dependencies.

available resources. However, if the pattern is the bottleneck, either the pattern may by optimized or it has to be replaced by a more scalable one.

In order to help decision making, validity constraints may be attached to a pattern. For instance, a round-robin pattern can be adequate for one or a few connected masters, for equivalent request load and for homogeneous processors. If at least one of these conditions is not met, another pattern should be considered, like for example a load-balancing pattern or DIET.

A collection can also be modified to optimize resources usage. For instance, if there is a lot of workers compared to the number of requests, it can be suitable to remove some workers to release resources. Last, more complex situations occur when an application contains several instances of the *master-worker* paradigm. In such a case, re-structuring a collection should be coordinated in order not to be to the detriment of other collections.

3.   A framework for adaptability

In a previous work [1, 6], we have studied how to make applications suit varying conditions relying on the notion of adaptability. This work led us to develop a generic component framework for adaptability, DYNACO. Benefiting from a joint work with the university of Pisa [1], this framework splits adaptability into four sub-functionalities: *1)* the framework has to be able to *observe* characteristics of the environment in order to trigger adaptability; *2)* when a change is detected, the framework has to *decide* an adaptation strategy according to observed measures; *3)* once a strategy has been decided, the framework has to *plan* actions to implement it; at last, *4)*, planned actions have to be *executed* synchronously with the execution of applicative code. On the left of Figure 2, each sub-functionality is captured by a FRACTAL component.

Rather than reimplementing the components of the framework specifically to each application, developers are encouraged to focus on application-specific issues, thanks to the reuse of existing generic engines. For instance, we have experimented 3 generic engines for the *decide* component: *1)* a JAVA virtual machine, such that the decision procedure is implemented with a general-purpose language, allows easy implementations of intuitive decision procedures; *2)* the JESS [10] expert system, such that the decision procedure is expressed with a domain-specific rule language (i.e. as a collection of ordered rules that looks like the following statement: *"decide a given strategy when an associated con-*

dition becomes true"), allows efficient implementations of complex rule-based decision procedures; and *3)* a genetic algorithm, such that the decision procedure is expressed as a function to optimize (e.g. the performance model of the application), allows to implement straightforwardly decision procedures when the application's behavior is well formalized, possibly with a higher runtime cost. As described, each engine proposes a different trade-off.

The same applies to the *plan* and *execute* components. For the former, for instance, a pattern matching based mapping from strategies to predefined plans suits well simple cases; while more sophisticated formalisms such as STRIPS [12] (developers only declare the collection of possible actions as pre- and post-conditions) may be relevant when developers cannot predefine plans by hand. Similarly, synchronizing adaptation actions with the applicative code depends mostly on the applicative programming model: we have proposed an algorithm (AFPAC [6]) for any SPMD application. Other algorithms could be used such as ASSIST [3] when using its *parmod* skeleton programming model.

The *observe* component does not adhere to the same design: *monitors* are facilities provided by the environment itself that are wrapped into adapter components, which gather, aggregate and preprocess raw measures and events to their expected formats. The whole *observe* component is almost independent from the application and does not need any particular specialization.

As on the right of Figure 2, application-specific code is captured in *policy*, *guide* and a collection of *actions*, which respectively specialize the *decide*, *plan* and *execute* components. Using generic engines in that way is what makes DYNACO highly generic and open, while it encourages effective code reuse.

4. Design choices for adaptability in the M-W paradigm

This section studies how to make use of an adaptability framework such as DYNACO in the *master-worker* paradigm. It analyzes two major design choices we have identified: the choice of the adaptability strategy and of the architecture. The discussion is done with respect to three criteria: modularity, accuracy, and scalability. *Modularity* measures the possibility to compound strategies such as at the collection level and at the pattern level. *Accuracy* stands for the kinds of allowed adaptations while *scalability* refers to the number of components in the collection.

4.1 Strategy level

The first choice concerns the way to logically design the adaptation strategy, which can be *monolithic, independent* or *coordinated*.

Considering a single *monolithic* strategy, the global strategy should handle any possible situation and adaptation for the whole collection. Especially, it should consistently handle the adaptation at the levels of the collection, the pattern and the pattern implementation. For instance, observing that the request queue lengthens, instantiating new workers may increase the heterogeneity of processors, such that the pattern should be replaced by a more suited one (e.g. switching from round-robin to DIET). A monolithic strategy is able to handle those two adaptations at once. Assuming now that the bottleneck is the pattern, which may not be able to perform better, not even with a different implementation nor with additional resources. Being aware of all of the implemented patterns, a monolithic strategy has sufficient knowledge to detect such a situation and prevent useless workers. Therefore, high accuracy is provided. However, the major drawback is poor modularity. Indeed, the tight entanglement between adaptations makes it particularly difficult to add incrementally the support for new patterns, as well as to maintain the strategy, as any local modification may have an impact on the whole strategy. Worse, in the case of a multi-collection application, adaptations for all of the collections have to be handled by a single strategy at the level of the whole application.

Rather than designing the strategy as a whole, it may be better to decompose it such that the specification of the strategy for each adaptation is close to what is adapted. Basically, in order to allow good modularization, 3 sub strategies would be designed: the first one, attached to the collection composite, adapts the number of workers; the second one, attached to the pattern, selects a convenient pattern; and the last one, attached to the pattern implementation, optimizes the pattern. Two alternatives can be derived from this compound strategy. Each sub strategy may be *independent* or otherwise it may be *coordinated*. In the former case, independence means that no explicit interaction occurs from one sub strategy to the others. The latter case allows explicit interactions between sub strategies such that they can coordinate the adaptations of the elements of the collection. Any technique can be used to implement the coordination, such as triggering adaptations from other adaptations (propagating adaptations) or running a negotiation protocol (agreeing on adaptations).

Focusing on the *independent* approach, let us consider first the above example of adding worker instances that increase heterogeneity, which may result from different processors or from different implementations. Independence implies that the pattern switches its implementation on its own when it observes that heterogeneity increases, once the collection (independently) has instantiated new workers. Thus, despite their independence, the sub strategies achieve together the same adaptations as the single monolithic strategy. However, that way of observing effects of adaptations is not always enough to implement accurate adaptations. Consider that the queue lengthens. An accurate strategy does not instantiate new workers if the pattern would not be able to dispatch requests at a sufficient pace; and it does not optimize the pattern if there can't be enough workers to handle requests. However, independence of the sub strategies prevents the collection from knowing whether the pattern would be

Strategy	Accuracy		Modularity	Scalability
	Collection	Application		
Monolithic	High	None	None	Low
Independent	Low	Low	High	High
Coordinated	High	High	High	High

Figure 3.   Summarized features of each alternative for the strategy level.

able or not to dispatch requests to additional workers; and it prevents the pattern from knowing whether the collection would be able to instantiate new workers. In such a situation, this strategy would desperately preserve the *status quo*, even if the collection would be able to perform better; while lowering accuracy may lead to instantiate useless workers or to over-optimize the pattern.

Last, the *coordinated* strategy promises to bring the advantages of the two other strategies without their drawbacks (Figure 3). It preserves compound strategies for modularity and scalability while letting a global vision to be built for accuracy. However, several adaptation modules have to be interconnected.

4.2   Achitecture level

The second design choice concerns the architecture of the adaptability. Two alternatives are identified: *centralized* and *distributed*.

A *centralized* architecture locates the whole adaptability management into a single location. With respect to the model presented in Section 2, it has to be into the membrane of the collection. Bindings are, nevertheless, present to enable it to control the whole collection. The *centralized* approach is compatible with all adaptation strategies described in Section 4.1. It also simplifies the implementation of the *coordinated* strategy as the communication between the different strategies may be embedded into the same adaptation framework. However, it raises an issue for the compound strategies with respect to the composition of components: the adaptation part of sub components needs to be injected into the adaptation part of the collection. Hence, the connection operator of the component model turns out to be more complex. As far as we know, there is no standard component models that permits it.

With a *distributed* architecture, the adaptability management is spread over the whole collection, and in particular in the membranes of the collection, of the pattern and of the pattern implementation components. The *distributed* architecture is not straightfowardly compatible with the *monolithic* strategy. However, it perfectly fits with the counpound strategies provided that the communications of the *coordinated* strategy are quite simply done through some ports. Considering the advantages of the *coordinated* strategy, we conclude that this strategy with a *distributed* architecture appears to be the best choice to deal with dynamic change in a collection.

4.3   Positionning

Only a couple of adaptability frameworks address the problem of coordinating and distributing adaptations. DYNACO is neutral as it does not prevent policies to coordinate on their own, but it does not provide any specific support.

Among the other frameworks, ACEEL [8] and PLASMA [11], are fairly close to the constructive approach defended here, i.e. building global adaptations as the collaboration of individual local adaptations. With our previous framework ACEEL, each component contacts other components before adapting, in order to ensure consistent and synchronized adaptation of the whole assembly. With PLASMA, components impose their adaptations to the other ones through a simpler propagation mechanism. The contract-driven approach of ASSIST [2] is different: considering a hierarchical component model, composite components divide their contract in order to assign recursively subcontracts to their sub components. Coordination of adaptation is enforced by the submission of contracts that are consistent with another. However, this approach requires composite components to have precise understanding of the composition of their immediate subcomponents, in order to devise subcontracts.

Those frameworks are however tied to the programming models for which they have been specifically designed, often restricted to a fixed collection of predefined adaptations; while focusing only on adaptability, DYNACO integrates gracefully to any programming model. DYNACO also allows to design more specific and adequate solutions for each programming paradigm than other general approaches. Hence, DYNACO is a better start point.

5.   Adapation example for a *master-worker* application

Based on the preceding analysis, this section discusses a design example for adaptability of a *master-worker* application. As outlined in Section 2.2, the adaptation aims at preventing the request queue from unacceptably growing, while making the queue contain enough requests to feed continuously the workers. In order to enforce that objective, we propose the following intuitive compound strategy, using the coordinated approach:

- **at the level of the collection:** if the request queue lengthens beyond a threshold, if the pattern is able to increase its dispatch rate accordingly and if there are available resources, then instantiate new workers; if the request queue shortens under a threshold, then terminate some workers.

- **at the level of the pattern:** if the number of masters or the variability of request durations increases above a threshold, or if the heterogeneity of workers

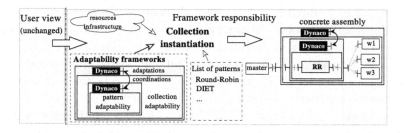

Figure 4.   Introducing dynamic management in the *master-worker* model.

increases beyond a threshold, then switch to the DIET pattern; otherwise, under a threshold switch to round-robin.

In this strategy, coordination (as it appears on Figure 4) occurs before the collection instantiates new workers. It actually asks the pattern whether it would be able to dispatch requests at a sufficient rate, for instance involving a contract renegotiation protocol. The length of the request queue cannot always be observed directly; lengthenings and shortenings can nevertheless be deduced from the comparison between arrival and service rates. Other observations are almost obvious. The example shows that the *coordinated* and *distributed* design suits well and that the necessary monitoring does not breach encapsulation.

Now that an adaptation strategy is designed, the issue is to consider the impact on the proposed M-W model. Achieving the objective of transparent dynamic management, there is no need to modify the model at the user view level. The collection instantiation process seems to be more appropriate to introduce an adaptability framework. A collection implementation, in particular the collection and pattern membranes, are determined at this stage. Adding adaptability framework as controllers in appropriate membranes appears to be straightforward. Then, only the implementation of collection and pattern components are concerned by the use of an adaptability framework. However, the diversity of resource infrastructures and resource management systems lead to various adaptability policies. For instance, a policy can be more constrained by resource availability when resource sharing is privileged, otherwise it can be more constrained by application requirements. As a consequence, similarly as for patterns, the framework has to do a selection from a set of adaptability implementations. Fortunately, the specificity of DYNACO to be component-based allows the use of different implementations. The *master-worker* model extended with adaptability support is presented in Figure 4.

6.   Conclusion

The paper analyses how to design dynamic adaptability support for component-based *master-worker* applications. Among the discussed possibilities, co-ordinating several distributed adaptations appears to be the best-suited solution with regard to modularity, scalability and accuracy. In addition, integrating adaptability at the level of the *master-worker* abstraction achieves the goal of hiding the management of execution resources from the developers' sight.

Among adaptability frameworks, none fully meets the requirements of our proposal. Its genericity and openness make DYNACO be the best start point. Based on the experience we gained in our previous work on ACEEL [8–9], we plan to extend DYNACO with specific support for the coordination of distributed adaptations, so that it meets the requirements. We will also evaluate the proposed model on synthetic *master-worker* benchmarks as well as the possibilities to write generic adaptation policies at the collection and application levels.

References

[1] M. Aldinucci, F. André, J. Buisson, S. Campa, M. Coppola, M. Danelutto, and C. Zoccolo. An abstract schema modelling adaptivity management. In Sergei Gorlatch and Marco Danelutto, editors, *Integrated Research in GRID Computing*, CoreGRID. Springer, 2007.

[2] M. Aldinucci, M. Danelutto, and M. Vanneschi. Autonomic qos in assist grid-aware components. In *14th Euromicro International Conference on Parallel, Distributed and Network-based Processing*, February 2006.

[3] M. Aldinucci, A. Petrocelli, E. Pistoletti, M. Torquati, M. Vanneschi, L. Veraldi, and C. Zoccolo. Dynamic reconfiguration of grid-aware applications in assist. In José C. Cunha and Pedro D. Medeiros, editors, *Proceedings of the 11th International Euro-Par Conference*, volume 3648 of *Lecture Notes in Computer Science*, pages 771–781, Lisbon, Portugal, September 2005. Springer.

[4] G. Antoniu, H. L. Bouziane, M. Jan, C. Pérez, and T. Priol. Combining data sharing with the master-worker paradigm in the common component architecture. In *The 15th IEEE International Symposium on High Performance Distributed Computing (HPDC)*, Paris, France, June 2006.

[5] H. L. Bouziane, C. Pérez, and T. Priol. Modeling and executing master-worker applications in component models. In *11th International Workshop on High-Level Parallel Programming Models and Supportive Environments (HIPS)*, Rhodes Island, Greece, April 2006.

[6] J. Buisson, F. André, and J.-L. Pazat. Afpac: Enforcing consistency during the adaptation of a parallel component. *Scalable Computing: Practice and Experience*, 7(3):83–95, September 2006. electronic journal (http://www.scpe.org/).

[7] E. Caron, F. Desprez, F. Lombard, J.M. Nicod, M. Quinson, and F. Suter. A Scalable Approach to Network Enabled Servers. In B. Monien and R. Feldmann, editors, *Proceedings of the 8th International EuroPar Conference*, volume 2400 of *Lecture Notes in Computer Science*, pages 907–910, Paderborn, Germany, August 2002. Springer-Verlag.

[8] D. Chefrour. *Plate-forme de composants logiciels pour la coordination des adaptations multiples en environnement dynamique*. PhD thesis, Université Rennes 1, November 2005.

[9] D. Chefrour and F. André. Développement d'applications en environnements mobiles à l'aide du modèle de composant adaptatif ACEEL. In *Langages et Modèles à Objets. Actes publiés dans la revue STI*, volume 9 of *série L'objet*, Vanne, France, 2003.

[10] Jess, the rule engine for the java platform. http://herzberg.ca.sandia.gov/jess/.

[11] O. Layaida and D. Hagimont. Designing self-adaptive multimedia applications through hierarchical reconfiguration. In L. Kutvonen and N. Alonistioti, editors, *DAIS'05*, volume 3543 of *LNCS*, pages 95–107. Springer, 2005.

[12] N. Nilsson and R. Fikes. STRIPS: a new approach to the application of theorem proving to problem solving. *Artificial Intelligence*, 2(3–4):189–208, 1971.

IV

COMMUNICATION AND NETWORKING

TOTAL EXCHANGE PERFORMANCE PREDICTION ON GRID ENVIRONMENTS

modeling and algorithmic issues

Luiz Angelo Steffenel and Emmanuel Jeannot
Université Nancy 2 / LORIA* - AlGorille Team
LORIA - Campus Scientifique - BP 239
54506 Vandoeuvre-lès-Nancy Cedex
France
Luiz-Angelo.Steffenel@univ-nancy2.fr
Emmanuel.Jeannot@loria.fr

Abstract   One of the most important collective communication patterns used in scientific applications is the *complete exchange*, also called *All-to-All*. Although efficient algorithms have been studied for specific networks, general solutions like those available in well-known MPI distributions (e.g. the MPI_Alltoall operation) are strongly influenced by the congestion of network resources. In this paper we address the problem of modeling the performance of *Total Exchange* communication operations in grid environments. Because traditional performance models are unable to predict the real completion time of an All-to-All operation, we try to cope with this problem by identifying the factors that can interfere in both local and distant transmissions. We observe that the traditional MPI_Alltoall implementation is not suited for grid environments, as it is both inefficient and hard to model. We focus therefore in an alternative algorithm for the total exchange redistribution problem. In our approach we perform communications in two different phases, aiming to minimize the number of communication steps through the wide-area network. This reduction has a direct impact on the performance modeling of the MPI_Alltoall operation, as we minimize the factors that interfere with wide-area communications. Hence, we are able to define an accurate performance modeling of a total exchange between two clusters.

Keywords: MPI, all-to-all, total exchange, network contention, performance modeling, computational grids, personalized many-to-many communications

---

*UMR 7503 - CNRS, INPL, INRIA, UHP, Nancy 2

1. Introduction

One of the most important collective communication patterns for scientific applications is the *total exchange* [1], in which each process holds n different data items that should be distributed among the n processes, including itself. An important example of this communication pattern is the All-to-All operation, where all messages have the same size m.

Generally, most All-to-All algorithms from well-known MPI distributions rely on direct point-to-point communications among the processes. Because all these communications are started simultaneously, the communication performance is strongly influenced by the saturation of network resources and subsequent loss of packets - the network contention. Further, when working in a grid, we must also face problem related to the heterogeneous communication environment, which behaves differently if message exchange are made locally or remotely.

In this paper we study different approaches to model the performance of the All-to-All collective operation in grid environments. Performance prediction can be extremely helpful on the development of application performance prediction frameworks such as PEMPIs [2], but also in the optimization of grid-aware collective communications (e.g.: LaPIe [3] and MagPIe [4]). We demonstrate that traditional algorithms for the MPI_Alltoall operation are hard to model because of the combined complexity of both local-area contention and wide-area latency.

This paper is organized as follows: Section 2 presents the problem of the total exchange and the challenges we face in a grid environment. Section 3 discusses the existing approaches to introduce the network contention in the performance models for the MPI_Alltoall operation. Section 4 extends the performance prediction problem to a grid environment. We propose a new algorithmic approach that helps minimizing the contention impact, and we validate its performance modeling against experimental data obtained on a grid network. Finally, Section 5 presents some conclusions and the future directions of our work.

2. Problem of Total Exchange between Two Clusters

We consider the following architecture (see Figure 1). Let there be two clusters $\mathcal{C}_1$ and $\mathcal{C}_2$ with respectively n_1 nodes and n_2 nodes. A network, called a backbone, interconnects the two clusters. We assume that a cluster use the same network card to communicate to one of its node or to a node of another cluster. Based on that topology inter cluster communications are never faster than communication within a cluster.

Let us suppose that an application is running and using both clusters (for example, a code coupling application). One part of the computation is performed on cluster $\mathcal{C}_1$ and the other part on cluster $\mathcal{C}_2$. During the application, data must be exchanged from $\mathcal{C}_1$ to $\mathcal{C}_2$ using the *all-*

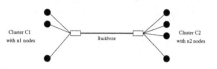

Figure 1. Architecture for the redistribution problem

toall pattern. *Alltoall* (also called total exchange) is defined in the MPI standard. It means that every node has to send some of its data to all the other nodes. Here we assume that the data to be transfer is different for each receiving node (if the data is the same, the routine is called an *allgather* and is less general that the studied case). Moreover we assume that the size of the data to exchange is the same for every pair of nodes (the case where the size is different is implemented by the *alltoallv* routine: it is more general than our case and will be studied in a future work). Altogether, this means that we will have to transfer $(n_1 + n_2)^2$ messages over different network environments. The data of all these messages are different but the size of the messages are the same and is given and called m (in bytes). Several MPI libraries (OpenMPI, MPICH2, etc.) implement the *allltoall* routine assuming that all the nodes are on the same clusters, which means that all communications have the same weight. However, in our case, some messages are transferred within a cluster (from a node of $\mathcal{C}_1$ to a node of $\mathcal{C}_1$ or from $\mathcal{C}_2$ to $\mathcal{C}_2$) or between the two clusters. In the first case, bandwidth and latency are faster than in the second case. Therefore, we need different tools to model the overall performance.

3. Modeling Network Contention

In the *All-to-All* operation, every process holds $m \times n$ data items that should be equally distributed among the n processes, including itself. The intensive communication among the processes can easily saturate the network, degrading the communication performance. Indeed, Chun [5] demonstrated that the overall execution time of intensive exchange collective communications is strongly dominated by the network contention and congestive packet loss, two aspects that are not easy to quantify. As a result, a major challenge on modeling the All-to-All operation in local-area networks is to represent the impact of network contention.

Unfortunately, most communication models like those presented by Christara *et al.* [1] and Pjesivac-Grbovic *et al.* [6] do not take into account the potential impacts of network contention. These works usually represent the All-to-All operation as parallel executions of the *personalized one-to-many* pattern [7], as presented by the linear model below, where α is the start-up time (the latency between the processes), $\frac{1}{\beta}$ is the bandwidth of the link, m represents the message size in bytes and n corresponds to the number of processes involved in the operation:

$$T = (n - 1) \times (\alpha + \beta m) \tag{1}$$

To correct the performance predictions, Bruck [8] suggested the use of a *slowdown factor*. Similarly, Clement *et al.* [9] introduced a technique that suggested a way to account contention in shared networks such as non-switched Ethernet, consisting in a contention factor γ proportional to the number of process. The use of a contention factor was supported by the work of Labarta *et al.* [10], that intent to approximate the behavior of the network contention by considering that if there are m messages ready to be transmitted, and only b available buses, then the messages are serialized in $\lceil \frac{m}{b} \rceil$ communication waves.

A slightly different approach was followed by Chun [5], who consider the contention as a component of the communication latency, resulting in the use of different latency values according to the message size. One drawback, however, it that this model does not take into account the number of messages passing in the network nor the link capacity, which is related to the occurrence of network contention.

3.1 Performance modeling in homogeneous clusters

To cope with this problem and to model the impact of contention on the All-to-All operation in cluster environments, we presented in [11] an approach inspired in the work from Clement *et al.* [9]. In our approach, the network contention depends mostly on the physical characteristics of the network (network cards, links, switches). Consequently, we can define a contention ratio γ that bounds the theoretical model from Equation 1 and the real performance of the network.

Our method differs from previous one by considering that communication times are not linear regarding the message size. Indeed, we observed that the communication time presents a non-linear behavior according to some factors such as MPU message segmentation, MPI transmission policy and switches maximum interconnection bandwidth.

Therefore, we augment the *contention ratio* model with a new parameter δ, which depends on the number of processes but also on a given message size M, as seen below. As a consequence, we are able to associate different equations (linear and affine) in order to help defining a more realistic performance model for the MPI_Alltoall operation in a given network, as illustrated in Figure 2.

$$T = \begin{cases} (n - 1) \times (\alpha + m\beta) \times \gamma & if \; m < M \\ (n - 1) \times ((\alpha + m\beta) \times \gamma + \delta) & if \; m \geq M \end{cases} \tag{2}$$

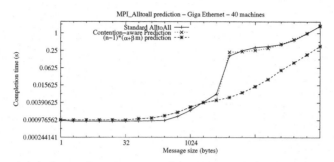

Figure 2. Measured and predicted performance for the standard MPI_Alltoall in a Gigabit Ethernet network

4. Performance Modeling on Grid Environments

As the previous model allows a quite accurate representation on the performance of local-area networks (see [11]), our first approach would be to estimate the communication time by composing both local (contention-aware) and remote communications.

Unfortunately, this simple strategy fails to represent the operation of the MPI_Alltoall in a grid. Hence, Figure 3 presents the completion time of the MPI_Alltoall implementation from OpenMPI in a grid with two clusters of 30 machines each. As stated above, we try to predict the communication performance by individually representing local and remote communication costs. To predict the performance of the local network (subjected to contention), we use $\gamma = 2.6887$ and $\delta = 0.005039$ as the contention signature of each local network (both clusters have similar characteristics under contention).

Actually, we observe that the local-area part plays a small role in the overall execution time, compared to the wide-area communication cost. Of course, one could try to define additional parameters for the wide-area communications, but the final model would be too complex to be useful in real situation. Instead, we addressed this problem by redefining the All-to-All problem against the challenges that characterize a grid environment.

4.1 Minimizing the impact of contention on the backbone

When dealing with wide-area networks, the most important factor to be considered is the time a message takes to be delivered. Indeed, in addition to the geographical distance, message are subjected to network protocols heterogeneity, message routing and transient interferences on the backbone.

Actually, popular algorithms for collective communications on grids (such as the ones implemented in PACX MPI [12] and MagPIe [4]) try to minimize communications over the wide-area network by defining a single coordinator in every cluster, which participates in the inter-cluster data transfers across the

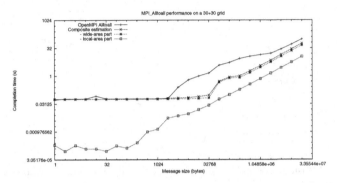

Figure 3. Measured and predicted performance for the standard MPI_Alltoall in a grid

wide-area backbone. By minimizing the number of WAN communication steps, we reduce the probability of inducing contention and accumulating transmission delays on the messages.

However, a single communication between each cluster is an approach inappropriate for the MPI_Alltoall operation. First, it induces additional communication steps to/from the cluster coordinator, which becomes a bottleneck. Second, this approach is not optimal concerning the usage of the wide-area bandwidth, as wide-area backbones are designed to support simultaneous transfers and simultaneous transfers [13]. Hence, in order to improve the performance in a WAN, we need to change the MPI_Alltoall algorithm strategy.

4.2 The $\mathcal{LG}$ algorithm

To cope with this problem, we try to minimize wide-area communication steps in a different way. Actually, most of the complexity of the All-to-All problem resides on the need to exchange *different* messages through different networks (local and distant). The traditional implementation of the MPI_Alltoall operation cannot differentiate these networks, leading to poor performances. However, if we assume that communications between clusters are slower than intra-clusters ones, it might be useful to collect data in the local level before sending it in parallel through the backbone, in a single communication step.

As a consequence, we propose in [14] a grid-aware solution which performs on two phases. In the first phase only local communications are performed. During this phase the total exchange is performed on local nodes on both cluster and extra buffers are prepared for the second (inter-cluster) phase. During the second phase data are exchanged between the clusters. Buffers that have been prepared during the first phase are sent directly to the corresponding nodes in order to complete the total exchange.

More precisely, our algorithm works as follow. Without loss of generality, let us assume that cluster $\mathcal{C}_1$ has less nodes than $\mathcal{C}_2$ ($n_1 \leq n_2$). Nodes are numbered from 0 to $n_1 + n_2 - 1$, with nodes from 0 to $n_1 - 1$ being on $\mathcal{C}_1$ and

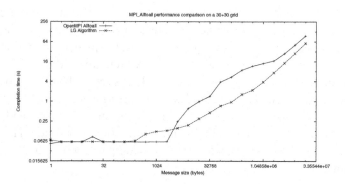

Figure 4.   Performance comparison between OpenMPI and $\mathcal{L}G$ algorithms

nodes from n_1 to $n_1 + n_2 - 1$ being on cluster $\mathcal{C}_2$. We call $\mathcal{M}_{i,j}$ the message (data) that has to be sent from node i to node j. For instance, the algorithm proceeds in two phases:

First phase During the first phase, we perform the local exchange: Process i sends $\mathcal{M}_{i,j}$ to process j, if i and j are on the same cluster. Then it prepares the buffers for the remote communications. On $\mathcal{C}_1$ data that have to be send to node j on $\mathcal{C}_2$ is first stored to node $j \bmod n_1$. Data to be sent from node i on $\mathcal{C}_2$ to node j on $\mathcal{C}_1$ is stored on node $\lfloor i/n_1 \rfloor \times n_1 + j$.

Second phase During the second phase only n_2 inter-cluster communications occurs. This phase is decomposed in $\lceil n_2/n_1 \rceil$ steps with at most n_1 communications each. Steps are numbered from 1 to $\lceil n_2/n_1 \rceil$ During step s node i of $\mathcal{C}_1$ exchange data stored in its local buffer with node $j = i + n_1 \times s$ on $\mathcal{C}_2$ (if $j < n_1 + n_2$). More precisely i sends $\mathcal{M}_{k,j}$ to j where $k \in [0, n_1]$ and j sends $\mathcal{M}_{k,i}$ to i where $k \in [n_1 \times s, n_1 \times s + n_1 - 1]$.

As our algorithm minimizes the number of inter-cluster communications between the clusters, we need only $2 \times \max(n_1, n_2)$ messages in both directions (against $2 \times n_1 \times n_2$ messages in the traditional algorithm). For instance, the exchange of data between two clusters with the same number of process will proceed in one single communication step of the second phase. Our algorithm is also wide-area optimal since it ensures that a data segment is transferred only once between two clusters separate by a wide-area link. Additionally, wide-area transmissions pack several messages together, reducing the impact of transient interferences on the backbone. Hence, Figure 4 presents a comparison between the traditional algorithm used by OpenMPI and the $\mathcal{L}G$ algorithm. We observe that $\mathcal{L}G$ improves the performance of the MPI_Alltoall operation, reaching over than 50% of performance improvement comparing to the traditional strategy.

4.3   Modeling approach

As shown above, the algorithm we propose to optimize All-to-All communications in a grid environment rely on the relative performances of both local and remote networks. Indeed, we extend the total exchange among nodes in the same cluster in order to reduce transmissions through the backbone.

This approach has two consequences for performance prediction: First, it prevents contention in the wide-area links, which are hard to model. Second, the transmission of messages packed together is less subjected to network interferences. For instance, we can design a performance model by composing local-area predictions obtained with our contention ratio model and wide-area predictions that can be easily obtained from traditional methods. Hence, an approximate model would consider the following parts, where $\mathcal{T}_{C_n}$ corresponds to Equation 2:

$$T = max(T_{\mathcal{C}_1}, T_{\mathcal{C}_2}) + \lceil n_2/n_1 \rceil \times (\alpha_w + \beta_w \times m \times n_1) \tag{3}$$

4.4   Experimental validation

To validate the algorithm we propose in this paper, this section presents our experiments to evaluate the performance of the MPI_Alltoall operation with two clusters connected through a backbone.

These experiments were conducted over two clusters of the Grid'5000 platform [1], one located in Nancy and one located in Rennes, approximately 1000 Km from each other. Both clusters are composed of identical nodes (dual Opteron 246, 2 GHz) locally connected by a Gigabit Ethernet network and interconnected by a private backbone of 10 Gbps. All nodes run Linux, with kernel 2.6.13 and OpenMPI 1.1.4. The measures were obtained with the *broadcast-barrier* approach [15].

To model the communication performance of both *inter-cluster* and *intra-cluster* communications we use the *parameterised LogP* model (*pLogP*) [4]. The *pLogP* parameters for both local and distant communications were obtained with the method described in [16]. To model the contention at the local level we used $\gamma = 2.6887$ and $\delta = 0.005039$ for $M >= 1KB$, parameters obtained from the method of the least squares as described in [11].

Therefore, in Figure 5 we compare the performance predictions obtained with Equation 3 against the effective completion time of the $\mathcal{L}G$ algorithm. We observe that prediction fit with a good accuracy to the real execution times, which is not possible with the traditional MPI_Alltoall algorithm. Indeed, the new algorithm minimizes the impact of distant communications, concentrating the contention problems at the local level. Because we are able to predict the performance of local communications even under contention, we can therefore establish an accurate performance model adapted to grid environments.

---

[1] *http://www.grid5000.org/*

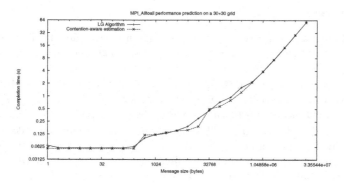

Figure 5. Performance predictions for the $\mathcal{L}G$ algorithm

5. Conclusions and Future Works

In this paper we address the problem of modeling the performance of *Total Exchange* communication operations in grid environments. Because traditional performance models are unable to predict the real completion time of an All-to-All operation, we try to cope with this problem by identifying the factors that can interfere in both local and distant transmissions. We observe that the traditional MPI_Alltoall implementation is not suited for grid environments, as it is both inefficient and hard to model. We focus therefore in an alternative algorithm for the total exchange redistribution problem. In our approach we perform communications in two different phases, aiming to minimize the number of communication steps through the wide-area network. This reduction has a direct impact on the performance modeling of the MPI_Alltoall operation, as we minimize the factors that interfere with wide-area communications.

In our future works we plan to extend the model to handle more complex distributions. First, we would like to consider achieving efficient *alltoall* communications with more than two clusters. This would allow efficient communications on general grid environments. Second, we would like to explore the problem of total exchange redistribution when messages have different sizes. This problem, represented by the *alltoallv* routine, is more general than our case and does requires adaptive scheduling techniques.

Acknowledgments

Experiments presented in this paper were carried out using the Grid'5000 experimental testbed, an initiative from the French Ministry of Research through the ACI GRID incentive action, INRIA, CNRS and RENATER and other contributing partners (see https://www.grid5000.fr).

References

[1] C. Christara, X. Ding and Ken Jackson. An efficient transposition algorithm for distributed memory computers. *Proc. of the High Performance Computing Systems and Applications*, pages 349-368, 1999.

[2] E. T. Midorikawa, H. M. Oliveira and J. M. Laine. PEMPIs: A New Metodology for Modeling and Prediction of MPI Programs Performance. *Proc. of the SBAC-PAD 2004*, IEEE Computer Society/Brazilian Computer Society, pages 254-261, 2004.

[3] L. A. Steffenel and G. Mounie. Scheduling Heuristics for Efficient Broadcast Operations on Grid Environments. *Proc. of the Performance Modeling, Evaluation and Optimization of Parallel and Distributed Systems Workshop - PMEO'06 (associated to IPDPS'06)*, IEEE Computer Society, April 2006.

[4] T. Kielmann, H. Bal, S. Gorlatch, K. Verstoep and R. Hofman. Network Performance-aware Collective Communication for Clustered Wide Area Systems. *J. Parallel Computing* **27**(11):1431-1456, 2001.

[5] A. T. T. Chun. Performance Studies of High-Speed Communication on Commodity Cluster. *PhD. Thesis*, University of Hong Kong, 2001.

[6] J. Pjesivac-Grbovic, T. Angskun, G. Bosilca, G. E. Fagg, E. Gabriel and J. J. Dongarra. Performance Analysis of MPI Collective Operations. *Proc. of the Wokshop on Performance Modeling, Evaluation and Optimisation for Parallel and Distributed Systems (PMEO), in IPDPS 2005*, 2005.

[7] S. L. Johnssonn and C-T. Ho. Optimum Broadcasting and Personalized Communication in Hypercubes. *IEEE Transactions on Computers* **38**(9):1249-1268, 1989.

[8] J. Bruck, C-T. Ho, S. Kipnis, E. Upfal and D. Weathersby. Efficient algorithms for all-to-all communications in multiport message-passing systems. *IEEE Transactions on Parallel and Distributed Systems* **8**(11):1143-1156, 1997.

[9] M. Clement, M. Steed and P. Crandall. Network performance modelling for PM clusters. *Proc. of Supercomputing*, 1996.

[10] J. Labarta, S. Girona, V. Pillet, T. Cortes and L. Gregoris. DiP: A parallel program development environment. *Proc. of the 2nd Euro-Par Conference*, vol. 2, pages 665-674, 1996.

[11] L.A. Steffenel. Modeling Network Contention Effects on AlltoAll Operations. in *Proc. of the IEEE Conference on Cluster Computing (CLUSTER 2006)*, September 2006.

[12] E. Gabriel, M. Resch, T. Beisel, and R. Keller. Distributed computing in a heterogeneous computing environment. In *Proc. of the Euro PVM/MPI 1998*. LNCS 1497, pages 180-187, 1998.

[13] H. Casanova. Network modeling issues for grid application scheduling. *International Journal of Foundations of Computer Science* **16**(2):45-162, 2005.

[14] E. Jeannot and L. A. Steffenel. Fast and Efficient Total Exchange on Two Clusters. Submitted to EuroPar'07 - 13th International Euro-Par Conference European Conference on Parallel and Distributed Computing.

[15] B. Supinski, N. Karonis. Accurately Measuring MPI Broadcasts in a Computational Grid. In *8th IEEE International Symposium on High Performance Distributed Computing (HPDC'99)*, 1999.

[16] T. Kielmann, H. Bal, and K. Verstoep. Fast measurement of LogP parameters for message passing platforms. In *4th Workshop on Runtime Systems for Parallel Programming*. LNCS Vol. 1800, pages 1176-1183, 2000.

SYNTHETIC COORDINATES FOR DISJOINT MULTIPATH ROUTING OVER THE INTERNET

Andrei Agapi, Thilo Kielmann, Henri E. Bal
Dept. of Computer Science, Vrije Universiteit
Amsterdam, The Netherlands
aagapi@few.vu.nl, kielmann@cs.vu.nl, bal@cs.vu.nl

Abstract   We address the problem of routing packets on multiple, router-disjoint, paths in the Internet using large-scale overlay networks. Multipath routing can improve Internet QoS, by routing around congestions. This can benefit interactive and other real-time applications.

One of the main problems with practically achieving router-disjoint multipath routing is the scalability limitation on the number of participating nodes in such an overlay network, caused by the large number of (expensive) topology probes required to discover relay nodes that provide high router-level path disjointness. To address this problem, we propose a novel, synthetic coordinates-based approach.

We evaluate our method against alternative strategies for finding router-level disjoint alternative paths. Additionally, we empirically evaluate the distribution of path diversity in the Internet.

Keywords: path disjointness, path similarity, Quality of Service, overlay networks

1. Introduction

Many Internet-based applications suffer from the lack of proper quality-of-service (QoS) provisioning. Examples are multimedia communication (telephony, video streaming), interactive systems (tele conferencing, games), as well as distributed scientific experiments, like the LOFAR distributed radio telescope.

It has been proposed [1, 8, 10] to improve the achievable QoS by using overlay networks that provide alternative paths, designed to circumvent performance bottlenecks within the Internet. Such overlay networks use (application-level) gateways to relay data around bottlenecks, using paths that are *disjoint* from the default path given by Internet routing. The idea is that alternative paths through relay gateways should *avoid* using as many routers from the default Internet path as possible, as to minimize correlation between congestion events on default and alternative paths. One of the main problems in practically applying this solution, generally not addressed by these systems, is scale: for large numbers of hosts within an overlay network and in lack of complete a priori knowledge of Internet topology underlying the overlay, identifying hosts that provide highly disjoint alternative paths becomes non-trivial.

In this paper, we propose to select such relays by path similarity, based on previously discovered relays. The idea is that if a relay is suitable for a given path, it is also likely to be good for other, similar paths. Paths can be similar when senders and receivers are respectivelly geographically close to each other and/or serviced by the same ISPs. Even if this is not the case, similar BGP-level connections between ISPs traversed for paths might yield the same relays to provide highly disjoint alternative paths. With our path similarity-based approach, exhaustive topology probing to search for good relays can be avoided.

We study measures of path similarity and propose an algorithm to select relays based on previously used, similar paths. We evaluated our approach using 200 PlanetLab nodes. Our evaluation shows that we can indeed quickly identify relay nodes that lead to paths that are highly disjoint from the default Internet routes. Specifically, the cost of our approach in number of topology probes is a small constant (e.g. about 20 traceroutes), independent of the total number of nodes in the overlay, N. Alternatively, as explained in our evaluation section, an *exhaustive* search for the best relay for a given path is $O(N)$. The performance of our constant-cost method (i.e. the disjointness provided by relays found), while worse than that of exhaustive search, significantly improves over random search with equal, constant cost.

2. Identifying Relays for Alternative Paths

We propose to use a synthetic coordinate system modeling Internet path diversity to overcome the above-mentioned scalability problems. Below, we denote by the default Internet path, or simply default path between a source s and a destination d, the set of routers that an IP package has to pass through when being routed between s and d on the Internet. We denote by alternative path between s and d, through a relay host r, the union of default paths (s, r) and (r, d). We define the disjointness of an alternative path as the number of routers in the default Internet path that are *not* part of the alternative path.

2.1 Synthetic Coordinates for Path Disjointness

Our approach is based on the idea of *path similarity*. The intuition behind is that many Internet paths exhibit similarity w.r.t. which relays provide them with good disjointness. For instance, a relay that is good for a path between New York and Amsterdam, is likely to also be good for a path between e.g. New Jersey and Brussels. In the following, we will try to evaluate this hypothesis and quantify the afore-mentioned probability.

When building a synthetic coordinate system for latency prediction ([7], [3]), distance is easy to measure, e.g., as the round-trip time between hosts. When modeling path disjointness provided by other peer nodes, "distance" is less obvious. For this purpose, we define path similarity between paths P1 and P2 as the probability that a relay that is good for P1 is also good for P2. This probability can be quantified in multiple ways, depending on the working definition of relay goodness. In this paper, we propose and evaluate 3 such similarity functions: SimKendall (based on Kendall rank correlation [12]), SimPearson (based on classic Pearson correlation) and SimEuclidian (based on Euclidian distance).

In all cases, a path's coordinates are derived as an N-tuple. Each tuple element represents the disjointness provided to that path by a relay. A consistent, randomly chosen relay set, RS, is used and maintained for determining coordinates for all paths. A path's coordinates can be derived by direct topology probing (e.g. using traceroute). For each path positioning, $2 * |RS| + 1$ topology probes (where $|RS|$ is the size of RS, typically about 10-20) are needed: 1 probe from source to each relay, 1 from each relay to destination, and 1 for the default path itself.

Once a path is positioned in the coordinate space this way, relays that were previously found to be good for paths close to ours in the path similarity space are also likely (with a probability given by the similarity function) to be good for our path. Path coordinates are calculated in the same manner for all versions of our algorithm; the difference is only in the way the path similarity between two paths is calculated (thus the distance function of the coordinate space). We detail the three similarity functions evaluated in the following.

2.2   Path Similarity Evaluation Functions

Kendall's rank correlation is a non-parametric measure of correlation between two sets of values, which gives the probability that any two corresponding pairs of values in the two sets are concordant (identically ordered). In our case, if we consider the two sets to be the disjointness values provided by the same, consistently ordered, set of relays for paths $P1$ and $P2$, the Kendall correlation gives the probability that if a relay $R1$ provides a better disjointness than $R2$ (note $R1 > R2$) for $P1$, we also have $R1 > R2$ for $P2$. Consequently, if a relay R provides high path disjointness for $P1$ relative to the entire set of relays used, it will also have a high rank, thus will be a good relay, for $P2$. We denote by *SimKendall(P1,P2,RS)*, the similarity between $P1$ and $P2$, through relay set RS, as given by the Kendall rank correlation test.

The second path similarity estimator we used, *SimPearson*, is perhaps the most commonly used correlation measure in statistics, based on linear regression. We considered Kendall in addition to the more classic, parametric, Pearson correlation, because it is distribution-free (not assuming the distribution of disjointness, as defined above, to be uniform), less sensitive to outliers and more accurate for small samples [2](which helps minimizing the number of probes needed for initial positioning).

SimKendall and *SimPearson* quantify the relative ordering of relays for the two paths, w.r.t. disjointness provided. Basically, we identify a path in the path disjointness space by the relative order of a consistent set of relays. While Pearson takes into consideration the actual disjointness values, Kendall only considers rank order. However, none takes into account the difference between the average values of the two disjointness sets (e.g. {5, 6, 7, 7} and {1, 2, 3, 3} are identic as far as they are concerned). This is on purpose, based on the following insight: while the actual number of routers from the direct path avoided by using a same relay may vary from path to path, we hypothesize that the "relative goodness" of relays is enough to characterize a path's positioning in the Internet w.r.t. path disjointness. This is true because the feature we are interested in is exactly reusing the best relays from similar paths. However, for comparison purposes, the last function takes into account the afore-mentioned difference. It is calculated based on the Euclidian distance in the space formed by the disjointnesses provided to a path by a consistent set of relays.

2.3   Relay Identification Algorithm

We store the needed information in a database (called PathCache) containing Internet paths, together with relays that provide high disjointness and respective disjointness values. Our current PathCache implementation is centralized but work is ongoing on a distributed version.

Figure 1 outlines a very simple, distributed algorithm that uses path similarity coordinates and PathCache to find good relays. Initially, RS, a set of random relays, is picked from all nodes of the overlay and published through a shared database. This set will act as a consistent random sample for path similarity calculations. Statistical studies [2]show that, for accurate calculation of correlations (Kendall), the minimum sample size should be between 10 and 20. This would thus also be a reference minimal size for RS. Making sure that the nodes in RS are alive is handled by a separate polling algorithm: if nodes in RS become unavailable, new random nodes are picked and published instead. In Fig. 1, when a node needs relays for a new path P, first the set $D(P, RS)$ containing disjointness values provided by relays in RS for path P is calculated ($2 * |RS| + 1$ topology probes required). This set represents the Path Diversity (PD) coordinates of path P. PathCache is then queried for the most similar paths for which PD coordinates have previously been published (a k-Nearest Neighbors query with distance function based on one of the similarity functions). The best relays that have been discovered so far for these paths are then used for our path.

As we can see, the algorithm relies on previously discovered relays. To ensure that the database is populated with good relays, several approaches are possible. For instance, each node can periodically randomly probe for good relays for random PathCache paths and publish them in PathCache. However, it is important to note that the search for better relays to populate PathCache can be done in parallel with queries, and need not be in real time. Conversely, relays found in this search are likely to benefit multiple queries in the future.

```
getDisjointRelaysPD(P)
    RS ← PathCache.getSampleRelaySet()
    Coord_p ← getDisjointnessSet(P, RS)    // 2 · |RS| traceroutes needed
    SimilarPaths ← PathCache.kNNQuery(Coord_p,SimFunction)
    DisjointRelays ← PathCache.pickTopRelays(SimilarPaths)
```

Figure 1. Sample use of PD coordinates to find good relay nodes.

3. Evaluation

To evaluate our system we used Internet topology traces obtained on a platform of about 200 geographically distributed PlanetLab nodes. We have fed these topology measurements into a trace-driven simulator of an overlay network, based on PlanetSim . Nodes ran the algorithm described above to derive their coordinates and find relays.

3.1 Quantifying Internet Path Diversity

In this section, we present an evaluation of the amount of path diversity inherent to the Internet. Specifically, we characterize the distribution of disjointness values provided to Internet paths by a single, third relay. Fig. 2.a) presents a cumulative distribution function of the disjointness ratio over about 400 random Internet paths using 150 random relay hosts. Here, we define the disjointness ratio as the ratio between the disjointness provided by a relay and the total length of the path (i.e. number of routers in it). We thus normalize for different path lengths. In the figure, the X axis represents disjointness ratio and Y the probability that the disjointness ratio provided by a random relay is $< X$.

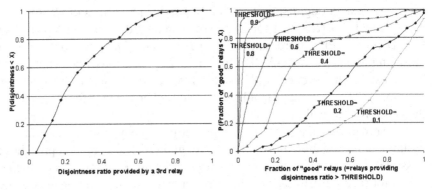

Figure 2. a) CDF of disjointness provided by a third relay to default Internet paths. b) CDFs for distributions of paths w.r.t. fraction of relays providing high disjointness.

We can see that the probability p that an alternative path through a random relay will *avoid less than* $r=49\%$ of the routers in the default path is of 81%. For $r=72\%$, $p=98\%$, whereas for $r=90\%$, $p=99.89\%$. These results suggest that indeed, for large system sizes, randomly looking for relays will perform poorly. Fig. 2.a) basically characterizes the probability distribution of disjointness provided by random relays, averaged over all paths. Depending on the Internet path, this distribution may vary. For instance, depending on the Autonomous Systems the ends belong to, good relays might be easier to find for some paths than for others. In this respect, Fig. 2.b) characterizes the distribution of Internet *paths* w.r.t. the number of good relays that exist for them. "Good" relays are defined as those that provide disjointness ratio larger than a certain threshold; CDFs for various values of this threshold are plotted. The X axis shows the fraction of "good" relays, given the respective THRESHOLD. We see that the CDF becomes very steep as THRESHOLD increases; for instance, if we consider good relays to be those providing disjointness ratio > 0.8, we note that for 77% of Internet paths, there exist less than 3% good relays.

3.2 Evaluation of Synthetic Coordinates

We now evaluate the performance of searching for good relays using path similarity-based synthetic coordinates. Fig. 3.a) shows CDFs of disjointness provided to paths by relays found with our heuristic. Performance is compared with the "optimal" algorithm (if knowledge of the complete relevant topology would be obtained and the absolute best relays would be picked) and the "random" algorithm, the latter using R random picks and choosing the best relay found, where R is the actual number of relays that are probed in our approach (basically the size of the RS set mentioned in section 2). This way, the two approaches are comparable in terms of cost in topology probes. Obviously, the optimal approach is much more expensive: $(2 * (N - 2) + 1$ probes needed to aquire topology information on all possible relays for a given path, N beeing the size of the network), but is plotted as a reference. From Fig. 3.a), we can see that our approach significantly improves on the quality of the relays found by random search. While our performance is sub-optimal, let us recall that we only require a low constant cost in topology probes as compared to the O(N) cost of the optimal approach. We evaluated our heuristic with the three similarity functions presented. As expected, especially the Kendall and Pearson metrics seem to perform well. This confirms our hypothesis that the order of the reference set of relays w.r.t. disjointness provided is a good heuristic in positioning Internet paths among each other in what path disjointness is concerned.

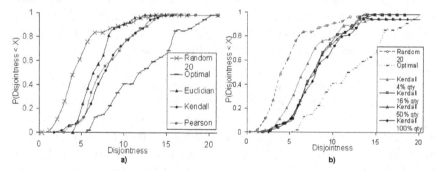

Figure 3. a) CDFs for disjointness distributions of relays found by our heuristic, with methods: Euclidian, Pearson, Kendall vs. random and optimal. b) CDFs for Kendall PathCache at relay quality levels: 4%, 16%, 50%, 100% vs. random, optimal.

The main parameters that can influence the performance of our approach are the similarity function used, $|RS|$, the PathCache "fill ratio" (i.e. number of paths that exist in PathCache) and what we call the PathCache "relay quality". This last parameter basically reflects the average quality of relays published for PathCache paths. As mentioned in subsection 2.3, a separate algorithm can optionally be employed in the background to improve the quality of relays published in PathCache, based on periodic random probes. We estimate a published path's "relay quality" as the number of random probes that were executed so far to derive its current relay set. PathCache's overall "relay quality" is an average of the relay qualities of the paths it contains. We found that search performance does not significantly depend on $|RS|$, as long as it is at least 10. Therefore, an accurate positioning can be done with about 20 traceroutes. Also, against statistics community guidelines, we found Kendall only marginally better than Pearson at small sample sizes.

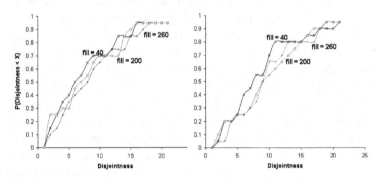

Figure 4. CDFs of average disjointness for relays returned by PathCache at various cache fills: 40, 200 and 260 paths. Similarity metrics: Kendall (left), Pearson (right).

Fig. 4 shows how the distribution of disjointness provided by returned relays varies at various PathCache fill ratios for both Kendall and Pearson similarity metrics. We can see that the quality of relays does improve as the cache contains more paths and that Kendall seems to be slightly more appropriate at large cache sizes than Pearson. As reference, CDFs in Fig. 3.a) were plotted at a fill ratio of 265 paths.

In Fig. 3.b), we evaluate PathCache at various average relay quality levels. We only present the Kendall evaluation, as the results for Pearson are very similar. Qualities are shown in percentages of total search space covered (100%=exhaustive search). Again, this is the background search done for a limited number of paths, not the search needed at query time for all paths. We see that relays returned by PathCache get better as average relay quality increases. However, even for very low relay qualities (lowest quality tried is 10 random samples per path), the improvement is consistent when compared to random search. The improvement increases slowly between 16% and 50% quality levels, becoming slightly more consistent as the quality approaches exhaustive search. A cause might be that, as seen in subsection 3.1, extremely good relays are relatively rare, thus hard to find in a large set of nodes without exhaustive search. Where our approach helps a lot is in quickly finding relays that were relatively good for similar paths, thus significantly improving over random search. This is useful, because we can imagine that continuous, long-lived random (or even exhaustive) searches can be conducted in the background for a limited number of paths that populate PathCache, benefiting all future path queries.

4.   Related Work

Recent work is focusing either on Internet topology discovery [9] or on using overlay networks for improving QoS via multipath routing [8, 1]. Resilient Overlay Networks (RON) [1] uses overlays for routing around congestions and network outages. RON and [8] rely on small overlay network sizes for which topology can be discovered by exhaustive probing. Therefore, we consider these approaches applications that could benefit from our scalable discovery of relays. Other work on QoS-improving overlays [10] is focusing on packet loss reduction via Forward Error Correction and alternative path routing rather than *discovery*. A *routing underlay* is suggested in [6], exposing topology information to overlays on top, avoiding redundant probing. The approach differs from ours as AS-level path inference, rather than path similarity, is employed.

[4] suggests a heuristic for finding good alternative paths in large systems. It considers paths at BGP- rather than router level. The approach relies on the *earliest divergence rule*, stating that BGP paths that diverge from the default path the earliest have a high chance of converging later. Compared to ours, this approach requires unbounded probing of candidate relay nodes and BGP information. RSIM [5] is a *node* similarity metric, used to *predict* path similarity. It is based on the number of common routers shared by paths from two sources to multiple destinations. In comparison, we directly estimate and employ path similarity. Using synthetic coordinates to faster predict Internet properties was extensively pursued ([7], [3]), however focusing on latency. To the best of our knowledge, we make the first attempt to derive and use synthetic coordinates for path disjointness prediction.

5.   Conclusions

Using alternative paths helps improving QoS of communication across the Internet. Such paths can be formed by using explicit relays among the nodes of an overlay network that lead communication around network bottlenecks. The crux of the approach is to identify a suitable relay that leads to a new path which is highly disjoint from the default path given by Internet routing. In small-scale systems, such relays can be identified by exhaustive search of the overlay network. Our work focuses on large-scale, possibly dynamic, systems (e.g. volunteer p2p networks), in which such exhaustive search can not be applied. We propose a technique that identifies good relays from the ones that have been suitable for similar paths in the recent past. Our evaluation on 200 PlanetLab nodes shows that we successfully identify suitable relays much faster than exhaustive search, with low, constant cost. We are currently investigating distributed storage mechanisms for path similarity data to enable a distributed PathCache implementation.

Acknowledgments

This work is partially supported by the *CoreGRID* Network of Excellence, funded by the European Commission's FP6 programme (contract IST-2002-004265).

References

[1] D. G. Andersen, H. Balakrishnan, M. F. Kaashoek, and R. Morris. Resilient overlay networks. In *Proceedings of ACM SOSP*, 2001.

[2] D.G. Bonett. Sample Size Requirements for Estimating Pearson, Kendall and Spearman Correlations In*Psychometrika*, 2000.

[3] R. Cox, F. Dabek, F. Kaashoek, J. Li, and R. Morris. Practical, distributed network coordinates. In *ACM SIGCOMM Computer Communication Review*, 2004.

[4] T. Fei, S. Tao, L. Gao, and R. Guerin. How to Select a Good Alternate Path in Large Peer-to-Peer Systems. In *Proceedings of IEEE INFOCOM*, 2006.

[5] N. Hu and P. Steenkiste. Quantifying Internet End-to-End Route Similarity. In*Passive and Active Measurement Conference (PAM)*, 2006.

[6] A. Nakao, L. Peterson, and A. Bavier. A routing underlay for overlay networks. In *Proceedings of ACM SIGCOMM*, 2003.

[7] T. S. E. Ng and H. Zhang. Predicting Internet network distance with coordinates-based approaches. In*Proceedings of IEEE INFOCOM*, 2002.

[8] T. Nguyen and A. Zakhor. Path diversity with forward error correction (PDF) system for packet switched networks. In *Proceedings of IEEE INFOCOM*, 2003.

[9] N. Spring, R. Mahajan, D. Wetherall, and T. Anderson. Measuring ISP topologies with Rocketfuel. In*IEEE/ACM Transactions on Networking*, 2004.

[10] L. Subramanian, I. Stoica, H. Balakrishnan, and R. H. Katz. OverQoS: An Overlay Based Architecture for Enhancing Internet QoS. In *Proc. NSDI*, 2004.

[11] B. Zhang, T. S. E. Ng, A. Nandi, R. Riedi, P. Druschel, and G. Wang. Measurement based analysis, modeling, and synthesis of the Internet delay space. In *Proceedings of ACM SIGCOMM on Internet measurement*, 2006.

[12] M.G Kendall. A New Measure of Rank Correlation. In*Biometrika, Vol. 30, No. 1/2, 81-93. Jun.*, 1938

ATOMIC COMMITMENT IN TRANSACTIONAL DHTS*

Monika Moser
Zuse Institute Berlin (ZIB)
Berlin, Germany
moser@zib.de

Seif Haridi
Royal Institute of Technology (KTH)
Stockholm, Sweden
haridi@kth.se

Abstract   We investigate the problem of atomic commit in transactional database systems built on top of Distributed Hash Tables. Therefore we present a framework for DHTs to provide strong data consistency and transactions on data stored in a decentralized way. To solve the atomic commit problem within distributed transactions, we propose to use an adaption of Paxos commit as a non-blocking algorithm. We exploit the symmetric replication technique existing in the DKS DHT to determine which nodes are necessary to execute the commit algorithm. By doing so, we achieve a lower number of communication rounds in contrast to applying traditional Three-Phase-Commit protocols. We also show how the proposed solution can cope with dynamism due to churn in DHTs. Our solution works correctly relying only on an inaccurate failure detection of node failure, what is necessary for systems running over the Internet.

Keywords: Atomic Commit, Database, Transactions, DHT, Paxos

---

*This research work is carried out under the SELFMAN project funded by the European Commission and the Network of Excellence Core-GRID funded by the European Commission.

1.   Introduction

DHTs provide the ability to store and lookup data in a fully decentralized manner. They can be utilized to build a distributed database on top of it. We consider such a database which provides the user with an interface to perform transactions on its data, and where all operations on distributed data are done in a transactional manner. For distributed transactions an atomic commit protocol is needed to guarantee that either all operations of the transaction take place or none of them. Only committed states are made visible. Another important mechanism of distributed transactional systems is concurrency control, which ensures that concurrent transactions cannot interfere with each other. We present a framework for having transactions on DHTs and consequently strong notion of data consistency in DHTs. Our focus in this paper is on the atomic commit problem.

A typical transaction is a sequence with an arbitrary number of operations on different items. This sequence of operations is enclosed by a *Begin of Transaction (BOT)* and an *End of Transaction (EOT)*. BOT signals that a client or application wants to start a transaction. The end of a transaction is marked with EOT. At this point the system has to ensure that either all of the operations contained in the transaction take place or none of them will affect the system. Therefore a node receiving EOT starts a distributed commit protocol where it determines whether all nodes, which are responsible for items that are involved in the transaction, can execute the operations. If all those nodes confirm that they can do so, the transaction will be committed.

We propose a solution for atomic commit which is based on the Paxos commit algorithm introduced in [6]. We show how it can be adapted for a DHT-based database. The Paxos commit algorithm defines different roles for nodes running the protocol. We use the specific structure and services of the DHT to determine which nodes have to act in which role. As DHTs are systems that are highly dynamic, we show how we can cope with the dynamism and when we have to fix the group of nodes involved in the protocol. Another advantage of the Paxos commit algorithm is that it can handle a number of failures among the nodes without relying on a perfect failure detector, which is an important property for distributed systems running on the Internet.

Outline.   Section 2 gives the problem description for this paper. In section 3 we describe the architecture of our system. Our approach for atomic commit in a transactional DHT-based database system is presented in 4. Section 5 lists some related work. As this paper summarizes some work in progress, we add an outlook on our future work to the final conclusions presented in 6.

2. Problem Description

DHTs are utilized to efficiently find data items stored in a P2P system. They use a hashing function to assign each data item consisting of (Key, Value) an identifier in a typically large identifier space. Each node that is part of the DHT is responsible for at least one subrange in the identifier space. Examples for DHTs are DKS [4], Chord [1], Chord# [2] and CAN [10].

There exist a number of storage systems which are built on DHTs, e.g. Bamboo[1] which is based on Pastry and DHash[2] which is based on Chord. Mostly items in such systems are replicated for a higher degree of availability and reliability. These systems are typically read-only storage systems.

Atomicity is one of the four ACID properties of a transaction. A transaction will be executed either completely or will have no effects on the data at all. Changes on data made by a transaction will be made persistent when it reaches its *commit point* at EOT. A transaction will either end with *commit* or with *abort*, in which case the data modifications are canceled, and the transaction has no effect. In distributed databases, items involved in a transaction may be spread over different nodes. There is one node that acts as the *Transaction Manager (TM)*, which is responsible for coordinating the transaction. Nodes that are responsible for items which are involved in the transaction are the *Transaction Participants (TP)*. A transaction can only be committed if each of the TPs is able to commit its part of the transaction. All TPs have to agree on the same outcome of the transaction. Well known solutions to this problem are *Two-Phase-Commit (2PC)* algorithms. In the first phase (voting phase) the TM initially asks all the TPs to prepare. The TPs answer whether they are prepared and were able to commit. In the second phase (decision phase) the TM tells the TPs to commit if all TPs are prepared and are able to make their changes durable. Figure 1 shows the possible states of a 2PC protocol with one Transaction Manager and two Transaction Participants.

One Problem with the basic 2PC is that it is a blocking protocol. If the TM fails in the decision phase (state Collecting), the TPs are not able to receive the outcome of the transaction and are blocked. A number of non-blocking algorithms were introduced. *Three-Phase-Commit (3PC)* algorithms introduce an extra phase to circumvent a blocking state. For DHT-based systems adding an extra phase might be very costly in terms of latencies, in particular if nodes are distributed worldwide. Most of them are also relying on timeouts, which might impact the performance for Internet-based systems with fluctuating link delays. We therefore use the Paxos based commit algorithm introduced in [6]. Instead of using an extra phase, votes of the TPs are sent to a number

---

[1] http://www.bamboo-dht.org/
[2] http://pdos.csail.mit.edu/chord/

154

Figure 1. State-charts for a 2-Phase-Commit Protocol with 2 Participants and 1 Transaction Manager

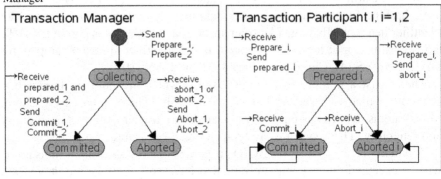

of so called acceptors. The non-blocking property is introduced at the cost of a higher number of messages, instead of an additional communication round. We think that in a P2P environment it is more important to reduce latency than reducing the number of messages sent, to achieve an acceptable performance. Besides the size of the messages needed for the protocol is small. Another important property of the Paxos commit protocol is that it does not rely on a perfect failure detector.

Next we will describe the architecture of the system for which our solution is designed for.

3. Architecture of the Transactional System

In DHT-based transactional database systems each node can act as TM and as TP. Clients and applications which invoke transactions are connected to arbitrary nodes in the DHT. Any such node will act as a TM for the transaction started by the associated client. During the commit phase all nodes which are responsible for an item that is involved in the transaction act as TPs. Items in our DHT are replicated. Our solution is illustrated with the symmetric replication scheme of the DKS DHT as mentioned below. With symmetric replication replicas can be accessed concurrently.

3.1 Symmetric Replication and Data Consistency

We consider symmetric replication as described in [5, 3]. The storage system replicates each item with the replication factor f. An identifier of an item is associated with $f - 1$ other identifiers. This corresponds to a partition of the identifier space of size N in $\frac{N}{f}$ equivalence classes. The identifiers for replicas of an item with identifier id are determined using the following function: $r_i(id) = (id + (i-1)\frac{N}{f}) mod N$, for $1 \leq i \leq f$. Using symmetric replication, items can be accessed concurrently by determining their associated identifiers.

Our system maintains strong consistency among operations on data by including at least a majority of replicas in these operations. All operations related to data enforce the invariant that a majority of replicas for a certain data item is up to date. A majority contains at least $\lfloor \frac{f}{2} \rfloor + 1$ replicas. As write and store operations are performed on a majority, a read operation includes a majority as well, to ensure to get the latest version of an item. As a consequence join, leave and node failure handling have to maintain the replication factor. Especially they have to ensure that the number of replicas never exceeds f. When a new node joins the system, it gets the data it will be responsible for, and then takes over the responsibility from the node formerly responsible for those items. There is no point where they are both responsible for the transfered items in order to ensure that the number of replicas for each item does not exceed f. When a node leaves, it transfers the responsibility for its items to its successor node and thus again does not change the number of replicas for an item. When a node failure is detected, another node in the system becomes responsible for this node's items. It will read the items from the remaining replicas. Here the number of replicas is restored to f after some time, but it does not increase the number of replicas

According to Brewer's conjecture [12], we will only be able to maintain availability until partitioned overlays merge. It is impossible to maintain consistency, availability and partition-tolerance at the same time. Our emphasis is on consistency.

3.2 System Properties

A DHT-based database system differs from a traditional distributed database system in a number of points that are important for the design of the commit algorithm. Traditional distributed database systems usually consist of a number of reliable nodes connected through a LAN. In contrast a DHT is built on unreliable nodes. The MTTF (Mean Time to Failure) of a node in a DHT system is typically much smaller. The need for a non-blocking atomic commit algorithm therefore is higher than in a traditional database system. Traditional database systems often are optimized for the failure-free case as failures occur quite seldom.

Another point is latency. In DHT-based database systems latencies are high due to the WAN communication paths and the routing structure of a DHT. A non-blocking atomic commit algorithm implemented in a DHT has to be low in the number of communication rounds to achieve acceptable performance.

The number of nodes involved in a transaction is typically much higher for a DHT-based system as items are distributed over a larger number of nodes. There are even two levels of distribution. Additionally distributed items are replicated and again spread over the whole system. The number of nodes involved in a transaction depends on the number of items which are part of the transaction. An atomic commit algorithm for a DHT therefore has to be scalable in the number of participants.

The failure model for a traditional database system is normally based on a crash-recovery process model. In contrast there are several possible failure models for DHT-based database systems. In this paper we consider a DHT database system that is based on a crash-stop process model. When a node crashes and later recovers, it joins as a new node. Therefore it does not need to remember any previously stored data, nor logs of uncommitted transactions. Here we rely on the majority of nodes holding replicas of items involved in ongoing transactions will survive. This is a consequence of our majority based consistency mechanisms.

The atomic commit algorithm we present in the next section assumes the crash-stop DHT model and symmetric replication. It is tailored for high latencies, high distribution of items and it can handle the failure of the TM.

4. Atomic Commit Protocol for a DHT

As mentioned above nodes of the DHT can act as TMs and as TPs. A client that invokes a transaction is connected to a node in the DHT. This node will be the TM for that particular transaction. Invoking a transaction will result in the creation of a transaction item, such that the key of the transaction item results in an identifier that belongs to the responsibility of the TM and which we refer to as the transaction-ID. This item will contain the result of the transaction and will be stored in the transaction manager and also symmetrically stored in the DHT.

As failures of nodes in DHTs may occur quite often, a non-blocking atomic commit protocol is needed. Gray and Lamport [6] introduce a commit protocol built on the Paxos consensus algorithm [8–9]. Our solution is an adaptation of this commit protocol to work for DHTs. The Paxos commit protocol uses a number of nodes that collect the votes of the TPs. These are called acceptors. In the case of a TM's failure the decision for the transaction can be requested from the associated set of acceptors. We adapt this protocol by having the set of nodes responsible for the replicated transaction item as our set of acceptors. Therefore the number of acceptors is determined by the replication factor of the whole system.

As mentioned above the Paxos commit algorithm provides an ability to circumvent the blocking problem of a Two-Phase-Commit protocol. In the next section we will briefly introduce the properties of the Paxos consensus algorithm and thereafter Paxos commit.

4.1   The Paxos Protocol

Paxos is an algorithm which guarantees uniform consensus. Consensus is necessary when a set of nodes has to decide on a common value. Uniform consensus satisfies the following properties: 1. *Uniform agreement*, which means that no two nodes decide differently, regardless of whether they fail after the decision was taken; 2. *Validity* describes the property that the value which is decided can only be a value that has been proposed by some node; 3. *Integrity*, meaning no node may decide twice and finally 4. *Termination*, every node eventually decides some value [7]. Paxos assumes an eventual leader election to guarantee termination. Eventual leader election can be built by using inaccurate failure detectors.

Paxos defines different roles for the nodes. There are *Proposers*, which propose a value, and *Acceptors*, which either accept a proposal or reject it in a way that guarantees uniform agreement. Paxos as described in [9] assumes that each node may act as both proposer and acceptor. In our solution presented below we use different nodes as proposers and acceptors.

The above mentioned properties of uniform agreement can be guaranteed by Paxos whenever a majority of acceptors is alive. That means, it tolerates the failure of F acceptors out of initially $2F + 1$ acceptors.

Paxos basically consists of two phases called the read and write phase. In the *read phase* a node makes a proposal and tries to get a promise that his value will be accepted by a majority or it gets a value that it must adopt for the write phase. In the *write phase* a node tries to impose the value resulting from the read phase on a majority of nodes. Either the read or write phase may fail. Proposals are ordered by proposal numbers. By using an eventual leader to coordinate different proposals, the algorithm will eventually terminate.

4.2   Atomic Commit with Paxos

Uniform consensus alone is not enough for solving atomic commit. Atomic commit has additional requirements on the value decided. If some node proposes abort or is perceived to have crashed by other nodes before a decision was taken, then all nodes have to decide on abort. To decide on commit, all nodes have to propose prepared.

In the Paxos Commit protocol [6] we have a set of acceptors, with a distinguished leader, and a set of proposers. The set of acceptors play the role of the coordinator and the set of proposers are those who have to decide in the atomic commit protocol.

Each proposer creates a separate instance of the Paxos algorithm with itself as the only proposer to decide on either prepared or abort. All instances share the same set of acceptors. It can be noted that the Paxos consensus can be optimized, because there is only one proposer for each instance. If a proposer fails, one of the acceptors, normally the leader, acts on behalf of that proposer in the particular Paxos instance and proposes abort.

Acceptors store the decisions of all proposers. Whenever an acceptor has collected all decisions, it sends commit or abort to the leader. A leader needs to receive the decision of a majority of acceptors to do the final decision. Thereafter the final abort/commit is sent to the initial proposers. If the leader fails by the eventual failure detector, another leader will take over and can extract the decision from a majority of acceptors and complete the protocol.

The state-chart of a proposer is similar to the state-chart of a TP in the original 2PC protocol, as shown in figure 1. Also the state-chart of an acceptor is similar to that of the TM, referring to the same figure. But instead of sending the decision commit to the participants, the acceptors send the outcome to the leader.

4.3   Adapted Paxos Commit for a DHT

Paxos is designed for a static environment with a fixed number of participants and acceptors. However each transaction involving items of a DHT has different nodes involved. Every node responsible for an item in a transaction becomes a TP for that particular transaction. In fact the TM initially does not know which nodes are TPs. The number of nodes varies according to whether or not the node is responsible for an item that is involved in the transaction. As mentioned earlier, each transaction has a certain transaction item. We therefore use a certain group of acceptors for each particular transaction, that can be easily determined from the transaction-ID of the transaction item, by using symmetric replication. The set of acceptors consists of the nodes responsible for a replica of the transaction item. One advantage is that we create a pseudo static group of acceptors. The group of acceptors is fixed temporarily by the TM just before the prepare request is sent to the TPs. With the prepare request the TM informs the nodes responsible for items in the transaction about the set of acceptors. When such a node receives the prepare request, it becomes a TP and starts its Paxos instance. It has to be noted that a node could be responsible for several items involved in the transaction. The TP runs a separate Paxos instance for each item it is responsible for.

At this stage the group of TPs and the group of acceptors are fixed. It will remain fixed during the atomic commit phase. If a node joins/leaves in a DHT, the responsibility of certain items has to be transferred. The transfer of the responsibility of items involved in an active commit protocol is deferred until the protocol instance terminates.

One modification to the Paxos commit is that the acceptors collect the votes from the TPs and classify them per item. When a majority of TPs holding a replica of an item votes prepared, the acceptors record a prepared vote for this specific item. If the decision is prepared for all items, the transaction commits.

When a TM knows the decision for the transaction, it can store this information in the transaction item. This item can then be replicated in the DHT just like regular data items. Whenever a TP does not receive the result of the transaction from the TM, it can query the result of the transaction by reading the transaction item stored in the DHT.

Another issue is garbage collection of transaction items. As information on previous transactions grows by time, garbage collection is needed to throw away information which is no longer needed. This can be done in different ways either by acknowledgment messages or expiry date associated with transaction items.

Most of the operations mentioned in this particular DHT-based Paxos commit are operations on a set of identifiers. This is supported efficiently by bulk operations in DHTs as described in the DKS system [5, 3].

5.   Related Work

In [11] Paxos is used to achieve consensus in DHTs. The authors present a middleware service called PaxonDHT, which provides a mean to guarantee strong consistency among a set or replicas. In contrast to PaxonDHT our work is providing an approach for atomic commit with replicas of several items involved.

OceanStore [13] provides the ability to concurrently update data stored in a global persistent data store. A master replica is required which consists of a set of nodes which run a Byzantine agreement protocol to cooperate with each other. In [13] the authors mention that transactions could be built on top of the API of OceanStore. Our work considers a system that provides transactions in its own interface and provides strong consistency among operations on data.

6.   Conclusion and Future Work

We presented a framework for having transactions on DHTs and consequently strong notion of data consistency in DHTs. We focus on the atomic commit problem. Our solution is based on the Paxos commit algorithm. We showed why Paxos commit is suitable for DHT-based systems and how we can adapt it for transactional DHT-based databases. Among nodes Paxos commit defines a set of acceptor and a set of proposers. Our approach uses the symmetric replication scheme for DHTs to determine a pseudo static group of acceptors. The non-blocking property of this commit protocol is important as failures in DHTs occur quite often. Another advantage is a lower number of communication rounds compared to traditional non-blocking algorithms in distributed database systems like Three-Phase-Commit. Paxos commit can handle a number of failures among the nodes which are involved in the atomic commit without violating the properties of atomic commit. Further we showed how to handle dynamism in a DHT due to churn. We defined the phases when it is necessary to fix the group of participants in the algorithm to enable a correct atomic commit.

There is a number of issues left that will be addressed in the future. We will investigate concurrency control for a DHT-based database system. An optimistic concurrency control seems reasonable for this scenario. One solution will be a timestamp based ordering. Further we will evaluate the whole architecture and specify the algorithms formally.

References

[1] I. Stoica, R. Morris, D. Karger, F. Kaashoek and H. Balakrishnan. Chord: A Scalable Peer-To-Peer Lookup Service for Internet Applications. *Proceedings of the 2001 ACM SIGCOMM Conference*, 2001, 149-160

[2] Thorsten Schütt, Florian Schintke and Alexander Reinefeld. Structured Overlay without Consistent Hashing: Empirical Results. *Proceedings of the Sixth Workshop on Global and Peer-to-Peer Computing (GP2PC'06)*, 2006

[3] A. Ghodsi. Distributed *k*-ary System: Algorithms for Distributed Hash Tables KTH. Doctoral Dissertation, KTH — Royal Institute of Technology, 2006

[4] L. Onana Alima, S. El-Ansary, P. Brand and S. Haridi. DKS (N, k, f): A Family of Low Communication, Scalable and Fault-Tolerant Infrastructures for P2P Applications. In *Proceedings of the 3st International Symposium on Cluster Computing and the Grid*, 2003

[5] A. Ghodsi, L. Alima and S. Haridi. Symmetric Replication for Structured Peer-to-Peer Systems. In *The 3rd Int Workshop on Databases, Information Systems and Peer-to-Peer Computing*, 2005

[6] J. Gray and L. Lamport. Consensus on transaction commit. In *ACM Trans. Database Syst.*, ACM Press, 2006, 31, 133-160

[7] R. Guerraoui and L. Rodrigues. Introduction to Reliable Distributed Programming. Springer-Verlag, 2006

[8] L. Lamport. Paxos Made Simple. 2001

[9] L. Lamport. The part-time parliament. In *ACM Trans. Comput. Syst.*, ACM Press, 1998, 16, 133-169

[10] S. Ratnasamy, P. Francis, M. Handley, R. Karp and S. Schenker. A scalable content-addressable network. In *SIGCOMM '01: Proceedings of the 2001 conference on Applications, technologies, architectures, and protocols for computer communications*, ACM Press, 2001, 161-172

[11] B. Temkow, A. Bosneag, X. Li and M. Brockmeyer. PaxonDHT: Achieving Consensus in Distributed Hash Tables. In *SAINT '06: Proceedings of the International Symposium on Applications on Internet, IEEE Computer Society*, 2006, 236-244

[12] S. Gilbert and N. Lynch. Brewer's conjecture and the feasibility of consistent, available, partition-tolerant web services. In *SIGACT News*, 2002

[13] J. Kubiatowicz , et al. OceanStore: An Architecture for Global-scale Persistent Storage. In *Proceedings of ACM ASPLOS*, 2000

V

JOBS, INFORMATION AND RESOURCES MANAGEMENT

INFORMATION QUALITY EVALUATION FOR GRID INFORMATION SERVICES

Wei Xing, Oscar Corcho, Carole Goble
School of Computer Science
University of Manchester
United Kingdom
wxing@cs.man.ac.uk
ocorcho@cs.man.ac.uk
carole@cs.man.ac.uk

Marios Dikaiakos
Department of Computer Science
University of Cyprus, Cyprus
mdd@cs.ucy.ac.cy

Abstract   The quality of the information provided by information services deployed in the EGEE production testbed differs from one system to another. Under the same conditions, the answers provided for the same query by different information services can be different. Developers of these services and of other services that are based on them must be aware of this fact and understand the capabilities and limitations of each information service in order to make appropriate decisions about which and how to use a specific information service. This paper proposes an evaluation framework for these information services and uses it to evaluate two deployed information services (BDII and RGMA) and one prototype that is under development (ActOn). We think that these experiments and their results can be helpful for information service developers, who can use them as a benchmark suite, and for developers of information-intensive applications that make use of these services.

Keywords: Grid, Grid Information Service, Information Quality, Evaluation

1.   Introduction and Motivation

Information Services are regarded as a vital component of Grid infrastructure. They address the challenging problem of discovery and monitoring of a variety of Grid resources, including services, hardware, software, etc. The quality of information provided by information systems affects the performance and the behaviour of other dependent Grid services. For instance, a Grid meta-scheduling service will not work optimally if the quality of the information used for decision making is poor; a Grid Resource Broker depends on the Grid resource information provided by the information services that it uses; etc.

There is little work on the evaluation of information quality of Grid information services. Most evaluation studies focus on performance measurement [1], evaluating scalability, overload, query response time, etc. Such measurements are based on the assumption that information quality is equal for different information services. However, this assumption does not hold in reality, since each information system has different mechanisms for collecting and processing information, and adopts different information models for storage and querying. We cover this in our experiments, which show that even for a simple query each system provides different results. For example, for the query *"find me Computing Elements which support the Biomed Virtual Organisation"* the two EGEE default information services, BDII and RGMA, gave 151 and 30 results respectively. Independently of the reasons for such differences, the main outcome from this simple test is that information quality of currently-deployed Grid information services has to be considered carefully.

The work described in this paper has several objectives. First, we want to obtain a **fair systematic approach to measure information quality of different Grid information services,** so that we can compare them and provide guidelines related to when each of them can be used. One challenge is related to the fact that different Grid information services have different information models to represent the same type of Grid resources: some of them use LDAP to represent that information and others use relational models, and the information that they store about each resource may also differ. Unlike information quality evaluation in other domains (such as Web search, where precision and recall measurements can be obtained by counting numbers of documents), the information objects in our evaluation are heterogeneous, both in the information model used and in its access API, what makes it hard to compare the outputs. We have proposed the use of a common information model to allow comparisons between these outputs, as explained in Section 3.2. Another challenge is related to the differences in the querying capabilities and expressiveness supported by each service, what makes it difficult to design a good set of relevant experiments for the evaluation. Some services allow making complex queries that relate information from different domains (*computing elements that sup-*

port a specific virtual organisation and a specific software environment) and others just provide simple querying functionalities. In our approach we have proposed a set of representative queries that may be issued by other middleware services or applications, with increasing levels of complexity.

Our second objective is to use our approach to **evaluate information quality of two EGEE information services (BDII and RGMA) and one prototype that is under development (ActOn)**. We will analyse the results from this evaluation and identify the reasons for obtaining them. These results can be used by developers working on these Grid information services, in order to improve them, and by developer of systems that are based on them.

The remaining of this paper is organised as follows. Section 2 describes the information systems to be evaluated. Section 3 introduces our evaluation framework, including the design rationale, the experiments, and the metrics to use for evaluation, together with details about how they are measured for each system. Section 4 describes the results of the experiments carried out, and provides some conclusions related to these results. Finally, Section 5 reflects about the lessons learnt in the design of this evaluation framework and gives references to additional performance tests that we have carried out.

2. Grid Information Services

Currently, there are several well-known and widely-used Grid information services: Monitoring and Discovery System (MDS), Berkeley DB Information Index (BDII), and RGMA [2–3]. These services are deployed in most Grid systems, such as Europe Data Grid, Crossgrid, and Open Science Grid, and widely used by Grid middleware and applications running on them. From these three services, we will select BDII and RGMA for our evaluation, since they are the default information services for the EGEE Grid. We do not include MDS because it is not used for Computing Elements (CEs) and Sites in EGEE and would make difficult to perform the comparison. Besides, BDII is based on MDS, with the same information model (information representation and access), hence the general results regarding information quality and recommendations obtained for BDII could be easily extrapolated to MDS. Besides these two services, we will evaluate our ontology-based information service (based on the ActOn [4] ontology-based integration architecture).

Berkeley DB Information Index (BDII) [2] is an improvement of MDS, the information service component of the Globus platform. It uses the MDS information model and access API and caches information with the Berkeley DB. Information about Grid resources is extracted by "information providers", software programs that collect and organise information from individual Grid entities, either by executing local operations or by contacting third-party information sources.

Relational Grid Monitoring Architecture (RGMA) [3] combines monitoring and information services based on a relational model, implemented with XML. It has been built in the context of the EU DataGrid project and implements the Grid Monitoring Architecture (GMA) proposed by the Open Grid Forum. GMA models the Grid information infrastructure with three types of components: information producers, information consumers, and a registry, which mediates the communication between them.

Active Ontology (ActOn)-based information service ActOn [4] is an ontology-based information integration system, developed by us, which can be used to maintain up-to-date information for dynamic, large-scale distributed systems. The ActOn architecture is comprised of a set of knowledge components, which represent knowledge from the application domain (e.g., the EGEE Grid) and from the information sources (e.g., RGMA and BDII servers); and software components, such as a metadata scheduler (MSch), an information source selector (ISS), a metadata cache (MC), and a set of information wrappers.

We will evaluate a deployment of the ActOn system that uses BDII and RGMA as information sources, and a Grid Ontology [5–6] as its information model, and has been deployed in the EGEE certificate and production testbeds.

3.   An evaluation framework for information quality in Grid information services

Information quality (IQ) can be defined as a measure of the value of the information provided by an information system to its users [7]. Quality is normally subjective and depends on the intended use of information. The authors in [7] distinguish a set of quality features (intrinsic, contextual, representational and accessibility IQ) and define different factors to be considered for each of them (accuracy, objectivity, reputation, relevancy, etc.).

The authors in [8] propose to focus on seven of these characteristics: completeness, accuracy, provenance, conformance to expectations, logical consistency and coherence, timeliness, and accessibility. We have selected three of them, namely *completeness*, *accuracy* and *conformance to expectations*.

We are not worried about the *provenance* of information, since we know clearly which are the information sources that we use in each moment and which are the information providers responsible for that information. We are not worried either about *accessibility*, since we assume that the systems work within a Grid security infrastructure (e.g., GSI), so that the information is accessible as long as the client has the rights to access it and knows the information model and API used by the corresponding information service.

With respect to the *logical consistency and coherence* and the *timeliness* of the information retrieved and aggregated from the information sources, these are features that will form part of our future evaluation work, and will be also considered in further developments of the ActOn-based information service. An example of why the first feature is important is the following: there are many cases where a computing element specifies that it gives support to MPI but does not comply with the requirements for running an MPI job, which are that it must be a CE server, must have an sshd service running on it, must have the libraries mpirun and libmpi.so in its file system, and must have at least two worker nodes. Information services like BDII or RGMA only store and provide the information that their information producers give them, without checking their consistency, hence they provide incorrect information due to this fact. As an example of the second feature, BDII normally updates the information that has been provided by its information sources every five or six minutes, what means that this information may be already inaccurate when a client requests it. Hence, having metadata about the lifetime and freshness of information in the information service is important.

Now we describe our information quality evaluation framework, including metrics to be used, the design rationale, and the experiments, together with details about how the metrics are obtained for each system.

3.1 Evaluation metrics

To check our three criteria, we want to know whether all information services obtain the same results when answering the same query, given the same conditions in the EGEE testbed. We also want to check how many of those answers are correct and how many of the existing answers are actually retrieved. This allows us to know whether the results provided by the services conform to the user expectations. To check this, we have selected two metrics commonly used in information retrieval: precision (The proportion of relevant information retrieved, out of all the information retrieved) and recall (the proportion of relevant information that is retrieved, out of all the relevant information available).

3.2 Experiment setup and design

Measurements are taken on the EGEE production testbed, which are accessed through the UI machines at the University of Manchester[1] and at the Institute of Physics of Belgrade[2]. A set of Java-based client software and Unix shell scripts have been developed to carry out the experiments and record their results. They are available at [6].

The key aspects upon which we compare different information services are their information model and the expressiveness of their query language. To

---

[1] ui.tier2.hep.manchester.ac.uk
[2] ce.phy.bg.ac.yu

evaluate these two features, we have proposed six representative queries that cover a wide range of Grid systems (hardware and software resources, middleware environment, services, applications, etc.) with increasing complexity:

- Query 1: Find all the Computing Elements (CEs) that support the BIO-MED Virtual Organisation (VO).

- Query 2: Find all the CEs that support the BIOMED VO and have more than 100 CPUs available.

- Query 3: Find all the CEs that support the MPI running environment.

- Query 4: Find all the CEs that support the BIOMED VO, have more than 100 CPUs available, and support the MPI running environment.

- Query 5: Find all the CEs where GATE (Geant4 Application for Tomographic Emission) can be run.

- Query 6: Find all the CEs that support the BIOMED VO, have more than 100 CPUs available, and where GATE can be run.

Table 1. An Example of the Query 1 in BDII, RGMA, and ActOn

Information Service	Query 1
BDII (LDAP Search)	```ldapsearch -x -H ldap://lcg-bdii.cern.ch:2170 -b mds-vo-name=local,o=grid '(&(objectClass=GlueVOView) (GlueVOViewLocalID=biomed))' GlueCEAccessControlBaseRule```
RGMA (SQL Query)	```select GlueCEVOViewUniqueID, Value from GlueCEVOViewAccessControlBaseRule WHERE Value='VO:biomed'```

ActOn (SPARQL Query)	```PREFIX egeeOnto: <http://www.cs.man.ac.uk/img/ontogrid#> SELECT ?ceid ?ceID ?VO```
	
	 ```WHERE ?ceid egeeOnto:CEUniqueID ?ceID . ?ceid egeeOnto:hasVO ?VO . OPTIONAL { ?ceid egeeOnto:VO ?ceID . FILTER (?vo = ''biomed'')}```

Each query has been translated into the query languages of the three information services. Table 1 shows an example for Query1. We use different clients to execute them and extract the results (e.g., ldapsearch for BDII, the gLite RGMA client tools for RGMA and a Java-based ActOn client for the ActOn-based information service).

Results are obtained in different manners. The result of a BDII query is a set of LDAP entries, of an RGMA query a set of table rows, and of an ActOn-based query a set of RDF triples. Figure 1 shows three different ways to show the same Grid resource (ce02.tier2.hep.manchester.ac.uk, an EGEE Computing

Element) in the three services evaluated. In our experiment we use each "Grid resource" obtained from a query as the basic unit for counting information, which will be used to calculate precision and recall.

Query results of BDII:
```
# biomed, ce02.tier2.hep.manchester.ac.uk:2119/jobmanager-lcgpbs-biomed, UKI-NORTHGRID-MAN-HEP, local, grid
dn: GlueVOViewLocalID=biomed,GlueCEUniqueID=ce02.tier2.hep.manchester.ac.uk:2119/jobmanager-lcgpbs-
biomed,mds-vo-name=UKI-NORTHGRID-MAN-HEP,mds-vo-name=local,o=grid
GlueCEAccessControlBaseRule: VO:biomed
```

Query results of RGMA:
```
+----------------------------------------------------------------------+
| GlueCEVOViewUniqueID                                       | Value    |
+----------------------------------------------------------------------+
|ce02.tier2.hep.manchester.ac.uk :2119/jobmanager-lcgpbs-biomed/biomed  | VO:biomed |
```

Query results of ActOn:
```
| ceid                                  | ceID                         | VO        |
| <http://img.cs.man.ac.uk/ontogrid1234423456>  | "ce02.tier2.hep.manchester.ac.uk" | "biomed" |
```

Figure 1. Results of BDII, RGMA, and ActOn for the the same Grid resource Computing Element at University of Manchester (ce02.manchester.ac.uk)

3.3 Experimental Results Measurement

In the experiment we examine the information retrieved for each of the six queries, so as to get their corresponding precision and recall measures.

Precision is easy to determine, since it can be computed manually by looking at the results obtained from each query. In all cases, we assume binary relevancy of information, that is, each piece of information retrieved is either relevant or irrelevant for the issued query.

Recall is more difficult to determine, due to the fact that the amount of information available in the EGEE production testbed changes frequently in these systems and there is no way to get accurate information about the actual state of the Grid resources that are available without using the information services that we are evaluating. To get a good approximation that can be used for our purposes, we execute each query 100 times, with a 4-minute interval between executions, that is, we monitor the testbed during 400 minutes. Then we use the highest value obtained from this 100 executions as the total number of relevant information to be used to calculate recall.

4. Evaluation Results and Conclusions

Tables 2, 3 and 4 provide the precision and recall measurements obtained after the execution of the previous experiments for the three information services:

BDII, RGMA and the ActOn-based information service. The values in the tables show the average of executing the queries 100 times.

Table 2. BDII Recall & Precision Measurement (100 times)

QueryNo.	Retrieved Info.	Relevant Info.	Precision	Recall
1	14,999	15,200	1	0.987
2	242,517	19,708	0.082	0.918
3	7174	7300	1	0.983
4	485034	4600	0.010	0.990
5	-	-	-	-
6	-	-	-	-

Table 3. RGMA Recall & Precision Measurement (100 times)

QueryNo.	Retrieved Info.	Relevant Info.	Precision	Recall
1	3417	15200	1	0.225
2	6321	6321	1	1
3	6568	7300	1	0.900
4	11245	4914	0.437	0.563
5	-	-	-	-
6	-	-	-	-

Table 4. ActOn Recall & Precision Measurement (100 times)

QueryNo.	Retrieved Info.	Relevant Info.	Precision	Recall
1	15200	15200	1	1
2	34100	34100	1	1
3	6568	7300	1	0.900
4	6568	7300	1	0.900
5	24	24	1	0.900
6	6	6	1	1

As a general comment, we can highlight the fact that BDII shows in general poor results with respect to recall and precision, while ActOn and RGMA present better results. This is mainly related to the repository that BDII uses (LDAP), which is too lightweight and hence provides weak information process and query capabilities; while RGMA's is based on relational databases and ActOn's is based on RDF, which both have better query capabilities.

Now we will analyse with more detail some of the system behaviours over specific queries, and derive more conclusions from these values:

BDII has weak query capabilities. Table 2 shows bad precision results for BDII in queries 2 and 4, while the results for queries 1 and 3 are excellent. This is related to its weak query ability. LDAP-based queries are string-based, and hence they cannot support queries over numerical values, such as "greater than or lower than". To improve this precision value, we need to fetch all information about CE CPUs as a string value first (as we have done to get these results), and then post-process (filter) the results on the client side. RGMA and the ActOn-based information service have better query abilities.

RGMA is not able to relate information available in different tables. Table 3 shows that RGMA has bad precision in query 4. It contains information to solve this query, but it comes from two different tables (GlueCE and GlueSubClusterSoftwareRunTimeEnvironment), and the query language used by RGMA does not allow joining both tables. Hence the situation is similar to the previous case: this problem can be solve on the client side by post-processing the results that have been obtained from each separate query.

RGMA is very sensitive to the registering and availability of information providers at a given point in time. Table 3 shows that RGMA has bad recall in query 1. This is because the amount of Computing Element producers that is available during the experiment is not always stable, due to the fact that either producers were not registered in the RGMA registry at that specific moment, or that the producers were not configured correctly or available at that point in time. BDII and the ActOn-based information service are more robust to this, due to the fact that they store information locally and do not depend on their information providers at the time of querying.

Some complex queries cannot be answered by one information service in isolation. Tables 2 and 3 show that BDII and RGMA can only answer the first four queries. They cannot answer queries 5 and 6 because their information providers cannot provide enough information and should be combined. This shows that the ability of BDII and RGMA to share their data resources is weak. On the other hand, the ActOn-based information service has the ability to adopt existing information sources as its information providers, and aggregate information from these information sources to answer such complex queries.

5. Lessons learned

We have gathered valuable lessons from our experience in designing the experiments for information quality measurement and conducting them on the

EGEE Grid testbed. Most of them are related to the fairness of the information quality measurement process.

First, **there are not standard domain-independent methods to measure information quality in information systems.** To design an experiment in a specific domain (e.g., Grid information services), we must design it according to that domain and the information needs of the information service users.

Second, **different information services use different information models, and usually provide different expressivity in their query languages or access APIs.** Hence a special effort has to be made in order to define clearly a fair way to perform measurements that takes into account these differences.

Acknowledgements

This work is supported by the EU FP6 OntoGrid project (FP6-511513), by the Marie Curie fellowship RSSGRID (FP6-2002-Mobility-5-006668), and by the EU FP6 CoreGrid Network of Excellence (FP6-004265). We also thank Pinar Alper (IMG group), Antun Balaz and Laurence Field (EGEE porject), Georges Da Costa and Anastasios Gounaris (CoreGrid WP2), for their comments.

References

[1] X. Zhang and J. Schopf, *Performance analysis of the globus toolkit monitoring and discovery service, mds2*, in the International Workshop on Middleware Performance (MP 2004), part of the 23rd International Performance Computing and Communications Workshop (IPCCC), April 2004.

[2] *Berkeley Database Information Index (BDII)*, http://lfield.home.cern.ch/lfield/cgi-bin/wiki.cgi?area=bdiipage=documentation.

[3] E. W. Team, *EDG RGMA*, www.marianne.in2p3.fr/datagrid/documentation/rgma-guide.pdf.

[4] W. Xing, O. Corcho, C. Goble, and M. Dikaiakos, *A Grid Information Service based on an Intelligent Information Integration Architecture*, in Europe Semantic Web Conference 2007 (ESWC-2007), 2007, Poster.

[5] M. Parkin, S. van den Burghe, O. Corcho, D. Snelling, and J. Brooke, *The Knowledge of the Grid: A Grid Ontology*, in Proceedings of the 6th Cracow Grid Workshop, Cracow, Poland, October 2006.

[6] *OntoGrid CVS*, http://www.ontogrid.net/ontogrid/downloads.jsp.

[7] R. Wang and D. Strong, *Beyond Accuracy: What Data Quality Means to Data Con-sumers*, Management Information Systems, vol. 12, no. 4, pp. 5 34, 1996.

[8] B. Hughes, *Metadata quality evaluation: Experience from the open language archives community*, in ICADL, 2004, pp. 320 329.

DESIGNING GENERAL, COMPOSABLE, AND MIDDLEWARE-INDEPENDENT GRID INFRASTRUCTURE TOOLS FOR MULTI-TIERED JOB MANAGEMENT*

Erik Elmroth, Peter Gardfjäll, Arvid Norberg,
Johan Tordsson, and Per-Olov Östberg
Dept. Computing Science and HPC2N, Umeå University, SE-901 87 Umeå, Sweden
{elmroth, peterg, arvid, tordsson, p-o}@cs.umu.se
http://www.gird.se

Abstract   We propose a multi-tiered architecture for middleware-independent Grid job management. The architecture consists of a number of services for well-defined tasks in the job management process, offering complete user-level isolation of service capabilities, multiple layers of abstraction, control, and fault tolerance. The middleware abstraction layer comprises components for targeted job submission, job control and resource discovery. The brokered job submission layer offers a Grid view on resources, including functionality for resource brokering and submission of jobs to selected resources. The reliable job submission layer includes components for fault tolerant execution of individual jobs and groups of independent jobs, respectively. The architecture is proposed as a composable set of tools rather than a monolithic solution, allowing users to select the individual components of interest. The prototype presented is implemented using the Globus Toolkit 4, integrated with the Globus Toolkit 4 and NorduGrid/ARC middlewares and based on existing and emerging Grid standards. A performance evaluation reveals that the overhead for resource discovery, brokering, middleware-specific format conversions, job monitoring, fault tolerance, and management of individual and groups of jobs is sufficiently small to motivate the use of the framework.

Keywords: Grid job management infrastructure, standards-based architecture, fault tolerance, middleware-independence, Grid ecosystem.

---

*Financial support has been received from The Swedish Research Council (VR) under contract number 621-2005-3667. This research was conducted using the resources of the High Performance Computing Center North (HPC2N).

1.   Introduction

We investigate designs for a standards-based, multi-tier job management framework that facilitates application development in heterogeneous Grid environments. The work is driven by the need for job management tools that:

- offer multiple levels of functionality abstraction,
- offer multiple levels of job control and fault tolerance,
- are independent of, and easily integrated with, Grid middlewares,
- can be used on a component-wise basis and at the same time offer a complete framework for more advanced functionality,

An overall objective of this work is to provide understanding of how to best develop such tools. Among architectural aspects of interest are, e.g., to what extent job management functionalities should be separated into individual components or combined into larger, more feature-rich components, taking into account both functionality and performance. As an integral part of the project, we also evaluate and contribute to current Grid standardization efforts for, e.g., data formats, interfaces and architectures. The evaluation of our approach will in the long term lead to the establishment of a set of general design recommendations.

Features of our prototype software include user-level isolation of service capabilities, a wide range of job management functionalities, such as basic submission, monitoring, and control of individual jobs; resource brokering; autonomous processing; and atomic management of sets of jobs. All services are designed to be middleware-independent with middleware integration performed by plug-ins in lower-level components. This enables both easy integration with different middlewares and transparent cross-middleware job submission and control.

The design and implementation of the framework rely on emerging Grid and Web service standards [3],[9],[2] and build on our own experiences from developing resource brokers and job submission services [6],[7],[8], Grid scheduling support systems [5], and the SweGrid Accounting System (SGAS) [10]. The framework is based on WSRF and implemented using the Globus Toolkit 4.

2.   A Model for Multi-Tiered Job Submission Architectures

In order to provide a highly flexible and customizable architecture, a basic design principle is to develop several small components, each designed to perform a single, well-defined task. Moreover, dependencies between components are kept to a minimum, and are well-defined in order to facilitate the use of alternative components. These principles are adopted with the overall idea that a specific middleware, or a specific user, should be able to make use of a subset of the components without having to adopt an entire, monolithic system [11].

We propose to organize the various components according to the following layered architecture.

Middleware Abstraction Layer.   Similar to the hardware abstraction layer of an operating system, the middleware abstraction layer provides the functionality of a set of middlewares while encapsulating the details of these. This construct allows other layers to access resources running different middlewares without any knowledge of their actual implementation details.

Brokered Job Submission Layer.   The brokered job submission layer offers fundamental capabilities such as resource discovery, resource selection and job submission, but without any fault tolerance mechanisms.

Reliable Job Submission Layer.   The reliable job submission layer provides a fault tolerant, reliable job submission. In this layer, individual jobs or groups of jobs are automatically processed according to a customizable protocol, which by default includes repeated submission and other failure handling mechanisms.

Advanced Job Submission & Application Layers.   Above the three previously mentioned layers, we foresee both an *advanced job submission layer*, comprising, e.g., workflow engines, and an *application layer*, comprising , e.g., Grid applications, portals, problem solving environments and workflow clients.

3.   The Grid Job Management Framework (GJMF)

Here follows a brief introduction to the GJMF, where the individual services and their respective roles in the framework are described.

The GJMF offers a set of services which combined constitute a multi-tiered job submission, control and management architecture. A mapping of the GJMF architecture to the proposed layered architecture is provided in Figure 1.

All services in the GJMF offer a user-level isolation of the service capabilities; a separate service component is instantiated for each user and only the owner of a service component is allowed to access the service capabilities. This means that the whole architecture supports a decentralized job management policy, and strives to optimize the performance for the individual user.

The services in the GJMF also utilize a local call structure, using local Java calls whenever possible for service-to-service interaction. This optimization is only possible when the interacting services are hosted in the same container.

The GJMF supports a dynamic one-to-many relationship model, where a higher-level service can switch between lower-level service instances to improve fault tolerance and performance.

178

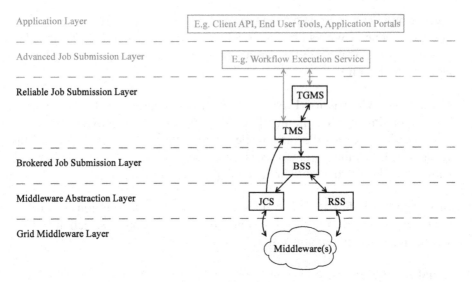

Figure 1. GJMF components mapped to their respective architectural layers.

As a note on terminology, there are two different types of job specifications used in the GJMF: abstract *task* specifications and concrete *job* specifications. Both are specified in JSDL [3], but vary in content. A job specification includes a reference to a computational resource to process the job, and therefore contains all information required to submit the job. A task specification contains all information required except a computational resource reference. The act of brokering, the matching of a job specification to a computational resource, thus transforms a task to a job.

Job Control Service (JCS). The JCS provides a functionality abstraction of the underlying middleware(s) and offers a platform- and middleware-independent job submission and control interface. The JCS operates on jobs and can submit, query, stop and remove jobs. The JCS also contains customization points for adding support for new middlewares and exposes information about jobs it controls through WSRF resource properties, which either can be explicitly queried or monitored for asynchronous notifications. Note that this functionality is offered regardless of underlying middleware, i.e., if a middleware does not support event callbacks the JCS explicitly retrieves the information required to provide the notifications. Currently, the JCS supports the GT4 and the ARC middlewares.

Resource Selection Service (RSS). The RSS is a resource selection service based on the OGSA Execution Management Services (OGSA EMS) [9]. The OGSA EMS specify a resource selection architecture consisting of two services, the Candidate Set Generator (CSG) and the Execution Planning Service (EPS).

The purpose of the CSG is to generate a candidate set, containing machines where the job *can* execute, whereas the EPS determines where the job *should* execute. Upon invocation, the EPS contacts the CSG for a list of candidate machines, reorders the list according to a previously known or explicitly provided set of rules and returns an *execution plan* to the caller.

The current OGSA EMS specification is incomplete, e.g., the interface of the CSG is yet to be determined. Due to this, the CSG and the EPS are in our implementation combined into one service - the RSS. The candidate set generation is implemented by dynamical discovery of available resources using a Grid information service, e.g., GT4 WS-MDS, and filtering of the identified resources against the requirements in the job description. The RSS contains a caching mechanism for Grid information, which alleviates the frequency of information service queries.

Brokering & Submission Service (BSS).   The BSS provides a functionality abstraction for brokered task submission. It receives a task (i.e., an abstract job specification) as input and retrieves an execution plan (a prioritized list of jobs) from the RSS. Next, the BSS uses a JCS to submit the job to the most suitable resource found in the execution plan. This process is repeated for each resource in the execution plan until a job submission has succeeded or the resource list has been exhausted. A client submitting a task to the BSS receives an EPR to a job WS-Resource in the JCS as a result. All further interaction with the job, e.g., status queries and job control is thus performed directly against the JCS.

Task Management Service (TMS).   The TMS provides a high-level service for automated processing of individual tasks, i.e., a user submits a task to the TMS which repeatedly sends the task to a known BSS until a resulting job is successfully executed or a maximum number of attempts have been made. Internally, the TMS contains a per-user job pool from which jobs are selected for sequential submission. The TMS job pool is of a configurable, limited size and acts as a task submission throttle. It is designed to limit both the memory requirements for the TMS and the flow of job submissions to the JCS. The job submission flow is also regulated via a congestion detection mechanism, where the TMS implements an incremental back-off behavior to limit BSS load in situations where the RSS is unable to locate any appropriate computational resources for the task. The TMS tracks job progress via the JCS and manages a state machine for each job, allowing it to handle failed jobs in an efficient manner. The TMS also contains customization points where the default behaviors for task selection, failure handling and state monitoring can be altered via Java plug-ins.

Task Group Management Service (TGMS). Like the TMS for individual tasks, the TGMS provides an automated, reliable submission solution for groups of tasks. The TGMS relies on the TMS for individual task submission and offers a convenient way to submit groups of independent tasks. Internally, the TGMS contains two levels of queues for each user. All task groups that contain unprocessed tasks are placed in a task group queue. Each task group queue, in turn, contains its own task queue. Tasks are selected for submission in two steps: first an active task group is selected, then a task from this task group is selected for submission. By default, tasks are resubmitted until they have reached a terminal state (i.e., succeeded or failed). A task group reaches a terminal state once all its tasks are processed. A task group can also be suspended, either explicitly by the user or implicitly by the service when it is no longer meaningful to continue to process the task group, e.g., when associated user credentials have expired. A suspended task group must be explicitly resumed to become active. The TGMS contains customization points for changing the default behaviors for task selection, failure handling and state monitoring.

Client API. The Client API is an integral part of the GJMF; it provides utility libraries and interfaces for creating tasks and task groups, translating job descriptions, customizing service behaviors, delegating credentials and contains service-level APIs for accessing all components in the GJMF. The purpose of the GJMF Client API is to provide easy-to-use programmable (Java) access to all parts of the GJMF.

For further information regarding the GJMF, including design documents and technical documentation of the services, see [12].

4.   Performance Evaluation

We evaluate the performance of the TGMS and the TMS by investigating the total cost imposed by the GJMF services compared to the total cost of using the native job submission mechanism of a Grid middleware, GT4 WS-GRAM (without performing resource discovery, brokering, fault recovery etc.).

In the reference tests with WS-GRAM, a client sequentially submits a set of jobs using the WS-GRAM Java API, delaying the submission of a job until the previous one has been successfully submitted. All jobs run the trivial /bin/true command and are executed on the Grid resources using the POSIX Fork mechanism. The jobs in a test are distributed evenly among the Grid resources using a round-robin mechanism. The WS-GRAM tests do not include any WS-MDS interaction. No job input or output files are transferred and no credentials are delegated to the submitted jobs. In each test, the total wall clock time is recorded. Tests are performed with selected numbers of jobs, ranging from 1 to 750.

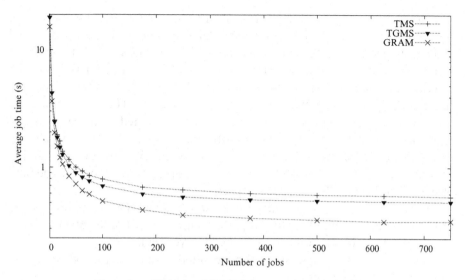

Figure 2.   GRAM and GJMF job processing performance.

The configuration of the GJMF tests is the same as for the WS-GRAM tests, with the following additions. For the TGMS tests, user credentials are delegated from the client to the service for each task group (each test). Delegation is also performed only once per test in the TMS case, as all jobs in a TMS test reuse the same delegated credentials. For both the TGMS and the TMS tests, the BSS performs resource discovery using the GT4 WS-MDS Grid information system and caches retrieved information for 60 seconds. In the TMS and TGMS tests, all services are co-located in the same container, to enable the use of local Java calls between the services, instead of (more costly) Web service invocations.

Test Environment.   The test environment includes four identical 2 GHz AMD Opteron CPU, 2 GB RAM machines, interconnected with a 100 Mbps Ethernet network, and running Ubuntu Linux 2.6 and Globus Toolkit 4.0.3.

In all tests, one machine runs the GJMF (or the WS-GRAM client) and the other three act as WS-GRAM/GT4 resources. For the GJMF tests, the RSS retrieves WS-MDS information from one of the three resources, which aggregates information about the other two.

Analysis.   Figure 2 illustrates the average time required to submit and execute a job for different number of jobs in the test. As seen in the figure, the TGMS offers a more efficient way to submit multiple tasks than the TMS. This is due to the fact that the TMS client performs one Web service invocation per task whereas the TGMS client only makes a single, albeit large, call to the TGMS. The TGMS client requires between 13 (1 task) and 16.6 seconds (750 tasks) to delegate credentials, invoke the Web service and get a reply. For the TMS, the initial Web service call takes roughly 13 seconds (as it is associated with dynamic class-loading, initialization and delegation of credentials), additional calls average between 0.4 and 0.6 seconds. For the GRAM client, the initial Web service invocation takes roughly 12 seconds. The additional TMS Web service calls quickly become the dominating factor as the number of jobs are increased. When using Web service calls between the TGMS and the TMS this factor is canceled out. Conversely, when co-located with the TMS and using local Java calls, the TGMS only suffers a negligible overhead penalty for using the TMS for task submission. In a test with 750 jobs, the average job time is roughly 0.35 seconds for WS-GRAM, and approximately 0.51 and 0.57 seconds for the TGMS and TMS, respectively.

As the WS-GRAM client and the JCS use the same GT4 client libraries, the difference between the WS-GRAM performance and that of the other services can be used as a direct measure of the GJMF overhead.

In the test cases considered, the time required to submit a job (or a task) can be divided into three parts.

1 The initialization time for GT4 Java clients. This includes time for class loading and run-time environment initialization. This time may vary with the system setup but is considered to be constant for all three test cases.

2 The time required to delegate credentials. This only applies to the GJMF tests, not the test of WS-GRAM. Even though delegated credentials are shared between jobs, the TMS is still slightly slower than the TGMS in terms of credential delegation. The TMS has to retrieve the delegated credential for each task, whereas the TGMS only retrieves the delegated credential once per test.

3 The Web service invocation time. This factor grows with the size of the messages exchanged and affects the TGMS, as a description of each individual task is included in the TGMS input message. The invocation time is constant for the TMS and WS-GRAM tests, as these services exchange fixed size messages.

Summary. When co-hosted in the same container, the GJMF services allots an overhead of roughly 0.2 seconds per task for large task groups (containing 750 tasks or more). The main part of this overhead is associated with Java class loading, delegation of credentials and initial Web service invocation. These factors result in larger average overheads for smaller task groups. For task groups containing 5 tasks, the average overhead per task is less than 1 second, and less than 0.5 seconds for 15 tasks. It should also be noted that, as jobs are submitted sequentially but executed in parallel, the submission time (including the GJMF overhead), is masked by the job execution time. Therefore, when using real world applications with longer job durations than those in the tests, the impact of the GJMF overhead is reduced.

5.   Related Work

We have identified a number of contributions that relate to this project in different ways. For example, the Gridbus [16] middleware includes a layered architecture for platform-independent Grid job management; the GridWay Metascheduler [13] offers reliable and autonomous execution of jobs; the Grid-Lab Grid Application Toolkit [1] provides a set of services to simplify Grid application development; GridSAM [15] offers a Web service-based job submission pipeline which provides middleware abstraction and uses JSDL job descriptions; P-GRADE [14] provides reliable, fault-tolerant parallel program execution on the grid; and GEMLCA [4] offers a layered architecture for running legacy applications through grid services. These contributions all include features which partially overlap the functionality available in the GJMF. However, our work distinguishes itself from these contributions by, in the same software, providing i) a composable service-based solution, ii) multiple levels of abstraction, iii) middleware-interoperability while building on emerging Grid service standards.

6.   Concluding Remarks

We propose a multi-tiered architecture for building general Grid infrastructure components and demonstrate the feasibility of the concept by implementing a prototype job management framework. The GJMF provides a standards-based, fault-tolerant job management environment where users may use parts of, or the entire framework, depending on their individual requirements. Furthermore, we demonstrate that the overhead incurred by using the framework is sufficiently small (approaching 0.2 seconds per job for larger groups of jobs) to motivate the practical use of such an architecture. Initial tests demonstrate that by proper methods, including reuse of delegated credentials, caching of Grid information and local Java invocations of co-located services, it is possible to implement an efficient service-based multi-tier framework for job management. Considering the extra functionality offered and the small additional overhead imposed, the GJMF framework is an attractive alternative to a pure WS-GRAM client for the submission and management of large numbers of jobs.

Acknowledgments

We are grateful to the anonymous referees for constructive comments that have contributed to the clarity of this paper.

References

[1] G. Allen, K. Davis, K. N. Dolkas, N. D. Doulamis, T. Goodale, T. Kielmann, A. Merzky, J. Nabrzyski, J. Pukacki, T. Radke, M. Russell, E. Seidel, J. Shalf, and I. Taylor. Enabling

applications on the Grid - a GridLab overview. *Int. J. High Perf. Comput. Appl.*, 17(4), 2003.

[2] S. Andreozzi, S. Burke, L. Field, S. Fisher, B. Kónya, M. Mambelli, J. M. Schopf, M. Viljoen, and A. Wilson. Glue schema specification version 1.2 draft 7. http://glueschema.forge.cnaf.infn.it/uploads/Spec/GLUEInfoModel_1_2_final.pdf, March 2007.

[3] A. Anjomshoaa, F. Brisard, M. Drescher, D. Fellows, A. Ly, A. S. McGough, D. Pulsipher, and A. Savva. Job Submission Description Language (JSDL) specification, version 1.0. http://www.ogf.org/documents/GFD.56.pdf, March 2007.

[4] T. Delaittre, T. Kiss, A. Goyeneche, G. Terstyanszky, S.Winter, and P. Kacsuk. GEMLCA: Running legacy code applications as Grid services. *Journal of Grid Computing*, 3(1 – 2):75 – 90, June 2005. ISSN: 1570-7873.

[5] E. Elmroth and P. Gardfjäll. Design and evaluation of a decentralized system for Grid-wide fairshare scheduling. In H. Stockinger, R. Buyya, and R. Perrott, editors, *e-Science 2005, First International Conference on e-Science and Grid Computing*, pages 221–229. IEEE CS Press, 2005.

[6] E. Elmroth and J. Tordsson. An interoperable, standards-based Grid resource broker and job submission service. In H. Stockinger, R. Buyya, and R. Perrott, editors, *e-Science 2005, First International Conference on e-Science and Grid Computing*, pages 212–220. IEEE CS Press, 2005.

[7] E. Elmroth and J. Tordsson. A standards-based Grid resource brokering service supporting advance reservations, coallocation and cross-Grid interoperability. Submitted to *Concurrency and Computation: Practice and Experience*, December 2006.

[8] E. Elmroth and J. Tordsson. Grid resource brokering algorithms enabling advance reservations and resource selection based on performance predictions. *Future Generation Computer Systems. The International Journal of Grid Computing: Theory, Methods and Applications*, 2007, to appear.

[9] I. Foster, H. Kishimoto, A. Savva, D. Berry, A. Grimshaw, B. Horn, F. Maciel, F. Siebenlist, R. Subramaniam, J. Treadwell, and J. Von Reich. The Open Grid Services Architecture, version 1.5. http://www.ogf.org/documents/GFD.80.pdf, March 2007.

[10] P. Gardfjäll, E. Elmroth, L. Johnsson, O. Mulmo, and T. Sandholm. Scalable Grid-wide capacity allocation with the SweGrid Accounting System (SGAS). Submitted to *Concurrency and Computation: Practice and Experience*, October 2006.

[11] Globus. An "Ecosystem" of Grid Components. http://www.globus.org/grid_software/ecology.php. March 2007.

[12] Grid Infrastructure Research & Development (GIRD). http://www.gird.se. March 2007.

[13] E. Huedo, R.S. Montero, and I.M. Llorente. A framework for adaptive execution on Grids. *Software - Practice and Experience*, 34(7):631–651, 2004.

[14] P. Kacsuk, G. Dózsa, J. Kovács, R. Lovas, N. Podhorszki, Z. Balaton, and G. Gombás. P-GRADE: a Grid programming environment. *Journal of Grid Computing*, 1(2):171 – 197, 2003.

[15] W. Lee, A. S. McGough, and J. Darlington. Performance evaluation of the GridSAM job submission and monitoring system. In *UK e-Science All Hands Meeting*, Nottingham, UK, 2005.

[16] S. Venugopal, R. Buyya, and L. Winton. A Grid service broker for scheduling e-Science applications on global data Grids. *Concurrency Computat. Pract. Exper.*, 18(6):685–699, May 2006.

AMON - A USER-FRIENDLY JOB MONITORING FOR THE GRID

Ralph Müller-Pfefferkorn, Reinhard Neumann, Thomas William
Center for Information Services and High Performance Computing (ZIH)
Technische Universität Dresden
D-01062 Dresden, Germany

Ralph.Mueller-Pfefferkorn@tu-dresden.de

Reinhard.Neumann@tu-dresden.de

Thomas.William@zih.tu-dresden.de

Abstract   To process large amounts of data, in some fields of science hundreds or thousands of single jobs are submitted into a Grid. Monitoring the enormous numbers of jobs and their resource usage in such environments (like the LCG/gLite middleware) effectively becomes an important issue for the users. Current tools in LCG / gLite provide only limited value to the user as they are often simple command line applications only. Keeping an eye on large number of jobs can thus become quite painful.

In this paper, the user-centric monitoring system AMon is presented that has been developed within the HEPCG project. It provides Grid users with useful and graphical information that helps her/him to understand the status of the jobs and their usage of resources. The latter enables the user to better recover from job failures.

Keywords: LCG, gLite, job monitoring, resource usage monitoring, R-GMA, visualisation, portal, GridSphere

1.   Introduction

One of the frontiers in Grid Computing is the processing of large amounts of data. The Large Hadron Collider Computing Grid (LCG) project aims to provide the particle physics community of the LHC collider at CERN with an environment to be able to analyse the petabytes of data that will be produced every year.

A typical analysis scenario in this context consists of several hundreds or thousands of jobs each just reading some small part of the data (one or several sets of collision events). Another scenario is the simulation of particle physics events that are written as event sets. Both scenarios have the common problem of tracking the status of the single jobs, either to simply inform the user about his/her jobs or to help him to react in case of problems.

Existing monitoring tools in the LCG/gLite environment provide just limited functionality. They are either command line tools that deliver text strings for every job - which is hard to evaluate in the case of hundreds of jobs and the information they provide is very limited (e.g. status only or just parts of the information necessary to track down problems). Other tools focus on the monitoring of the hardware or the services in the Grid, which is not the information the user wants and needs.

Outside of gLite there are also ongoing efforts on monitoring. But most of them focus rather on infrastructure than on a user-centric job monitoring. Mon-ALisa [1] is a comprehensive system that can collect a variety of monitoring information. Currently, it focus mainly on hardware, network and service information to monitor the Grid infrastructure but it also allows to gather application specific information.

The High Energy Particle Physics Community Grid project[1] (HEPCG) [2] of the German D-Grid Initiative [3] wants to contribute to the functionality the LCG-Grid provides to physicists. One major goal is to improve the monitoring of jobs and their resource usage in a user centric way. This is meant to serve users who submit jobs as well as resource providers. For the latter the usage of their resources will be analysed for Grid management and planning.

The first section of this paper illustrates the goals of the monitoring system and provides an overview of its architecture. The following sections describe the single components in more details. At the end the status is described and an outlook will be given on further developments and features.

[1] funded by the German Federal Ministry of Education and Research (BMBF) under Grant No. 01AK802C

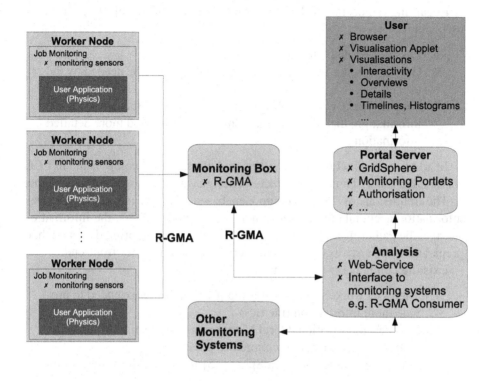

Figure 1. Architecture of the Job and Resource Usage Monitoring System

2. Goals and Architecture

The main goal of the developments is the creation of a job and resource usage monitoring that is focused on the user needs, where user means both the job submitter and the resource provider. It should be able to answer typical user (job submitter) questions regarding her/his jobs: What is the status of my job - still running, done, crashed? What about the memory consumption of my jobs? What is the CPU usage? Is there any critical entity in consumption of the resource? Such and more information can indicate problems or help in the case of unsuccessfully finished jobs. And, in general, these are information that the users are accustomed to have at their desktop computers.

On the other side it should help the resource providers to get an overview of what is going on on their machines. In the case of problems related to jobs and their resource usage the monitoring should support the site administrators in tracking them. And last but not least with the information they should be enabled to draw consequences from the usage of their resources - for planning and designing the Grid infrastructure.

Regarding the design of the monitoring there are other objectives from the users point of view:

1. Easy access and handling
2. Only limited knowledge about monitoring should be needed by the user
3. Support users with graphical representations of the pre-analysed information, that allow interaction to get further and more detailed information

In addition, the inclusion of existing and already used components in LCG was another point. Thus, an architectural design was setup as illustrated in figure 1: The architecture of AMon is component based. There is a separation between information accumulation on the single worker nodes (WN), the information storage, the gathering and analysis of the distributed monitoring data, and their preparation and visualisation for the user embedded in a user front-end.

Existing components that are used in AMon are:

1. The LCG worker node monitoring [6], which was extended to provide more information (metrics)
2. R-GMA, the Relational Grid Monitoring Architecture [4] as information system to store the monitoring data
3. The portal framework GridSphere [5] to embed the visualisation into

The information gathering, analysis and visualisation are new developments. They are independent of gLite as Web Services, portal technology and Java for graphics were used. A generic interface even allows to plug-in other systems for information gathering than R-GMA to AMon.

The next sections will describe the single components in more detail.

3. Visualisation and User Frontend

As the focus of AMon is on the user needs the description is started with the user front-end.

Web browsers are a common and known tool for most computer users. Thus, the access to the monitoring information is browser based. GridSphere [5], a JSR 168 compliant portal framework especially designed for Grid needs, is the integrating platform for the user interaction and the visualisation of the data. GridSphere already provides needed functionality like user management and Login/Logout. Additionally, with the GridPortlets package - a collection of portlets and services - Grid functionality like credential retrieval is available.

AMonVisualiser consists of a set of portlets (small Java classes that are plugged-in into the portal) and services (Java classes that provide tasks). If the user asks for monitoring information in a portlet, a services contacts the analysis

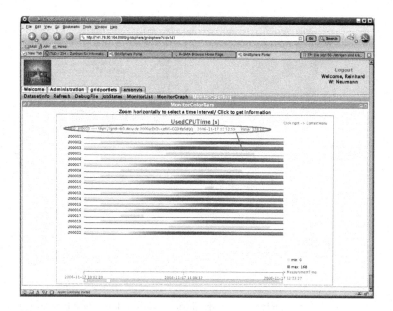

Figure 2. The monitoring is integrated into GridSphere. Here a example graph of the temporal development of an information (the CPU usage of the jobs). The red line and ellipse illustrate the interactivity - clicking in the display reveals more information. The ability to zoom in and out of the data is denoted by the scrollbars of the display.

service AMonAnalyser (see section 4) for the latest data. The visualisation itself is implemented as Java applets, that are fed with the data from AMonAnalyser and run in the users browser.

Visualisation is not just understood as putting data into static histograms. The visualisation provides the user with graphical representations of the information by allowing interactivity. Clicking on histograms, time lines or other charts will serve the user with detailed information about the chosen item, will lead to displays with extended information or allow to zoom into the data. Examples of displays are the temporal development of e.g. the CPU usage of the jobs or their memory consumption or their I/O (available metrics see section 5). Other charts may give summaries of metrics of their derivatives (see figures 2 and 3).

4. Information Gathering and Pre-Analysis

The second component - the analysis service AMonAnalyser - gathers the information from the distributed monitoring services and prepares them for the visualisation. As the amount of monitoring information can be quite significant this step is separated from the visualisation. It is setup as a Web Service running in an Tomcat application server [10] and Apache-Axis [9] environment.

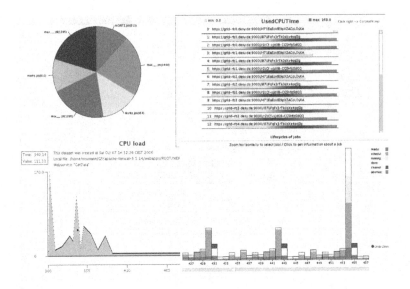

Figure 3. Examples of other displays for various kinds of information

This service is contacted by the visualisation. The monitoring data are transfered as SOAP messages. Inside SOAP they are packed into a table structure, where each row corresponds to a measurement at a certain time and each column represents a metric.

On the other side, AMonAnalyser provides a generic interface to monitoring systems. Currently, it is able to read out the R-GMA tables using an R-GMA consumer from the LCG worker node monitoring (see section 5) and the gLite Logging&Bookkeeping [11]. Access to other monitoring systems, like the Ganglia monitoring [8] is under development.

5. Information Accumulation and Storage

The LCG worker node monitoring [6] allows the users to start small job monitoring applications on the worker nodes. The user just has to set an environment variable to switch it on. Then, Python based scripts collect information about the status of the job.

The original version only provided information about wall clock time, CPU time and real, virtual and total memory usage of the job. The system was extended to provide more useful metrics that help the user not only to get an overview of his jobs but also help him to get hints to track down reasons for possible problems or errors. Table 1 lists all available metrics.

The architecture was changed such, that new metrics/sensors can be easily added. With the same environment variable as in the original version the user can now switch on all or single sensors. Additionally, the time intervals in

Category	Metrics
General	job ID; user name; the names of the resource broker, the computing element and the WN; job ID on WN
CPU	WallClockTime; UsedCPUTime; load averages
Memory Storage	real, virtual, total, and free memory; free and total swap space free space on home, temporary and work directory; summary of file system properties
File I/O	I/O rates for every file access of the application
Network	received and transmitted network

Table 1. Available metrics of the extended LCG worker node monitoring

which the information are collected are variable and configurable by the user. The default is to publish the data more often at the beginning of a job and then increase the time interval as the job is running. Nevertheless, the new version is fully backwards compatible - meaning that installing it will not need any other changes on the worker node compared to the original version.

The collected data are written to R-GMA, the Relational Grid Monitoring Architecture [4], which is used in LCG/gLite to store monitoring data. R-GMA is a kind of a distributed relational database, where monitoring data are stored in tables. It implements the OGF standard GMA, which is based on a producer-consumer-registry design. The existing table of the original LCG worker node monitoring (JobMonitor) was kept for backwards compatibility, the new metrics are stored in a new table.

6. Status and Future Work

The first prototype of the full system was finished at the end of 2006. A front-end and a analyser server are provided at the Technische Universiät Dresden (ZIH) for the HEPCG users to test the whole system.

As R-GMA does not provide any kind of authorisation currently, a authorisation mechanism using VOMS [7] is under development. It retrieves the user credentials from an MyProxy server and contacts an VOMS server for the users authorisation. Such, the access to the monitoring data is regulated. Resource providers are allowed to access their sites data only, job submitters can see the data of their jobs only, a VO manager has access rights to all data.

Work is also going on to provide access to other monitoring systems (like the already mentioned Ganglia [8]) or to the gLite Logging&Bookkeeping Web Service directly (instead of the R-GMA L&B data).

Better analysis algorithms for the data will be implemented, especially for resource usage data for resource providers. Such analysis algorithms will provide the users with improved information especially to realise critical conditions. A simple example is to show the ratio of the used CPU time and the wall clock time, which could point to "hanging" jobs.

A continuous effort is going into the development of new visualisations and the improvement of the existing ones. So, the main intention is to provide the users with a helpful, sophisticated and novel tool that supports them in their daily work in the Grid.

References

[1] I.C. Legrand, H.B.H.B. Newman, R. Voicu, C. Cirstoiu, C. Grigoras, M. Toarta, C. Dobre, : MonALISA: An Agent based, Dynamic Service System to Monitor, Control and Optimize Grid based Applications, CHEP 2004, Interlaken, Switzerland, September 2004

[2] HEPCG, High Energy Physics Community Grid (2005), *http://www.hepcg.org*

[3] D-Grid. The D-Grid Initiative (2005), *http://www.hepcg.org/index.php?id=1&L=1*

[4] R. Byrom, et al.: Fault Tolerance in the R-GMA Information and Monitoring System. In: European Grid Conference 2005. Volume 2470 of LNCS., Amsterdam/ Netherlands, Springer-Verlag Berlin Heidelberg New York (2005) 751-760

[5] J. Novotny, M. Russell, O. Wehrens: GridSphere - A Portal Framework for Building Collaborations (2005), *http://www.gridsphere.org:80/gridsphere/gridsphere?cid= publications.*

[6] L. Field, F. Naz, et al.: User level tools documentation (2006), *http://goc.grid.sinica .edu.tw/gocwiki/User tools.*

[7] R. Alfieri, R. Cecchini, V. Ciaschini, Luca dell'Agnello, A. Frohner, K. Lörentey, F. Spataro: From gridmap-file to VOMS: managing authorization in a Grid environment. In: Future Generation Computer Systems, v.21 n.4, p.549-558, April 2005

[8] M. L. Massie, B. N. Chun, and D. E. Culler: The Ganglia Distributed Monitoring System: Design, Implementation, and Experience., Parallel Computing, Vol. 30, Issue 7, July 2004.

[9] The Apache Software Foundation: Apache axis - a soap engine (2006), *http://ws.apache.org/axis/.*

[10] The Apache Software Foundation: Apache tomcat - a servlet container (2006), *http://tomcat.apache.org/.*

[11] D. Kouril et al.: Distributed Tracking, Storage, and Re-use of Job State Information on the Grid, In: Proceedings of CHEP04, Interlaken, Switzerland, 27 Sept.-1 Oct. 2004.

CO-ALLOCATING COMPUTE AND NETWORK RESOURCES - BANDWIDTH ON DEMAND IN THE VIOLA TESTBED

Thomas Eickermann, Lidia Westphal
Central Institute for Applied Mathematics
Research Centre Jülich,
52425 Jülich, Germany
{th.eickermann, l.kirtchakova}@fz-juelich.de

Oliver Wäldrich, Wolfgang Ziegler
Department of Bioinformatics
Fraunhofer Institute SCAI
53754 Sankt Augustin, Germany
{oliver.waeldrich, wolfgang.ziegler}@scai.fraunhofer.de

Christoph Barz, Markus Pilz
University of Bonn
D-53125 Bonn, Germany
{barz, pilz}@cs.uni-bonn.de

Abstract   Distributed applications or workflows need to access and use compute, storage and network resources simultaneously or chronologically coordinated respectively. Examples are distributed multi-physics simulations that use the combined computational performance and data storage of multiple clusters. A coordinated reservation and allocation of the resources is a prerequisite for the efficient use of such resources. This contribution describes the components of a system that provides Grid users with this functionality. The Grid middleware UNICORE is extended to access a MetaScheduling Service (MSS) performing orchestration of resources of different administrative domains, using advance reservation capability of local resource management systems (RMS) - including network connections for which ARGON serves as RMS. ARGON leverages Bandwidth on Demand, a cornerstone of next generation Grid enabled optical networks rendering the network to a first class Grid resource.

Keywords: Grid, advance reservation, Bandwidth on demand, ARGON, UNICORE

1. Introduction and Overview

Advanced applications usually benefit from the existence of different, heterogeneous resources available in Grids. Being able to select among multiple resources allows the end-user to execute the individual components of his application using the most appropriate resources available. Examples of such applications are distributed multi-physics simulations where multiple resources are needed at the same time, or complex workflows where the resources are needed with some timely dependencies [13].

Additionally, having distributed applications and data, there is also a need for dedicated QoS of the network connections between the resources to support efficient execution of the applications. However, to make efficient use of the resources we need reservation mechanisms that guarantee the availability of the selected resources including the network at the time they are needed to execute application components or a component of a workflow. Without reservation there is only a best effort approach to execute applications across multiple resources without a chance of coordination. Having reservation mechanisms allows to completely planning the execution of an application or workflow if the timely dependencies are given by the user. In the VIOLA [17] project we created a UNICORE based Grid testbed on top of an optical network.

This testbed provides solutions to the problems addressed above: the orchestration of resources of different sites belonging to different administrative domains is done by a MetaScheduling Service (MSS) [18]. This service is responsible for the negotiation of agreements on resource usage with the individual local resource management systems. The agreements are made using WS-Agreement [1] developed by the GRAAP [9]working group of the Global Grid Forum [8]. The agreements made basically are Service Level Agreements on the advance reservation of the resources needed for an application or a workflow [19]. The local resource management systems finally include the advance reservation in their individual schedules. Extending this approach to network resources as done in VIOLA allows user or application driven selection and reservation of network connections with dedicated QoS based on evolving network technologies.

2. Architecture

2.1 The UNICORE Environment and Extension of the Client

The Grid-system UNICORE [15] is being developed since 1998 and is used in various projects and production environments, mainly in Europe and Japan. UNICORE is based on a three-tier architecture, consisting of (1) a Java-Client as the user-interface to the Grid, (2) server-components at the UNICORE-sites that provide the secure access of the user to the UNICORE Grid and manage the userÕs jobs and finally (3) the target systems which execute those jobs (see Figure 1).

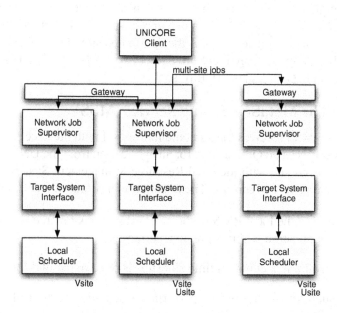

Figure 1. UNICORE Architecture

The standard UNICORE software offers extended workflow support. UNI-CORE jobs are composed of subjobs that can be executed on the same or different resources (called vsites). Dependencies between those subjobs can be specified, forcing them to be executed in a particular order. In addition to that, conditional execution and control statements allow to build loops of subjobs. However, UNICORE has no build-in capabilities to make advance reservations or to provide synchronous access to distributed resources.

Within VIOLA, this feature has been added via a UNICORE Client-plugin that accesses an external MetaScheduling Service. The plugin provides a GUI that lets the user specify his job including the number of processes to run on which target systems and the required bandwidth between them. Based on this information, the client requests a reservation from the MSS. Once the reservation has been made by the MSS, it is processed like any other UNICORE job. A job may consist of a number of subjobs Ð one for each target system that is requested. Users can retrieve output, monitor or cancel the job.

In the current version, the plugin is tailored to the needs of distributed simula-tions using the metacomputing-enabled MPI-implementation Me-taMPICH [3]. Using it, the user not only specifies the resources needed but also further

MetaMPICH-related information allowing the plugin to perform additional tasks, as e.g. distributing the different types of MetaMPICH tasks (compute tasks, network router tasks, I/O server tasks) onto the requested cluster nodes based on various policies and generating a MetaMPICH configuration file.

The plugin is designed and implemented in a modular fashion, allowing easy adaptation to other types of distributed application, not based on MetaMPICH. An example under consideration is the distributed simulation of crystal growth in the VIOLA application TechSim. Here, two MPI-applications are coupled via MpCCI [10] using plain TCP/IP sockets.

2.2 The MetaScheduling Service (MSS)

Once the MSS receives the agreement proposal with the necessary information on resources and QoS needed for an application from the UNICORE client it starts to negotiate with the local Resource Management Systems (RMS) of these resources (see Figure 2). The negotiation has four main phases:

1 querying the local RMS of the selected systems for free slots to execute the application within a preview period

2 determining a common time slot (this is done in parallel for all RMS)

3 if such a time-slot exists, perform a reservation request of this slot on behalf of the user.
   otherwise
   restart the query with a later start time of the preview period

4 check whether the reservation was made for the correct time slot on all systems (because local job requests might interfere),
   if yes
   we are done;
   otherwise
   restart the query with a later start time of the preview period.

If no common time-slot within the local RMSŌs specific look-ahead times can be identified, an error is reported to the user. The pseudo-code of the co-allocation algorithm is depicted in Listing 1. The successful negotiation and reservation is sent back as agreement to the UNICORE client which then processes the job as usual. When the job starts at the negotiated common starting time the MSS collects the IP addresses of the participating machines (this information may not be available at an earlier time as the local scheduling system might assign the job to different nodes than planned at the time of submission)

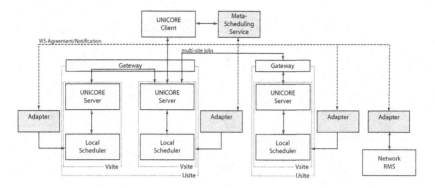

Figure 2. Architecture of the VIOLA MetaScheduling Environment

and communicates them to the network RMS which in turn is then able to manage the end-to-end connections with the requested QoS.

```
set n = number of requested resources
set resources [1..n] = requested resources
set properties [1..n] = requested property per resource  # number of nodes, bandwidth,
                                                         # time,...
set freeSlots [1..n] = null                              # start time of free slots
set endOfPreviewWindow = false
set nextStartupTime = currentTime+someMinutes           # the starting point when
                                                        # looking for free slots

while (endOfPreviewWindow = false) do {

  for 1..n do in parallel {
    freeSlots[i] = ResourceAvailableAt(resources[i], properties[i], nextStartupTime)
  }

  for 1..n do {
    set needNext = false
    if (nextStartupTime != freeSlots[i]) then {
      if (freeSlots[i] != null) then {
        if (nextStartupTime < freeSlot[i]) then {
          set nextStartupTime = freeSlots[i]
          set needNext = true
        }
      } else {
        set endOfPreviewWindow = true
      }
    }
  }
}

if ((needNext = false) & (endOfPreviewWindow = false)) then return
  freeSlots[1] else return "no common slot found"
```

Listing 1: Pseudo code of the common timeslot negotiation algorithm

2.3 Advance Network Reservation

Taking a look at the Grid as a geographically distributed set of resources comprising computing and storage for users and their applications, the connecting network infrastructure becomes important. While sites are usually connected by IP best effort technologies, the coordination of high performance resources like meta-computing brings new requirements and challenges to the network.

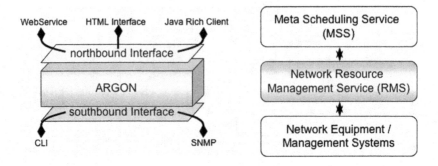

Figure 3. North- and sourthbound Interfaces of ARGON

A siteÕs Internet connectivity is usually tailored to the bandwidth demands of the well-known interactive Internet applications like e-mail and web traffic. It is assumed that coupling clusters to efficiently use computing and storage resources from multiple sites requires high bandwidth (e.g. in terms of multiple Gbit/s) and low delay (e.g. as low as possible) connections with virtually exclusively usage characteristics. The idea of QoS in the network domain has been apparent for many years [11], [4]. In addition, the VIOLA project provides an in advance reservation interface which allows to connect sites on demand with high speed, low delay connections.

These premium connectivity services can be invoked by the Meta-Scheduling Service in order to provide on demand the required network QoS for multi-site jobs. The following section presents a brief overview of the developed network RMS ARGON [2](Allocation and Reservation in Grid-enabled Optic Networks) including the advance reservation capable interface for the Grid application layer offering connectivity services with a specified QoS on top of the optical network between the Grid sites in the VIOLA network. Figure 3 shows the north- and southbound interfaces of ARGON.

ARGON is designed to provide a set of network related services to the Grid community, e.g. advance reservations can be requested by the upper layer (e.g. MSS). This includes the instantaneous setup of network connections if the requested resources are available for the specified span of time. At this level ARGON tries to hide the details of the network technologies, i.e. the user or application specifies QoS requirements for a service and describes the service endpoints.

ARGON maps abstract premium connectivity services to specific layer 2 and layer 3 network services via MPLS as well as point-to-point connectivity services via GMPLS. Beside the details of a single service, a set of services can be bundled in a single request for reservation. Hence, a reservation may consist of several services with chronological dependencies which may themselves consist of several connections as a basis for the service. Consequently, the whole reservation can be regarded as a transaction: All services contained are accepted, rejected or postponed as a whole. This also applies for malleable reservations where the overall service of the reservation can be stretched or compressed in the same way. The idea of malleable reservations is sketched in Figure 4. A data amount has to be transferred and according to the present resource allocation and reservation parameters, ARGON can choose an appropriate duration and capacity frame to schedule the service.

In order to allow for automated resource coordination and provisioning, the northbound interface is implemented as a WebService and accessible via SOAP [14]. The interface currently consists of five message types for reservation of resources, cancellation of reservations, query of reservation related information, availability information and the binding of additional information for provisioning purposes. Availability information and binding of provisioning information are especially important for the co-allocation of resources via the MSS. The availability request helps to find a common time slot for cluster and network resources.

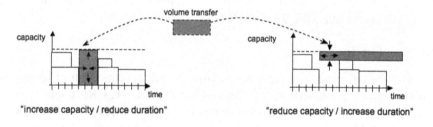

Figure 4. Malleable Reservations

A late binding of provisioning information allows for the MetaScheduling Service and the local scheduling systems respectively appointing the cluster nodes used for a reservation just in time before the provisioning. At the time of reservation only the service endpoint (e.g. provider or consumer edge router), but not the identity of the cluster nodes needs to be known. The provisioning information may consist of ports of the router to which the cluster nodes are attached and/or IP addresses.

The southbound interface of ARGON to the network components uses standard network management protocols Ð if available Ð to initiate MPLS/GMPLS based signalling to control both the MPLS and the GMPLS domain. At the time of writing, the primary interfaces to the network equipment use either a Command Line Interface (CLI) Ð which is not only vendor specific but also version dependent Ð and SNMP if possible. It is also envisioned to integrate vendor specific management interfaces that support XML message transfer with a higher layer of abstraction. In the context of MPLS two services are favoured by ARGON: A layer 3 based tunnel service and VPLS. The layer 3 based tunnel service utilizes MPLS traffic engineered point-to-point tunnels which convey IP packets.

One of the next topics for the network RMS ARGON includes the challenge of multi-domain reservations (east-/westbound interface). This topic includes the interaction between multiple ARGON systems or other network RMS like UCLP [16], G-lamda [6] and DRAC [5] which provide similar ideas to build next generations Grid enabled optical networks.

The core of ARGON utilizes the network topology information to compute the possible paths in the network to realize and plan the requested services in advance. Although the network equipment in the VIOLA testbed allows for traffic engineering, in on demand and in advance reservations must be handled by ARGON. Protocols used for traffic engineering Ð like OSPF-TE and RSVP-TE Ð provide means for instantaneous path computation and signalling within the network components. Pre-planning of future capacity usage is therefore left to the core of ARGON which supervises the resource usage in the underlying network layers like MPLS and GMPLS.

3. Outlook

The current version of the VIOLA Grid testbed expects the user to describe the resource demands of his application using the UNICORE client and do a pre-selection of resources satisfying this demand. However, we are working on several other projects to have applications providing this information. Annotating applications with the knowledge about their requirements will allow to make the resource pre-selection process more automatic and disburden the user from this task.

The communication of the MSS with the other components of the system is based on WS-Agreement. WS-Agreement version 1 does not support re-negotiation of agreements already accepted an extended version with richer negotiation capabilities is under preparation. Once this version becomes available we will switch to the new version. In the FP6 funded project UniGrids, a WS-based version of UNICORE is under development. A tighter integration of the MSS into the UNICORE system is currently under development in the European PHOSPHORUS [12] project and will be based on UNICORE 6. The PHOSPHORUS project is targeting on a better integration of Grid resources, Grid middleware and the network resources. PHOSPHORUS will also establish a bandwidth on demand service on top of the European GÉANT [7] and the National Research Networks of the project partners.

Acknowledgments

Some of the work reported in this paper is funded by the German Federal Ministry of Education and Research through the VIOLA project under grant #01AK605L. This paper also includes work carried out jointly within the Core-GRID Network of Excellence funded by the European Commission's IST programme under grant #004265.

References

[1] A. Andrieux, K. Czajkowski, A. Dan, K. Keahey, H. Ludwig, T. Nakata, J. Pruyne, J. Rofrano, S. Tuecke, and M. Xu. Web Services Agreement Specification (WS-Agreement), March 2007. 15 Mar 2007 <https://forge.gridforum.org/sf/docman/do/downloadDocument/projects.graap-wg/docman.root.current_drafts/doc6091/>.

[2] ARGON - Allocation and Reservation in Grid-enabled Optic Networks. VIOLA Project Report, March 2006 <http://www.viola-testbed.de/>.

[3] B. Bierbaum, C. Clauss, Th. Eickermann, L. Kirtchakova, A. Krechel, S. Springstubbe, O. Wäldrich, Ph.Wieder, and W. Ziegler. Reliable Orchestration of distributed MPI-Applications in a UNICORE-based Grid with MetaMPICH and MetaScheduling. In *Proc. of the EuroPVM/MPI 2006*, volume 4192 of *Lecture Notes in Computer Science*, pages 174 – 183. Springer, 2006.

[4] S. Chen and K. Nahrstedt. An Overview of Quality-of-Service Routing for Next Generation High-Speed Networks: Problems and Solutions. In *IEEE Network, Special Issue on Transmission and Distribution of Digital Video*, volume 12, No 6, pages 64–79. IEEE Communications Society, 1998.

[5] Dynamic Resource Allocation Controller (DRAC). March 2007 <http://www.nortel.com/drac/>.

[6] G-lambda Project. March 2007 <http://www.g-lambda.net/>.

[7] GÉANT – The pan-European research and education network. Mar 2007 <http://www.geant.net/>.

[8] GGF – The Open Grid Forum. Mar 2007 <http://www.ogf.org>.

[9] Grid Resource Allocation Agreement Protocol Working Group. Mar 2007 <https://forge.gridforum.org/projects/graap-wg/>.

[10] MPCCI - Multidisciplinary Simulations through Code-Coupling. Mar 2007 <http://www.scai.fraunhofer.de/mpcci.html/>.

[11] P. Paul and S. V. Raghavan. Survey of QoS Routing. In *Proceedings of the 15th international conference on Computer communication*, Mumbai, Maharashtra, India, 2000.

[12] PHOSPHORUS - Lambda User Controlled Infrastructure for European Research. Mar 2007 <http://www.phosphorus.pl/>.

[13] G. Quecke and W. Ziegler. MeSch – An Approach to Resource Management in a Distributed Environment. In *Proc. of 1st IEEE/ACM International Workshop on Grid Com-*

puting (Grid 2000), volume 1971 of *Lecture Notes in Computer Science*, pages 47–54. Springer, 2000.

[14] Simple Object Access Protocol Specification. SOAP Specification version 1.2. Web site, 2007. Online: <http://www.w3.org/TR/soap12/>.

[15] A. Streit, D. Erwin, Th. Lippert, D. Mallmann, R. Menday, M. Rambadt, M. Riedel, M. Romberg, B. Schuller, and Ph. Wieder. UNICORE - From Project Results to Production Grids. In L. Grandinetti, editor, *Grid Computing: The New Frontiers of High Performance Processing, Advances in Parallel Computing 14*. Elsevier, 2005.

[16] User-controlled LightPaths. March 2007 <http://www.canarie.ca/canet4/uclp/>.

[17] VIOLA – Vertically Integrated Optical Testbed for Large Application in DFN. Mar 2007 <http://www.viola-testbed.de/>.

[18] O. Wäldrich, Ph.Wieder, and W. Ziegler. A Meta-scheduling Service for Co-allocating Arbitrary Types of Resources. In *Proc. of the Second Grid Resource Management Workshop (GRMWS'05) in conjunction with the Sixth International Conference on Parallel Processing and Applied Mathematics (PPAM 2005)*, volume 3911 of *Lecture Notes in Computer Science*, pages 782–791, Poznan, Poland, September 11–14, 2006. Springer.

[19] Ph. Wieder, O. Wäldrich, R. Yahyapour, and W. Ziegler. Improving Workflow execution through SLA-based Advance Reservation. In *Intregrated Research in Grid Computing, CoreGRID Integration Workshop*, pages 333 – 344, Krakow, Poland, 2006. ISBN: 83-915141-6-1.

VI

PROGRAMMING METHODOLOGIES

ADDING METADATA TO ORC TO SUPPORT REASONING ABOUT GRID PROGRAMS*

Marco Aldinucci
Dept. Computer Science – University of Pisa – Italy
aldinuc@di.unipi.it

Marco Danelutto
Dept. Computer Science – University of Pisa – Italy
marcod@di.unipi.it

Peter Kilpatrick
Dept. Computer Science – Queen's University Belfast – UK
p.kilpatrick@qub.ac.uk

Abstract   Following earlier work demonstrating the utility of Orc as a means of specifying and reasoning about grid applications we propose the enhancement of such specifications with metadata that provide a means to extend an Orc specification with implementation oriented information. We argue that such specifications provide a useful refinement step in allowing reasoning about implementation related issues ahead of actual implementation or even prototyping. As examples, we demonstrate how such extended specifications can be used for investigating security related issues and for evaluating the cost of handling grid resource faults. The approach emphasises a semi-formal style of reasoning that makes maximum use of programmer domain knowledge and experience.

Keywords: Orc, grid, metadata, fault handling, security.

*This research is carried out under the FP6 Network of Excellence CoreGRID funded by the European Commission (Contract IST-2002-004265).

1.   Introduction

Grid computing is intended to enable the development of both industrial and scientific applications on an unprecedented scale in terms of computing power and ubiquity. These applications are supposed to transparently handle dynamicity and heterogeneity of computing platforms [11] and they often exploit some flavour of component programming model. Component technology focuses (by its very nature) on the decoupled development of modules implementing single features [1, 4, 5], that should then be arranged and connected to realize the application. While several frameworks for developing grid-oriented components exist or are under design [7–8], the models to reason about their orchestration are still inadequate. Although a model for orchestration should necessarily subsume a notion of component/module behaviour, it can be specified along a spectrum of abstraction levels: from the full implementation itself to the fully logic/algebraic description. Currently, most of the effort is concentrated on the ends of the spectrum, which are far from the designer's viewpoint. For example, BPEL [6] is a recognized standard for orchestration of Web Services, but it is designed for machine processing and is therefore not suitable for supporting human "abstract reasoning" about orchestration. At the other extreme, π-calculus is a well-recognized formal tool for reasoning about distributed programs [12], but it comes with a heavyweight formal framework typically outside the interest and experience of system designers.

In earlier work we explored the use of Orc [10] as a means of specifying and reasoning about grid computations. Orc was developed as a notation for describing the orchestration of distributed systems, rather than the core computations themselves. Orc's primitive is the *site* which may be used to abstract basic computations. A site call returns a single value or remains silent. Site calls may be combined using three composition operators (plus recursion):

Sequential : $A > x > B(x)$. For each output, x, from A execute an instance of B taking x as parameter. If x is not used in B write $A \gg B$.

Parallel : $A \mid B$. The output is the interleaved outputs from each of A and B.

Asymmetric parallel : $A \; where \; x \; :\in B$. Execute A and B in parallel until A needs x. Take the first x delivered by B and terminate the remaining execution of B while A continues.

We believe that Orc lies in the middle ground of the spectrum of orchestration description: as described in previous work [3], Orc appears to be a suitable candidate to reason about certain non-functional properties (e.g. fault-tolerance) of the grid-oriented *muskel* system [2]. In this paper we present a further step along the same path. We enrich Orc with *metadata* to describe non-functional properties such as deployment information. This could be used, for example, to describe the mapping of application parts (e.g. components, modules) onto a grid platform. The approach is consistent with the current trend of keeping decoupled the functional and non-functional aspects of an application. We believe that the use of metadata introduces a new dimension for reasoning about the orchestration of a distributed system by allowing a narrowing of the focus from the very general case. We expect this approach can be gracefully extended in order to allow reasoning – at design time – about several static invariants of the final implementation.

2. Orc metadata

A generic Orc program, as described in [10], is a set of Orc *definitions* followed by an Orc *goal expression*. The goal expression is the expression to be evaluated when executing the program. Assume $S = \{s_1, \ldots, s_s\}$ is the set of *sites* used in the program, i.e. the set of all the sites *called* during the evaluation of the goal expression (the set does not include the pre-defined sites, such as *if* and *Rtimer*, as they are assumed to be available at any user defined site), and $\mathcal{E} = \{e_0, \ldots, e_e\}$ is the set including the goal expression (e_0) and all the "head" expressions appearing in the left hand sides of Orc definitions.

The set of *metadata* associated with an Orc program may be defined as the set: $\mathcal{M} = \{\mu_1, \ldots, \mu_n\}$ where $\mu_i = \langle t_j, md_k \rangle$ with $t_j \in S \cup \mathcal{E}$ and $md_k = f(p_1, \ldots, p_{n_k})$. f is a generic "functor" (represented by an identifier) and p_i are generic "parameters" (variables, ground values, etc.). The metadata md_k are not further defined as, in general, metadata structure depends on the kind of metadata to be represented. In the following, examples of such metadata are presented.

As is usual, the semantics of Orc is not affected when *meta*data is taken into account. Rather, the introduction of metadata provides a means to restrict the set of actual implementations which satisfy an Orc specification and thereby eases the burden of reasoning about properties of the specification. For example, restrictions can be placed on the relative physical placement of Orc sites in such a way that conclusions can be drawn about their interaction which would not be possible in the general case.

Suppose one wishes to reason about Orc program site "placement", i.e. about information concerning the relative positioning of Orc sites with respect to a given set of *physical resources* potentially able to host one or more Orc sites. Let $\mathcal{R} = \{r_1, \ldots, r_r\}$ be the set of available physical resources. Then, given a program with $S = \{siteA, siteB\}$ we can consider adding to the program metadata such as $\mathcal{M} = \{\langle siteA, loc(r_1) \rangle, \langle siteB, loc(r_2) \rangle\}$ modelling the situation where $siteA$ and $siteB$ are placed on distinct processing resources. Define also the auxiliary function $location(x) : S \times \mathcal{E} \rightarrow \mathcal{R}$ as the function returning the location of a site/expression and consider a metadata set *ground* if it contains location tuples relative to *all* the sites in the program (that is, all sites have been allocated to a processor).

loc metadata can be used to support reasoning about the "communication costs" of Orc programs. For example, the cost of a communication with respect to the placement of the sites involved can be characterized by distinguishing cases:

$$k_{Comm} = \begin{cases} k_{nonloc} & if\ location(s_1) \neq location(s_2) \\ k_{loc} & otherwise \end{cases}$$

where s_1 and s_2 are the source and destination sites of the communication, respectively and, typically, $k_{nonloc} \gg k_{loc}$.

Consider now a second example of metadata. Suppose "secure" and "insecure" site locations are to be represented. Secure locations can be reached through trusted network segments and can therefore be communicated with while taking no particular care; insecure locations are not trusted, and can be reached only by passing through untrusted network segments, therefore requiring some kind of explicit data encryption to guarantee security. This representation can be achieved by simply adding to the metadata tuples such as $\langle s_i, trusted() \rangle$ or $\langle s_i, untrusted() \rangle$. Then a costing model for communications that takes into account that transmission of encrypted data may cost significantly more than transmission of plain data can be devised.

$$k_{SecComm} = \begin{cases} k_{InSecComm} & if\ \langle s_1, untrusted() \rangle \in \mathcal{M} \\ & \vee \langle s_2, untrusted() \rangle \in \mathcal{M} \\ k_{Comm} & otherwise \end{cases}$$

2.1 Generating metadata

So far the metadata considered have been identified explicitly by the user. In some cases he/she may not wish, or indeed be able, to supply all of the metadata and so it may be appropriate to allow generation of metadata from partial metadata supplied by the user. For example, suppose the user provides only partial location metadata, e.g. metadata relative to the goal expression location and/or metadata relative to the location of the components of the topmost parallel command found in the Orc program execution. Metadata information available can be used to infer ground location metadata (i.e. location metadata for all $s \in \mathcal{S}$) as follows. Consider two cases: in the first (*completely distributed* strategy) it is assumed that each time a new site in the Orc program is encountered, the site is "allocated" on a location that is distinct from the locations already used. In the second case (*conservative* strategy) new sites are allocated in the same location as their parent (w.r.t. the syntactic structure of the Orc program), unless the user/programmer specifies something different in the provided metadata.

More formally, in the first case, we can state that when an Orc definition such as $E \triangleq f \mid g, E \triangleq f(x)$ where $x :\in g, E \triangleq f \gg g$ or $E \triangleq f > x > g$ is considered, both the metadata $\langle f, loc(freshLoc(\mathcal{M})) \rangle$ and $\langle g, loc(freshLoc(\mathcal{M})) \rangle$

are added to $\mathcal{M}$. In the second case, the same Orc definitions will lead to insertion in the set $\mathcal{M}$ of the new metadata $\langle f, location(E) \rangle$ and $\langle g, location(E) \rangle$ (provided the user did not explicitly supply site metadata information for f and g).

Example To illustrate the use of metadata, consider the following description of a classical task farm (embarrassingly parallel computation):

$$farm(pgm, nw) \triangleq tasksource \mid resultsink \mid workers(pgm, nw)$$
$$workers(pgm, nw) \triangleq \mid i : 1 \leq i \leq nw : worker_i(pgm)$$
$$worker(pgm) \triangleq tasksource > t > pgm > y > resultsink(y) \gg worker(pgm)$$

A typical goal for this program will be of the form $farm(myPgm, 10)$. Suppose the user provides the metadata:

$$\forall i \in [1, nw] \langle worker_i, loc(PE_i) \rangle \in \mathcal{M}$$
$$\langle farm(myPgm, 10), strategy(fullyDistributed) \rangle \in \mathcal{M}$$

where $strategy(fullyDistributed)$ means the user explicitly requires that a "completely distributed implementation" be used. An attempt to infer metadata about the goal expression identifies $location(farm(myPgm, 10)) = \bot$ but, as the strategy requested by the user is *fullyDistributed* and as $farm(pgm, nw)$ is defined as a parallel command, the following metadata is added to $\mathcal{M}$:

$$\langle tasksource, loc(freshLoc(\mathcal{M})) \rangle$$
$$\langle resultsink, loc(freshLoc(\mathcal{M})) \rangle$$
$$\langle workers(pgm, nw), loc(freshLoc(\mathcal{M})) \rangle.$$

Next, expanding the *workers* term, gives the term

$$\mid i : 1 \leq i \leq nw : worker_i(pgm)$$

but in this case metadata relative to *worker*$_i$ has already been supplied by the user. At this point

$$\mathcal{M} = \{ \langle tasksource, loc(freshLoc(\mathcal{M})) \rangle, \langle resultsink, loc(freshLoc(\mathcal{M})) \rangle,$$
$$\langle workers(pgm, nw), loc(freshLoc(\mathcal{M})) \rangle, \langle worker_1, loc(PE_1) \rangle, \ldots,$$
$$\langle worker_{nw}, loc(PE_{nw}) \rangle \}$$

and therefore is *ground* w.r.t. the program.

Thus, in addition to the location metadata provided by the user it was possible to derive the fact that the locations of *tasksource* and *resultsink* are distinct and, in addition, are different from the locations of each *worker*$_i$. Suppose now that the user has also inserted the metadata item $\langle PE_2, untrusted() \rangle$ in addition to those already mentioned. That is, one of the placement locations is untrusted. This raises the issue of how it can be determined whether or not a communication must be performed in a secure way. This information may be inferred from the available metadata as follows. Let functions $source(C)$ denote a site "sending" data and $sink(C)$ denote a site "receiving" data in communication C. Then C *must* be secured iff

$$source(C) = X \wedge sink(C) = Y \wedge \langle X, loc(LX) \rangle \in \mathcal{M} \wedge \langle Y, loc(LY) \rangle \in \mathcal{M}$$
$$\wedge (\langle LX, untrusted() \rangle \in \mathcal{M} \vee \langle LY, untrusted() \rangle \in \mathcal{M}).$$

Thus, for the farm example above, the metadata $\langle worker_2, PE_2 \rangle$ and $\langle PE_2, untrusted() \rangle$ and the definition

$$worker_2(pgm) \triangleq tasksource > t > pgm > y > resultsink \gg worker_2(pgm)$$

together with the metadata $\langle tasksource, loc(TS) \rangle$, $\langle resultsink, loc(RS) \rangle$, $\langle TS, trusted() \rangle$, $\langle RS, trusted() \rangle$ lead to the conclusion that the communications represented in the Orc code by $tasksource > t > pgm.compute(t)$ and by $pgm.compute(t) > y > resultsink$ within $worker_2$ must be secured.

It is worth pointing out that the metadata considered here is typical of the information needed when running grid applications. For example, constraints such as the *loc* ones can be generated to force code (that is, sites) to be executed on processing elements having particular features, and information such as that modelled by *untrusted* metadata can be used to denote those cluster nodes that happen to be outside a given network administrative domain and may therefore be more easily subject to "man in the middle" attacks or to some other kind of security related leaks.

3. Metadata exploitation

In this section we consider two alternative versions of a tool and use their Orc specifications together with metadata to analyse their performance and security properties. muskel [9] is a skeleton-based parallel programming environment written in Java. muskel converts a user program to a data flow graph which is stored in a *taskpool*. Program input is handled as an input token to a fresh copy of the data flow graph placed in the taskpool. Fireable instructions (*tasks*) in the taskpool are computed by a set of *remote worker* processors that are recruited for the job. Each remote worker is under the supervision of a *control thread* that accesses the *taskpool*, sends a task to its worker and places the result in the *resultpool*.

The first version of muskel considered here includes a *manager* that is responsible for recruitment of remote workers, their allocation to control threads and the handling of remote worker failure. This represents the original (centralized) version of muskel, but the presence of such a manager was seen as a potential single point of failure. [3] describes how the original specification was analysed and modified to obtain a revised (decentralized) version in which this single point of failure was removed by making each control thread responsible for its own remote worker recruitment. Here, using metadata, we examine the efficiency implications of such a policy change. The Orc model of the decentralized version is given in Figure 1; the Orc model of the centralized version can be found in [3].

$systemDistribManager(pgm, tasks, contract, G, t) \triangleq$
$\quad taskpool.add(tasks) \mid i : 1 \leq i \leq contract : ctrlthread_i(pgm, t, G)$

$ctrlthread_i(pgm, t, G) \triangleq discover(G, pgm) > rw > ctrlprocess(pgm, rw, t, G)$

$discover(G, pgm) \triangleq let(rw)$ where $rw :\in |_{g \in G}\ g.can\_execute(pgm)$

$ctrlprocess(pgm, rw, t, G) \triangleq taskpool.get > tk >$
$\quad (\ \ $ if $valid \gg resultpool.add(r) \gg ctrlprocess(pgm, rw, t, G)$
$\quad \mid$ if $\neg valid \gg taskpool.add(tk)$
$\qquad\qquad\qquad \mid discover(G, pgm) > w >$
$\qquad\qquad\qquad\qquad ctrlprocess(pgm, w, t, G) \qquad)$
$\qquad$ where $(valid, r) :\in$
$\qquad (\ \ remoteworker(pgm, tk) > r > let(true, r)$
$\qquad \mid Rtimer(t) \gg let(false, 0) \quad)$

Figure 1. Decentralized manager `muskel` specification in Orc.

3.1 Comparison of communication costs

In comparing the two versions of `muskel`, as is typical in such studies, the focus will be on the "steady state" performance, that is, the typical activity of a control thread when it is processing tasks. There are two possibilities: the task is processed normally and the result placed in the *resultpool* or the remote worker fails and the control thread requires a new worker. In analysing the specifications a conservative placement strategy will be assumed; that is, the sub-parts of an entity are assumed to be co-located with their parent unless otherwise stated. Given the following metadata supplied by the developer:

$\forall rw_i \in G.\langle rw_i, loc(PE_i)\rangle \in \mathcal{M}$

$\langle system, loc(C)\rangle \in \mathcal{M}$

$\langle system(myPgm, tasks, 10, G, 50), strategy(conservative)\rangle \in \mathcal{M}$

the rules for propagation and the strategy adopted ensure that the following metadata are present for both versions:

$\langle rw_i, loc(PE_i)\rangle, \langle ctrlthread_i, loc(C)\rangle, \langle taskpool, loc(C)\rangle, \langle resultpool, loc(C)\rangle,$
$\langle rworkerpool, loc(C)\rangle.$

In addition, for the decentralized version, $\langle cntrlprocess, loc(C)\rangle$ is present.

Normal processing For the centralized version, examination of the definition of *cntrlthread* shows that in the case of a normal calculation the following sequence of actions will occur:

$taskpool.get > tk > remw(pgm, tk) > r > let(true, r) \gg resultpool.add(r).$

Using the metadata, and reasoning in the same way as in the farm example, it can be seen that the communication of the task *tk* to the remote worker and the subsequent return of the result r to the control thread represent non-local communications; all other communications in this sequence are local.

Similar analysis of the decentralized version reveals an identical series of actions for normal processing and an identical pattern of communications. Naturally then, similar results from the two versions for normal processing would be expected, and indeed this is borne out by experiment - see section 4.

Fault processing Now consider the situation where a remote worker fails during the processing of a task. In both versions the *Rtimer* timeout occurs, the task being processed is returned to the *taskpool* and a new worker is recruited. In the centralized version the following sequence of events occurs:

$$taskpool.get \gg Rtimer(t) \gg let(false, 0) \gg taskpool.add(tk) \gg$$
$$rworkerpool.get(remw)$$

while in the decentralized version the events are effectively:

$$taskpool.get \gg Rtimer(t) \gg let(false, 0) \gg taskpool.add(tk) \gg$$
$$rw.can\_execute(pgm) > rw > let(g)$$

where rw is the first site in G to respond.

Analysis of these sequences together with the metadata reveals that the comparison reduces to the local communication to the *rworkerpool* in the centralized version versus the non-local call to the remote site *rw* in the decentralized version. This comparison would suggest that, in the case of fault handling, the centralized version would be faster than the decentralized version and, again, this is borne out by experiment.

3.2   Comparison of security costs

Consider now the issue of security. Suppose that one of the remote workers, say rw_2, is in a non-trusted location (that is $\langle PE_2, untrusted() \rangle \in \mathcal{M}$). The implications of this can be determined by analysing the specification together with the metadata. In this case, as $\langle rw_2, loc(PE_2) \rangle \in \mathcal{M}$ we can conclude that $cntrlthread_2$ will be affected (while it is operating with its initially allocated remote worker) to the extent that the communications to and from its remote worker must be secured. This prompts reworking of the specification to split the control threads into two parallel sets: those requiring secure communications and those operating exclusively in trusted environments. In this way the effect, and hence cost, of securing communications can be minimised. Experimental results in section 4 illustrate the cost of securing the communications with differing numbers of control threads.

4.   Experimental results

We ran several experiments, on a distributed configuration of Linux machines, aimed at verifying that the results obtained from analysis of the Orc specifications of `muskel` together with metadata are consistent with practice.

We first verified that centralized and decentralized manager versions of `muskel` perform the same (up to a reasonable percentage difference) when no faults occur in the resources used for remote program execution. We ran the same `muskel` program with both the centralized and the decentralized `muskel` implementation, using up to 4 processing elements for the remote macro data flow interpreter instances: we obtained differences in completion time not exceeding 1.6% (1.05% average).

Then we considered remote resource failure. We measured the time spent in handling a single fault in several runs on both centralized and decentralized `muskel` versions. The distributed version takes longer to handle a single fault, as expected looking at the Orc models of the two implementations: 128.4 vs. 114.4 msecs, average. Finally, we attempted to verify the effectiveness of limiting secure mechanism usage to communications involving

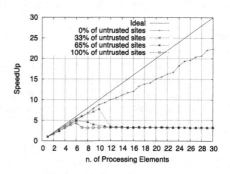

Figure 2.   Comparison of runs involving different percentages of *untrusted* locations

untrusted nodes, which may be identified by examination of the Orc specifications with associated metadata. Figure 2 shows the completion time of a `muskel` program whose remote worker sites are running on a variable mix of *trusted* and *untrusted* locations. The greater the number of remote interpreters exploited using secure mechanisms, the lower the performance values that are achieved. Therefore, restricting the classification of insecure nodes by analysis of metadata results in better efficiency on the target architecture.

5.   Conclusions

We have shown how, by associating metadata with an Orc specification, we can reason about the specification and that this reasoning carries through to the actual grid code which implements the specification. In particular, we considered how user provided metadata can be associated with the Orc model of a real structured grid programming environment (`muskel`) and showed how this could be used to perform qualitative performance comparison between two different versions of the programming environment, as well as to determine how the overhead introduced by security techniques can be minimized. We compared these theoretical results with actual experimental results and verified that they qualitatively match. Thus, the availability of an Orc model on which to "hang" the metadata allows metadata to be exploited *before* the actual implementation is available. We are currently working to formalize and automate the techniques discussed here. In particular, we are aiming to implement tools to support the metadata propagation and reasoning procedures adopted. It should be noted, however, that the whole approach, based on Orc, as described here and in [3] encourages the use of *semi*-formal reasoning to support program development (both program design and refinement). (Thus, for example, the equivalence of Orc specifications and the `muskel` implementations is not formally proven.) We believe this approach has the potential to reduce substantially experimentation by allowing the exploration of alternatives prior to costly implementation and *without* recourse to full-blown formal treatment.

References

[1] M. Aldinucci, S. Campa, M. Coppola, M. Danelutto, D. Laforenza, D. Puppin, L. Scarponi, M. Vanneschi, and C. Zoccolo. Components for high performance grid programming in grid.it. *Proc. of the Intl. Workshop on Component Models and Systems for Grid Applications*, CoreGRID series, pages 19–38, Saint-Malo, France, Jan. 2005. Springer.

[2] M. Aldinucci and M. Danelutto. Algorithmic skeletons meeting grids. *Parallel Computing*, 32(7):449–462, 2006. DOI:10.1016/j.parco.2006.04.001.

[3] M. Aldinucci, M. Danelutto, and P. Kilpatrick. Management in distributed systems: a semi-formal approach. TR-07-05, Univ. of Pisa, Dept. of Comp. Science, Feb. 2007.

[4] M. Alt, J. Dünnweber, J. Müller, and S. Gorlatch. HOCs: Higher-order components for grids. In *Component Models and Systems for Grid Applications*, CoreGRID series, pages 157–166. Springer, Jan. 2005.

[5] F. Baude, D. Caromel, and M. Morel. On hierarchical, parallel and distributed components for grid programming. *Proc. of the Intl. Workshop on Component Models and Systems for Grid Applications*, CoreGRID series, pages 97–108, Jan. 2005. Springer.

[6] Business Process Execution Language for Web Services version 1.1, 2007. http://www-128.ibm.com/developerworks/library/specification/ws-bpel/.

[7] The Common Component Architecture Forum, 2007. http://www.cca-forum.org/.

[8] CoreGRID NoE deliverable series, Institute on Programming Model. *Deliverable D.PM.04 – Basic Features of the Grid Component Model (assessed)*, Feb. 2007.

[9] M. Danelutto and P. Dazzi. Joint structured/non structured parallelism exploitation through data flow. *Proc. of ICCS: Intl. Conference on Computational Science, WS on Practical Aspects of High-level Parallel Programming*, LNCS, Reading, UK, May 2006. Springer.

[10] J. Misra and W. R. Cook. Computation orchestration: A basis for a wide-area computing. *Software and Systems Modeling*, 2006. DOI 10.1007/s10270-006-0012-1.

[11] Next Generation GRIDs Expert Group. *Future for European Grids: GRIDs and Service Oriented Knowledge Utilities. Vision and Research Directions 2010 and Beyond*, http://cordis.europa.eu/ist/grids/ngg.htm, 2006.

[12] H. Smith and P. Fingar. Workflow is just a pi process. *BPTrends*, pages 1–36, 2004.

A FRAMEWORK FOR ANALYSIS OF LEGACY CODE MIGRATION TO GRID ENVIRONMENT

Srujan Kumar Enaganti, Anish Damodaran and Anirban Chakrabarti
Software Engineering and Technology Laboratory,
Infosys Technologies Limited,
bangalore, India
Srujan_Enaganti@infosys.com
Anish_Damodaran@infosys.com
Anirban_Chakrabarti@infosys.com

Abstract   Enterprises are looking at Grid computing as a technology of enormous potential. However, there are several issues which require immediate attention before Grid can become an important component of the IT infrastructure. One such issue is migration of legacy applications to the Grid environment. In such cases, it becomes imperative to understand whether the application performance would significantly improve on migration. In this paper an attempt is made to provide a systematic framework called the Grid Application Migration Framework (GAMF) for handling the migration process. The framework consists of Grid Code Analyzer (GCA), an independently deployable component which generates a Directed Acyclic Graph (DAG). The paper also proposes a DAG reducer algorithm for reducing the DAG. The framework is tested with several proprietary and open source C as well as Java codes. In the paper, we take three sample open source applications and demonstrate the usefulness of the framework. Finally, a small sample is analyzed and recoded to show that validity of the proposed mechanisms.

Keywords: Legacy Code Migration, Grid Environment, Gridizability, Application Engineering, Parallel Programming, Grid Code Analyzer, Clusters, Simulator.

1.   Introduction

Last few years have witnessed a surge of interest in the area of Grid computing. The e-science community and enterprises, especially those in fields of Life Sciences, Energy, Finance, and Retail are realizing the potential of Grid computing and investing heavily on Grid deployment. Designing, developing and migrating legacy enterprise applications to Grid has become critical for successful Grid adoption. Migrating legacy applications to Grid assumes special importance as many applications like analytical applications, back end applications and applications dealing with huge data are being seen as prime candidates for Grid deployment for high performance and throughput. Migration typically involves significant investments in terms of domain knowledge and specialists judgments on application analysis and re-engineering. However, to take Grid to the enterprises efforts need to be undertaken to analyze the performance of the legacy code running in a Grid-based infrastructure. The approach described in this paper attempts to fill the void through the Grid Application Migration Framework (GAMF). The framework accepts a legacy code as input; analyzes it and then runs the analyzed code through a simulator. The performance of the application can be tested and re-engineering decisions can be made.

1.1   Background

The research in the area of parallel programming and Application Engineering can be broadly divided into three main categories: designing parallel applications, analyzing existing applications, and scheduling parallel application tasks. The research in the first category has led to the development of programming languages like parallel C/C++ and data parallel directives like High Performance Fortran. Specifications and libraries like Message Passing Interface (MPI)[1] and Parallel Virtual Machines(PVM)[2] are frequently used to execute parallel programs on clusters. The programming constructs, such as P-threads or more recently OpenMP [3], are used in writing multi-threaded or concurrent programs in SMP systems. The second relevant category of research concentrated on analyzing program dependencies and program execution patterns for more efficient program writing. The efforts resulted in the development of efficient techniques for program analysis like dependency analysis, loop analysis, pointer analysis, and so on, in different programming languages. The third category of research looks at efficient ways of scheduling and clustering parallel tasks to a distributed infrastructure. There are several clustering techniques like DSC[4], EZ[5], and scheduling techniques like ETF [6]are widely deployed. In [7], the authors provide a comprehensive overview of different scheduling and clustering techniques available in literature.

1.2 Motivation & Objectives

When we look at the issue of migrating applications to the Grid system, all the issues mentioned in the previous sub-section come to the fore. Before re-engineering any legacy applications to the Grid infrastructure, the amount of performance benefit one gets when one converts a legacy application to a Grid specific application needs to be analyzed. Applications in enterprises have a lot of complexities in terms of data, module between different components. Before an application is migrated to a Grid environment, it can be parallelized after taking into account the application level dependencies (see Table 1) so that the performance can be improved by distributing the application across the Grid. In our search for solution to the legacy code migration problem, we came across some standalone research. However, there is a dearth of a complete solution to address this important problem. Some of the well-known work includes Parallax[8], PYRROS[9], P-Grade[10], CASCH[11] etc. After analyzing the space, we found that a framework is needed to be developed which analyzes enterprise applications and provides inputs for re-engineering, which formed the motivation for this paper.

The objectives of the paper include (i) To propose a systematic framework for analysis of legacy code migration on to a Grid environment, (ii) To analyze sample applications using the proposed framework, (iii) To validate the framework by implementing it on a sample code. The organization of the paper is as follows: In Section 2, we describe an overview of the GAMF framework. In Section 3 we describe the results of simulation and sample implementation. Finally we conclude and provide pointers for future work in Section 4.

2. Grid Application Migration Framework

The work described in this paper consists of an end-to-end framework with three components, namely, Grid Code Analyzer, DAG reduction algorithms, and the Grid Simulator, which together form a framework to assess the gridizability of an application. The Grid Code Analyzer (GCA) component analyzes and profiles the source code and binary of a program through static and execution analysis. The GCA component takes a legacy program written in C as input and generates a Directed Acyclic Graph (DAG) which depicts both task and data dependencies among the components of the program. The DAG consists of nodes and edges where nodes indicate the processing times of different virtual blocks (see Table 1) of the program. The edges indicate the communication cost between the blocks. However, the DAG creates a large number of nodes which may hamper analysis. Therefore, we have designed a DAG Reduction algorithm which acts on the DAG to create a reduced DAG. The reduced DAG is then passed through a clustering algorithm like EZ or DSC to create tasks which indicate parallel tasks that can be put onto the Grid infrastructure. Finally, the

Table 1.   Important Definitions

Name	Definition
Dependency	Dependency is created when one portion of an application depends on another for its execution
Loop	It refers to situation in which there is a bidirectional dependency between two nodes in a DAG
Virtual Block	It is the minimum granular block that ensures that resultant graph is a DAG, i.e. without any loops
memmap	It is a data structure (implemented as an AVL tree) that maintains an updatable record of memory allocated on heap during the execution of legacy application.
Instrument String	Instrument strings are functions that represent different dependencies. They store information required to create the dependencies.
Node Weight(u_i)	In this paper, we have taken it as the CPU time taken to execute it (calculated by making C system calls). The term u_i is used to refer to the weight of node n_i.
Edge Weight(w_{ij})	In this paper, we have taken it as the cost of communication between processors executing the codes. w_{ij} is the weight of edge connecting nodes n_i and n_j. If no such edge exists, it is to be taken as zero
Dag Reducer(β)	It is normalizing factor with which each edge-weight is divided before the DAG is passed to DAG reducer algorithm. Hence, it defines the amount a DAG is reduced by the algorithm.

Grid Simulator (GS) simulates the actual Grid execution by taking the reduced clustered task graph as input and schedules the tasks on different processors in the Grid. The performance data is then analyzed to study the benefits of porting the application to Grid. The framework helps specialists to make informed decisions during the migration process.

2.1   Grid Code Analyzer(GCA)

The two components of GCA are Static Analyzer and Dynamic Analyzer (Details in [12]). *Static Analyzer* consists of two main components: Parser and Code Instrumentor. Static analyzer uses a parser to parse the code and represent them in the Symbol Table. The Symbol Table maintains the details of the various symbols like types, constants, functions and variables declared in the program. The Code Instrumentor instruments the code once the dependencies have been established and instrument strings are inserted into the source code to be used during dynamic analysis. *The Dynamic Analyzer* collects the runtime information of a program according to the instrumented strings placed in the code. The Dynamic Analyzer uses the symbol table from the static analysis to process the instrumented code. A DAG is constructed where nodes represent the block execution times while edges represent data flow between these blocks. In addition, data in the form of files, data sources, network etc. can be tracked and modeled in the DAG.

2.2   Sample Application Profiling

As mentioned in the previous section, GCA is a useful tool for profiling applications for the purpose of grid-enabling them. As part of the exercise, we have selected 25 different applications from different domains with varying sizes. We have selected two open source applications[13] and one proprietary application among them for illustrative purpose throughout the paper. The applications are described in Table 2.

Table 2.   Description of Algorithms

App Name	Description	App Feature
App 1	Path Finding Algorithm	Memory and CPU intensive
App 2	Password Quality Identifier	Highly compute intensive
App 3	Reflection of spheres in space	Compute intensive

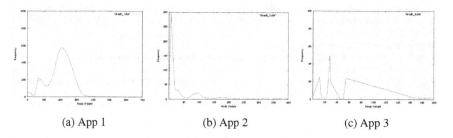

(a) App 1   (b) App 2   (c) App 3

Figure 1.   DAG Profiles for three sample applications

Let us illustrate the output of the GCA tool. Figure 1 shows the output of the GCA tool run over App 1 to App 3. The applications mentioned in Table 2 are then profiled using the GCA tool. The node weights are then plotted as shown in figures 1(a) to 1(c). The profiles of the applications show that the node weights follow multi-modal distribution. The application profiles show that there are a large number of nodes having low weights and a relatively smaller number of nodes having larger node weights. For example in figure 4a, there are an insignificant number of nodes with weight more than 400 and hence the curve dies down there after. This is intuitive as applications are loaded with statements or functions which take very little CPU time, like the initialization or assignment statements. Figures 1(b) and 1(c) also show similar trend as nodes with larger node weights tend to zero after some node weight. The above results imply that the computationally smaller functions may not have significant effect on the final performance of the application. A small application may have 1000-2000 nodes which require significant time to analyze. As most of these nodes have little or no effect on the ultimate performance, there is a need to design DAG Reduction algorithm. This motivates us to design a DAG reduction algorithm based on combining the smaller functions with the larger ones without performance degradation.

2.3   DAG Reduction Algorithm

The next step of the GAMF is the DAG reduction algorithm. The DAG reduction algorithm creates a reduced DAG by combining nodes so that the weight of the combined node is greater than that of a threshold value T. The threshold value is computed by dividing the maximum edge weight of the DAG by the DAG Reducer (β) (see Table 1).

Merging Function
Step 1: Sort the node weights (u_i) in ascending order.
Step 2: Select the node with lowest weight. Call the Loop Checking Function (Node, Parent) to check if a loop is created when the node is combined with its predecessor. In case of multiple predecessors, one of them is picked randomly.
(a) In case a loop is detected: The combination is rejected
(b) In case of no loop: The node is combined with the parent and a single combined node is created
Step 3: The new weight of the combined node is calculated by adding the node's weight with the parent's
Step 4: The node list is re-sorted
Step 5: Carry Step 2-4, until all the nodes having weights less than T are traversed
Loop Checking Function (Node, Parent)
Check whether there is any incoming edge to Node from any node N, such that predecessor of N is Parent node.

Figure 2.   DAG Reduction Algorithm

The principle behind the DAG reduction algorithm is quite intuitive. It reduces the DAG by removing the smaller nodes from the DAG which have less significant effect on the overall performance of the application. The reduction is carried out and the DAG Reducer (β) is varied by increasing the Granularity (g)[14] and Coarse Granularity (c) parameters so that a trade-off between performance and scalability (running time) of the algorithm can be achieved. Since all the blocks on DAG nodes whose weights are less than T have relatively low execution time, the algorithm merges them with each of the incident nodes. The intuition behind such an action is that the block is small and can be relocated in the incident blocks or the calling block. By doing so, we want to make sure that Coarse Granularity of resultant graph is greater than one. It can be proved that if coarse granularity is greater than one, granularity will also exceed one. A. Gerasoulis and T. Yang have proved that for any coarse grain graph (c > 1), there is a optimal clustering followed by scheduling that makes the parallel time of execution on a fully connected grid at most two times the optimal parallel time [14]. Hence, by making sure that coarse granularity is greater than one, we make sure that we can get suboptimal solution for parallelizing the application on to a fully connected grid.

2.4   Clustering & Grid Simulator(GS)

Clustering is the step that succeeds Reduction during application analysis. The reduced DAG obtained by application of Reduction algorithm is handed to the clustering algorithm for creating clusters. Clusters provide indication of the possible parallel codes by grouping the nodes of the DAG. We used Edge-Zeroing (EZ) for our purpose [5]. EZ algorithm successively performs edge-zeroings of edges in the decreasing order of their weights making sure that at every step parallel time to execute the resultant DAG obtained after zeroing is less than the parallel time taken before doing zeroing. Since edge weights are quantified by communication cost, zeroing an edge can be considered equivalent to allocating two nodes of the edge on the same processor for more optimal performance. Parallel time is calculated by calculating the same assuming that there are as many processors as the number of clusters formed in the DAG. The latter is the same as calculation of critical path of the DAG with clusters. Finally a clustered DAG is resulted to be used for further analysis. The third component of the GAMF is the Grid Simulator (GS). GS takes the clustered graph as input and simulates its performance on a grid consisting of processors which are fully connected. Grid Infrastructure is modeled by processors, links, and data elements. Processors are defined having a specific processing power, while links have been modeled having a specific link capacity. The processing powers, link capacities of processors and links are given as input to simulator along with the DAG(s). Different scheduling algorithms like Round Robin, Priority based, Match Making have also been implemented to schedule jobs among processors. However, noting the specific requirements in our case, we decided to build the simulator using JavaSim [15].

3.   Results

The three sample applications were analyzed using the GAMF framework. Two parameters have been used for evaluation purposes: (i)Performance Gain (PG) indicates the performance gain achieved by means of parallelization and it is calculated as the ratio of the running time of the sequential application to the parallelized one. (ii)Reduction Ratio(RR) defines the amount of reduction that can be achieved using the β parameter and is calculated as the ratio of the number of DAG nodes before to number of nodes after the reduction process. There is a big difference between parameters β and RR. While β is an input parameter, RR is the actual reduction that can be achieved.

3.1   Simulation Results - Performance Gain

The Performance Gain(PG) for the 3 sample applications are varied with the β value. For App 1, which is very memory and compute intensive,the

Performance Gain is very significant, the max value reaches around 40. A β value of 0.7 provides a good trade-off. The result is shown in figure 3(a).

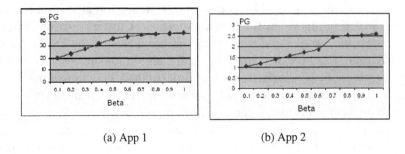

(a) App 1   (b) App 2

Figure 3.   PG Variation for (a) App 1 and (b) App 2

Now, we come to App 2's Performance Gain. This is a compute intensive program with the maximum gain attained around 2.5 due to lots of dependencies in the program. A β value of 0.7 is a good trade-off. Please note the difference in the values of between App 1 and App 2. As App 1 is a memory intensive program, several high cost edges exist which get reduced in case of low β resulting in significant loss of information. Therefore, for high edge graphs or memory intensive programs, it is advisable to keep β close to 1. Now, we look at App 3. This is a compute intensive program with good parallelization scope as is evident from a high gain of 11. A β value of 0.5 provides a good trade-off.

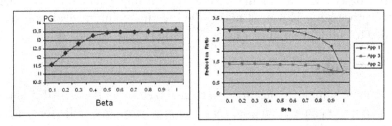

Figure 4.   PG Variation for App 3   *Figure 5.*   Variation of RR with β

3.2   Simulation Results - Reduction Ratio

Figure 5 shows the variation of the Reduction Ratio of the three sample applications with β. The trends are more or less similar here. For low values of β the Reduction Ratio does not change significantly. The change is really significant as the β value reaches close to 1. If we look at the figure(s) 3, we will find that it is in the low values of β where the maximum increase in Performance Gain takes place. The figure 3, therefore, is significant. It shows that with slight decrease in the β value, a significant reduction is achieved to the extent of nearly 50-70%. After the initial reduction, decreasing β further causes only slight reduction. However, while the initial sets of reduction lend itself slightly to the Performance Gain, the latter reduction (though small in comparison) has more significant effect. The reason is that the reduction of β at higher values reduces the high cost nodes resulting in more tangible effect on the ultimate performance. Therefore, figures 3, 4 and 5 motivate us in designing a β at 0.7 which causes a significant reduction, since the running time of EZ clustering algorithm is of the order of $O(v(e+v))$ where e indicates the number of edges and v indicates the number of nodes.

3.3   Sample Implementation

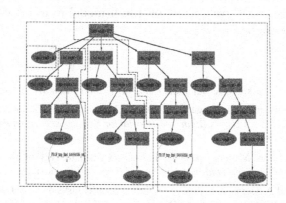

Figure 6.   The formation of Different Clusters

The next phase is to validate the results of the analysis through actual implementation. Implementation based on the technique mentioned in the paper has been carried on for several proprietary codes and the results are within 10-15% of that provided by the simulator. The output is then passed through the DAG Reducer and the clustering algorithms. The resultant output is as shown in figure 6. The algorithm creates four clusters. Running the output through the simulator with equal performing node shows that a four node grid will achieve a Performance Gain of 3.26. The program was re-written using simple MPI libraries and the actual performance came to about 3.19 which is reasonably close to the simulation result.

4.   Conclusions

Migration of legacy applications to the Grid environment is an important and challenging problem. It is challenging as holistic solutions are not available in this domain. This paper is an effort to fill the void. In this paper, we have proposed a Grid Application Migration Framework (GAMF) which consists of three independently deployable components: Grid Code Analyzer (GCA), DAG Reducer/Cluster Generator (DAGRCG) and Grid Simulator (GS). As part of DAGRCG, we have proposed a DAG Reduction algorithm which can reduce

DAGs by 50-70% with very little performance degradation. Reduction and Cluster Generation are two separate independent tasks themselves, we embedded them in one single component for the convenience of using it directly after GCA and prior to GS. The framework can predict the performance of applications with very high accuracy and is very useful for analysis of Grid application migration.The framework discussed in this paper is part of an ongoing project on Application Engineering. In addition, other efforts which will be taken up in near future are:(i)Inclusion of more legacy applications like COBOL, PL1 into the fold of GAMF. (ii)Data parallelization through data splitting for speeding up applications. (iii)Development of a ROI model to identify the economic viability of the migration process.

References

[1] W. Gropp, E. Lusk and A. Skjellum. *Using MPI, 2nd edition* MIT Press, Nov 1999.

[2] A. Geist, A. Beguelin, J. Dongarra, W. Jiang, R. Manchek, and V. Sunderam. *PVM: Parallel Virtual Machine - A User's Guide and Tutorial for Networked Parallel Programming* MIT Press, May 1994.

[3] L. Dagum and R. Menon. OpenMP: An Industry-Standard API for Shared-Memory Programming *IEEE Computational Science and Engineering* vol. 5, no. 1, Jan 1998.

[4] T. Yang and A. Gerasoulis. DSC: Scheduling parallel tasks on an unbounded number of processors. *IEEE Trans. Parallel Distrib. Syst.*, vol. 5, no. 9 pages 951-967, Sept 1994.

[5] V. Sarkar. *Patitioning and Scheduling Parallel Programs for Multiprocessors* May 1989.

[6] J.J. Hwang, Y-C. Chow, F.D. Anger and C.Y. Lee. Scheduling precedence graphs in systems with interprocessor communication times. *SIAM J. Comput.*, vol. 18, Apr 1989.

[7] Y-K. Kwok and I. Ahmed. Static Scheduling Algorithms for Allocating Directed Task Graphs to Multiprocessors. *ACM Computing Surveys*, vol. 31, no. 4, Dec 1999.

[8] T.G. Lewis and H. El-Rewini. Parallax: A Tool for Parallel Program Scheduling. *IEEE Parallel and Distributed Technology*, vol. 1, no. 3, pages 62-72, May 1993.

[9] T. Yang and A. Gerasoulis. PYRROS: Static Task Scheduling and Code Generation for Message-Passing Multiprocessors. *Proc. 6th ACM Int'l Conf. SuperComputing*, pages 428-433, ACM Press, New York, 1992.

[10] P-Grade Team. Parallel Grid Runtime and Application Development Environment. *User's Manual Version 8.4.2*, http://www.lpds.sztaki.hu/ smith/pgrade-manual/manual.html, accessed on 21st April, 2006.

[11] I. Ahmed, Y-K. Kwok, M-Y. Wu, and W. Shu. *CASCH: A Tool for Computer-Aided Scheduling* IEEE Concurrency, Oct 2000.

[12] R. Nallan, A. Chakrabarti, S. Sengupta, and A. Upadhyay. A Systematic Approach for Application Migration in a Grid Computing Environment. *Asia Pacific Services Computing Conf.(APSCC)*, China, Dec 2006.

[13] http://www.acm.inf.ethz.ch/ProblemSetArchive/B_EU_SWERC/1998/index.html.

[14] A.Gerasoulis and T. Yang. On the granularity and clustering of directed acyclic task graphs. *IEEE Transactions on Parallel and Distributed Systems*, vol. 4, no. 6, June 1993.

[15] Javasim available at http://javasim.ncl.ac.uk/

SIMPLIFYING GRID APPLICATION PROGRAMMING USING WEB-ENABLED CODE TRANSFER TOOLS

Cătălin L. Dumitrescu, Jan Dünnweber, Philipp Lüdeking, Sergei Gorlatch
Department of Mathematics and Computer Science, University of Münster, Germany
CoreGRID Institute on Programming Models
{dumitres,duennweb,muli,gorlatch}@uni-muenster.de

Ioan Raicu
Department of Computer Science, University of Chicago, USA

Ian Foster
Department of Computer Science, University of Chicago, USA
Mathematics and Computer Science Division, Argonne National Laboratory, USA
{iraicu,foster}@cs.uchicago.edu

Abstract   This paper deals with one of the fundamental properties of grid computing – transferring code between grid nodes and executing it remotely on heterogeneous hosts. Contemporary middleware relies for this purpose on Web Services, which makes application programs complicated and low-level and requires much additional expertise from programmers. We compare two mechanisms for grid application programming with regard to their handling of code transfer – the de-facto standard WS-GRAM in Globus and the higher-level approach based on HOCs (Higher-Order Components). We study the advantages and problems of each approach using a real-world application case study – the sequent alignment problem from bioinformatics. Our experiments show the trade-off between reduced development costs and software complexity when HOCs are used and the higher performance of the applications on the grid when using WS-GRAM.

Keywords: Distributed Systems, Resource Management, Service Level Agreements

This research work was supported in part under the FP6 Network of Excellence CoreGRID funded by the European Commission (Contract IST-2002-004265).

1. Introduction

Grids aim to provide a transparent access to large-scale computing, networking, and storage resources. A fundamental property of grid applications is the transfer of not only data but also executable code between the nodes of the grid. Contemporary middleware, for example the Globus Toolkit, relies on Web Services for this purpose, such that a typical grid application usually consists of two parts: a) an operational part that handles computations in a parallel and distributed manner, and b) a declarative part which includes resource specifications, interface definitions, deployment descriptors etc., in an XML-based format; it describes, e. g., how to encode a program for transmission and how to invoke code on a remote host. Therefore, grid application programming remains a quite low-level, complicated task that requires from the programmer much additional expertise beyond his particular application area.

In this paper, we study and compare two approaches to grid application programming with regard to how they manage the aspect of code transfer:

- The first approach is the Globus Resource Allocation Manager (WS-GRAM [2]) which is currently the most often used solution. In WS-GRAM, code is packaged as a job which is a Web service parameter of a special type. Each job carries an executable program, packaged together with a description of the parameters this program expects and the program's requirements concerning the processors and libraries available on the execution platform. WS-GRAM extends the Web service standards (WSDL and SOAP [15]) by a descriptive XML-based language RSL [2] for job definitions, since usually the types used for the parameters of Web services are plain data types rather than executable programs. Contrary to the static interface of a Web service, users upload RSL definitions to the service at runtime.

- The second approach seeks to raise the level of programming abstraction by relying on Higher-Order Components (HOCs [6]). HOCs are application-level components: they provide implementations of typical, recurrently used coordination patterns in parallel applications. HOC users implement only application-specific operations and pass them to the HOCs as code parameters. The Service Architecture for HOCs (HOC-SA [3]) is currently a Globus incubator project [4]. Using HOCs, the work of application programmers and the amount of code transferred in the grid is fairly reduced, because much work is done by HOC-SA.

In the remainder of the paper, we compare the process of grid application programming using these two approaches: WS-GRAM and HOC-SA. After describing the general properties of the both approaches in Section 2, we consider in Section 3 a particular application example - detection of similarities in genome sequences - and present how this application is implemented using each of the two approaches. In Section 4, we describe the results of extensive experiments with the genome sequence application which demonstrate the performance and the development costs of the application when using WS-GRAM and HOC-SA. We discuss related work and conclude in Section 5.

2. Grid Programming with WS-GRAM and the HOC-SA

From the user's viewpoint, a possibility to request the processing of application tasks over the Internet instead of only downloading application data is probably the feature which makes the grid most distinct from the Web.

2.1 Code transfer and Web services

The technology enabling the remote processing of application tasks is currently Web services in most grid middleware systems. Web services were created with the aim of increasing the interoperability among heterogeneous platforms by handling the exchange of data over the network using portable formats. The parameters accepted by a Web service must be encoded in an XML document. For any Web service this document must adhere to an XML Schema which the service developer writes into the WSDL description of the service interface [15]. However, Web services were not designed to exchange executable code. There is no representation for executable code in the XML Schema format. Therefore, Web service developers must declare code as plain data skipping the context information about the code, i. e., the information about how to invoke the code from within another program is potentially not available to the execution host, as explained in the following.

Generally, there are two different types of code a client can upload to a server in a distributed system: a self-contained program or a part of a program. Both types must be invoked in a different manner. In the case that clients upload a self-contained program, the context information required to invoke this program consists of the data format and sequence of the program input. Moreover the libraries, command line arguments, environment variables and also parameters like, e. g., the number of MPI processes used in the program must be communicated to the executing server. A Java class containing its own main method also falls under the category of self-contained programs: it is a portable binary that requires the same context information for remote execution as a native binary program.

In the second case, if the code uploaded by a client is only a part of a program, it must be a well-defined entity in the full program, e. g., a class or block which contains one or multiple procedure definitions. To insert this entity remotely into the proper context, the executing server requires information about the code format (source or binary) and programming language, which is not necessarily the case for self-contained programs, as these are either in a binary format or scripts that can be interpreted by the remote shell. To execute non-self-contained code remotely, the interface for accessing this code within the server-side context, i. e., the signatures of the procedures inside, must be declared in a file available to the execution host which must assign proper variable types to input and output. Both, command line options and interfaces have no standard representation in XML Schema making it difficult to define Web service interfaces for transferring any code, full or partial programs.

Thus, the code transfer problem that we address in this paper originates from the fact that the context information of a local code, i. e., the required information on how to execute it, is potentially lost when the code is transferred as a Web service parameter from one context (e. g., a client program) to another.

2.2 Web-enabled Code Transfer with WS-GRAM

Fig. 1 shows how the WS-GRAM service of Globus avoids the potential loss of information discussed above, when full programs are transferred: The client code (left in the figure) contains a call to WS-GRAM where application code is submitted as a job to the execution hosts. The shaded hexagons in the WS-GRAM job represent processes connected by arrows representing message exchange.

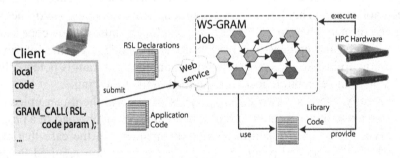

Figure 1.   Code Transfer via Job submission in WS-GRAM

Besides the application code, the client sends one RSL declaration per job. The programmer must write these declarations to provide the information about how to invoke the transferred code to the execution hosts. RSL files are uploaded by WS-GRAM users at runtime together with the code described therein. RSL belongs to the declarative part of a WS-GRAM application and extends the static configuration which any Web service-based software requires (WSDD & WSDL [15]). While the introduction of RSL to the Web service configuration enables the use of different kinds of executable code as Web service parameters, WS-GRAM requires users to be familiar both with the service configuration and with RSL. In Fig. 1, there is one RSL declaration document per application unit (transferred in a single submission, typically a class).

2.3 Web-enabled Code Transfer with HOC-SA

Higher-Order Components (HOCs) handle the platform-specific work automatically (data format conversions etc.) and require only the application-specific pieces of code being sent to them. This principle is depicted in Fig. 2: The client runs an application that uses a HOC which executes on the remote High-Performance Computers (HPC) with code parameters provided by the client. The HOC - Service Architecture (HOC-SA) provides a solution for code transfer in which only a part of a program is sent over the network. While the generic components (HOCs) are pre-installed, the application-specific code parameters are transferred on demand (i. e., at runtime as explained in the following). HOC-SA adds to WS-GRAM two elements, the Code Service and the Remote Code Loader. However, HOC-SA makes the situation simpler for the user as compared to WS-GRAM, since the upload of code (step ① in Fig. 2) is decoupled from using the code (step ②), as explained in the next paragraph.

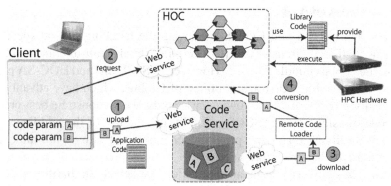

Figure 2. Code Transfer to a component (HOC) via the HOC-SA

In the upload step ①, the application code is intermediately stored in the Code Service, a Web service connected to a database (via OGSA-DAI [11]). Identifiers specified by the user (Ⓐ and Ⓑ in the figure) are linked to the uploaded code, making it a code parameter. Users can pass a code parameter to a HOC by referring to its identifier. Both HOCs and their code parameters can be reused in many different applications. The code parameter transfer (lower part of the client-side code) is not necessarily contained in the client application, but becomes rather an administrative action: HOC-SA includes a Web-based portal allowing programmers to browse the Code Service and check if a code parameter with the required functionality is available: if not, then a new code parameter can be stored using our portal (or hand-written code). Thus, in the HOC-SA, code transfer is separated from the application code, such that both Code Service and Remote Code Loader are not visible to the programmer.

In the HOC(A,B)-call in step ②, no code is transferred. It is an ordinary Web service request that is served by a HOC. HOCs execute recurring communication patterns (the pattern in Fig. 2 is called wavefront [3]; see Section 3 for an example). For transparently inserting code parameters into appropriate positions in the pattern implementation, the HOC-SA performs two steps invisible to the application programmer: in the download step ③, the code that the identifiers refer to is transferred to the HPC hardware (which is more than one host, in case of a distributed HOC implementation). The conversion step ④ is performed by the Remote Code Loader which is locally placed on the execution host(s) and makes the downloaded code parameters executable there. This conversion is done by cast operations which assign the code parameters their proper types. The type of HOC being used also determines the type of the code parameters (e. g. a certain class definition), such that RSL for describing HOC code parameters is unnecessary. In Fig. 2, the application code is much smaller than in Fig. 1 since it represents only a piece of a program (HOC parameters)

3. Application case study for the HOC-SA and WS-GRAM

Both WS-GRAM and HOC-SA delegate the handling of grid-specific requirements like file transfer and (to a certain extend) fault-tolerance and security to the Globus middleware [5]. However, WS-GRAM and HOC-SA provide different means for code transfer on top of Globus, which have advantages in different scenarios. In the following case study, we demonstrate best practices for code transfer, using HOCs for simplifying the use of the middleware and using WS-GRAM for giving programmer more control over the middleware and potentially better performance.

As a case study, we present an application that detects similarities in genome sequences. Although there are already many implementations for genome sequence alignment, our component-based solution features exchangeable processing modes, such that the same distributed procedure is employed to detect different kinds of similarities. The implementation is based on the Alignment HOC (a GRAM-based variant without code parameters is shown in Section 4). It fills a scoring matrix that rates differences between character sequence pairs: each matrix element holds the result of a user-defined scoring function applied to the two input subsequences, delimited by the element's indices. Besides the scoring function, the Alignment HOC has two more code parameters: the alignment function and the traceback function. The alignment function is used to iterate over the sequences and compute the scores, i. e., the users are in control over the computation order allowing them, e. g., to run a parallel schema. Eventually, the traceback operation is applied to the scoring matrix to produce the result (e. g., this is often a path through the matrix). While the code parameters allow users to run any kind of sequence rating with the Alignment HOC, a standard Smith & Waterman alignment [13] can be computed without writing any code parameter, since the Alignment HOC provides a default scoring, alignment and traceback function for this purpose.

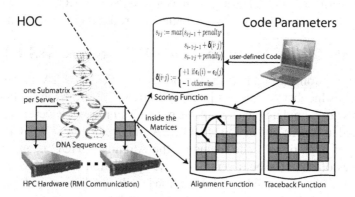

Figure 3. Computation Schema of the Alignment HOC for DNA Similarity Detection

As shown in Fig. 3, the Alignment HOC is a distributed component which uses RMI for dispatching parts of its input to multiple RMI servers (they are to be launched by the user in advance). For our example application, we specified a scoring and a traceback function that search for circular permutations [14]. While the default alignment function of the Alignment HOC allows for any kind of data dependences (even among non-neighboring input elements) and works sequentially, we implemented an alignment function that executes the parallel processing schema known as the wavefront pattern [3]. It partitions the matrix into submatrices which are positioned along the matrix antidiagonals and form a wavefront. The submatrices are processed by the servers which need no synchronization, since the wavefront pattern guarantees that there are data dependences only inside the submatrices but not amongst them. While the computations proceed through the matrix, there is a varying number of parallel processes active, as shown in the processing schema in Fig. 2. The alignment function is an example for code reuse (and, thus, reduced code transfer costs) in the HOC-SA: it can be used as a code parameter in different applications (with potentially different HOCs), even in applications of the wavefront pattern that neither process genome data nor use RMI servers.

For implementing the sequential processing inside the code parameters, we used the JAligner library [10]. As shown in Section 2.3, the HOC-SA provides to each HOC a specific library code in a server-sided repository. The Alignment HOC, e. g., has access to JAligner, allowing us to use it without transferring it to the servers ourselves.

The decision to choose one particular code transfer technology depends on the relation between application-independent parts that can be handled by a HOC and the size of the code parameters. An advantage of using HOC-SA, is that it has a relatively small footprint, i. e., can outsource tasks to remote machines which do not run Globus containers of their own. If the target environment has the Globus container installed on every node per default, it is always worth to consider using both WS-GRAM and HOC-SA. In the next section, we compare the two technologies regarding their performance.

4. Performance Comparison: HOC-SA vs. WS-GRAM

In this section, we compare the performance of the HOC-SA implementation as a Globus Incubator project [4] with WS-GRAM [2] from the Globus Toolkit.

We use two implementations of the genome similarity detection application described in Sec. 3: one on top of HOC-SA and one on top of WS-GRAM. The amount of operational code including the Alignment HOC is approximately 18K lines of code for both versions. The application-specific code, i. e., the part the user writes in the HOC-SA version is only 400 lines of code long. Since the Alignment HOC is an application-independent component, it is typically pre-installed in a server-side repository in the HOC-SA. Therefore, HOC-SA reduces the network traffic at startup of our application by factor 45.

All our tests were generated and submitted by means of the DiPerF tool in ServMark [1], a specialized tool for grid performance evaluation. HOC-SA was installed on grid nodes at the University of Chicago, with the following characteristics: Dual-Intel Xeon(TM) 3.0 GHz with Hyper-threading, 2.0 Gb of Memory and 100Mb/s network connectivity. Clients were deployed on the PlanetLab nodes [12], which are Linux PCs connected to the PlanetLab overlay network with worldwide distribution. Most nodes are connected via 100 Mb/s network links (some still have 10Mb/s links) over a wide-area network (WAN), have processor speeds exceeding 1.0 GHz IA32 Pentium III processors, and at least 512 MB RAM.

Our metrics used for quantifying the performance of the two implementations are as follows: (1) execution time (response) is the average time elapsed from job submission to finish; (2) throughput quantifies the number of computations that terminated and returned a result (i. e., completed requests) of the service per second, and (3) load represents the number of clients that use the service concurrently at a certain moment in time.

Figure 4 captures the performance WS-GRAM and HOC-SA in terms of response time. In some of experiments, the performance of WS-GRAM was up to two times higher than the performance of HOC-SA. We explain this by the highly optimized processing of repeated requests in WS-GRAM (e. g., via caching). On average, WS-GRAM showed lower variations for response time; the spikes can be explained by the temporal incapacity of the service to serve all requests, caused by the communication with the OGSA-DAI and the RMI servers. The performance of HOC-SA improves when the Code service and the RMI servers are placed in the same LAN and depends on the LAN

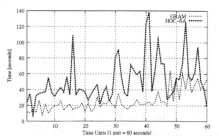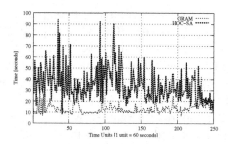

Figure 4. GRAM and HOC-SA response time in seconds on the dual Xenon processor with 40 (left) and 20 (right) clients running in PlanetLab for 1800 (left) or 3600 seconds (right)

capabilities [8]. Thus, the use of the HOC-SA Code service and Remote Code Loader for code transfer comes at a certain cost when the resources are widely dispersed.

However, we also measured that WS-GRAM, while delivering better response times, caused a processor load that was on average 20% higher than in the HOC-SA scenario. Thus, HOC-SA can provide a higher availability (in terms of responsiveness), when the number of concurrent clients rises.

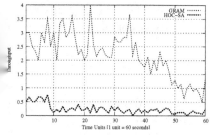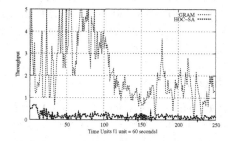

Figure 5. GRAM and HOC-SA throughput on the dual Xenon processor with at most 40 (left) and 20 (right) clients running on PlanetLab. Tunable parameters: starts a new client every 30 (left) and 180 (right) seconds, each client runs for 1800 (left) and 3600 (right) seconds

Figure 5 shows that the performance of WS-GRAM in terms of throughput is up to three times higher as in HOC-SA. This is explained by the use of gridFTP instead of SOAP for transferring the sequence files in the WS-GRAM version.

5. Conclusions and Related Work

This paper has compared two approaches to grid application programming – WS-GRAM and HOC-SA – with regard to how they handle code transfer over the network and its execution on the grid nodes. For our experiments we used a real-world application, which is successfully used in bioinformatics: this program recently scanned the genome database ProDom [14] and found pattern matches that were not known previously [8].

An important advantage of HOC-SA is that it frees the user from writing any declarative code. The traditional declaration of communicated data and code in grid applications becomes unnecessary due to pre-built components and a special portal. HOC-SA also allows users to perform code transfer by accessing the Code Service directly from within the application code. Other grid portal projects, e. g. , Ganga [7] and gridPort [9], also support the transfer of code. But these projects cannot be used for building new applications: their purpose is the placement of existing applications onto grid nodes. Ganga and gridPort also do not allow to submit to the grid application code that has data dependencies.

In our experiments, HOC-SA demonstrated an advantage of simplified application programming and reduced network traffic. If an application performs computations that are so time-consuming that they justify the costs for handling every part of them with hand-tuned code, then WS-GRAM is probably the best choice for implementing it. Since the time costs of most grid applications depend on the amounts of data being processed, a HOC that provides a distributed processing schema can help speeding up these applications by increasing the number of execution nodes. Thus, HOC-SA proves to be a viable extension to WS-GRAM in today's grids. Grid applications can also benefit from both technologies, HOC-SA and WS-GRAM, simultaneously: WS-GRAM can transfer a HOC together with its code parameters or any other self-contained part of a HOC-SA application.

References

[1] C. Dumitrescu, A. Iosup, I. Raicu, M. Ripeanu. ServMark: A Distributed Grid Testing Framework, 2006. http://dev.globus.org/wiki/Incubator/ServMark.

[2] K. Czajkowski, I. Foster, C. Kesselman et al.. A Resource Management Architecture for Metacomputing Systems . In *IPPS/PDP'98 Workshop*, pages 62–82, 1998.

[3] J. Dünnweber et al. Adaptable parallel components for Grid programming. *Integrated Research in GRID Computing*, pages 43–59. Springer Verlag, 2006.

[4] J. Dünnweber, P. Lüdeking, C. L. Dumitrescu, E. Argollo, and S. Gorlatch. The HOC-SA Globus Incubator Project. Web page: http://dev.globus.org/incubator/hoc-sa/, 2006.

[5] I. Foster and C. Kesselman. Globus Toolkit *Supercomputer Journal*, 11(2):115–128, 1997.

[6] S. Gorlatch and J. Dünnweber. From Grid Middleware to Grid Applications: Bridging the Gap with HOCs. In *Future Generation Grids*, pages 299–306. Springer Verlag, 2005.

[7] K. Harrison et al. Ganga: a Grid User Interface for Distributed Analysis. In S. J. Cox, editor, *Proceedings of Fifth UK e-Science All-Hands Meeting*. EPSRC, 2006.

[8] P. Luedeking. MS thesis: Proteine sequence analysis in the Grid with the HOC-SA, 2006.

[9] Maytal Dahan et al. Grid Portal Toolkit 3 (gridport). In *Proceedings of the 13th HPDC*, pages 272–273, Washington, DC, USA, 2004. IEEE.

[10] A. Moustafa. The JAligner library http://jaligner.sourceforge.net, 2007

[11] Grid Data Access and Integration OGSA-DAI www.ogsadai.org.uk, 2007

[12] L. Peterson et al. A Blueprint for Introducing Disruptive Technology into the Internet. In *Proceedings of the ACM HotNets)*, October 2002.

[13] T. F. Smith and M. S. Waterman. Identification of common molecular subsequences. *Journal of Molecular Biology*, 147:195–197, 1981.

[14] J. Weiner, G. Thomas, and E. Bornberg-Bauer. Rapid Motif-based Prediction of Circular Permutations in Multi-domain Proteins. *Bioinformatics*, 21:932 – 937, 2005.

[15] W3C: . XML protocol recommendations, http://www.w3.org/2002/ws, 2002.

VII

WORKFLOW MANAGEMENT

TOWARDS A LIGHT-WEIGHT WORKFLOW ENGINE IN THE ASKALON GRID ENVIRONMENT

Jun Qin, Marek Wieczorek, Kassian Plankensteiner, Thomas Fahringer
Institute of Computer Science, University of Innsbruck
Technikerstraße 21a, A-6020 Innsbruck, Austria
{jerry,marek,kassian,tf}@dps.uibk.ac.at

Abstract   Workflow scheduling and execution belong to the most difficult problems in the Grid computing research area. Instead of using a full-ahead planning to schedule workflows, which requires precise predictions of task execution time, file transfer time and Grid site status during the workflow execution, we propose a light-weight workflow engine for the ASKALON Grid environment, which uses just in-time scheduling based on automatically generated performance predictions and task prioritization. An extensive survey of the related work is discussed. The architecture of the proposed workflow engine and some preliminary results are presented.

Keywords: Grid Workflow, Enactment Engine, Scheduling, Performance

1.   Introduction

Grid computing has become a major paradigm for parallel processing. Workflow scheduling and execution in a computational environment is a difficult optimization problem, which is NP-complete [6] in most of its variants. To make a schedule effective and feasible is particularly challenging in case of Grid environments, which are usually large, highly dynamic and unreliable distributed environments. The ASKALON Grid environment [4], which is the main Grid application development and computing environment for the Austrian Grid infrastructure [1], uses full-ahead planning to schedule workflows in the Grid. It applies rescheduling to make the workflow processing more dynamic, and uses advance reservation to improve the predictability and feasibility of the scheduling [15]. The full-ahead scheduling is proved to be a reasonable approach, which shows an advantage over just in-time scheduling techniques, especially for a certain class of *highly unbalanced workflows* [14]. However, in order to benefit from a full-ahead scheduling approach, reliable predictions for task execution time, data transfer time, and grid resource status during the whole workflow execution are required. The experience we gained with executing workflows in Austrian Grid [1] using ASKALON shows that these assumptions may not always be fulfilled, due to short execution times, highly unpredictable overheads, and task failures. Based on these observations, the profit coming from sophisticated and time consuming scheduling techniques seems to be rather debatable, and a simpler but more dynamic workflow scheduling and execution approach is required.

In this paper, we propose a light-weight workflow engine, tightly coupled with a just in-time scheduler, which applies automatically generated performance feedback and one-step-ahead workflow analysis to optimize workflow executions in Grid environments.

2.   Past Experience

In ASKALON, the scientific workflows are specified in the Abstract Grid Workflow Language (AGWL) [5]. AGWL allows for a concise and expressive representation of workflows, based on a set of control flow constructs including basic constructs (sequence, parallel, dag), sequential and parallel loops (while, dowhile, for, forEach, parallelFor, parallelForEach), as well as conditional branches (if, switch). At the atomic level, AGWL workflows consist of explicitly defined *tasks* and *data transfers*. Data transfers are defined by means of *data ports* assigned to tasks and workflow constructs. Tasks in workflows can be of different types, referred to as *activity types*. The activity types are mapped to concrete activity implementations during workflow execution. Currently, we have one activity implementation associated with a given activity type on a specific Grid site, which means that activities of an activity type in most cases have the same execution time on a resource. The tasks are executed on Grid sites, using Globus Toolkit and local resource managers like OpenPBS. In the rest of the paper, the *execution time* of a task will describe only the effective execution time of a task on a Grid site, and the *environmental overhead* will describe the time needed by Globus Toolkit and the local resource manager to start up the job. Due to the lack of enough experimental data, the *data transfer time* and the related overhead have not been analyzed by us.

Since October 2006, we have executed 901 workflows of 15 different applications on the Austrian Grid using ASKALON. The workflows consisted of 46773 task executions, 752 of which failed. We based our study on the 34993 successfully finished tasks for which we had a full execution record stored in the database.

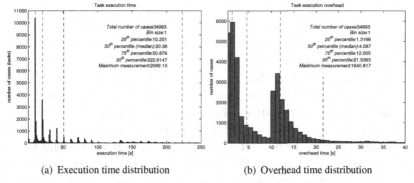

(a) Execution time distribution   (b) Overhead time distribution

Figure 1.   Execution and overhead time distribution

The histograms in Fig. 1 show the distribution of the execution time and the overhead time among the executed tasks. The dashed vertical lines represent the 25th, the 50th, the 75th, and the 95th percentile, respectively. As we can see, nearly all the execution times are concentrated around certain values which represent typical execution times for different activity types on different resources. The overhead time has a two-modal distribution, clearly because of two predominant configurations of the Globus Toolkit on different sites.

Fig. 2 shows the ratio between the overhead time and the execution time for different tasks. The overhead was equal in average to around 15% of the effective execution time, however very often it was equal or even higher than the effective execution time. The peaks around the arguments of 40%, 60%, and 100% represent the sets of tasks with very short execution time and relatively high overhead.

The presented results show that most of the tasks executed in ASKALON were rather short (shorter than 4 minutes, in most cases shorter than 1 minute). The environmental overhead time, which was usually between 1 and 5 seconds or between 10 and 20 seconds, in 50% of the cases was greater than 15% of the effective execution time. When running workflows consisting of such short

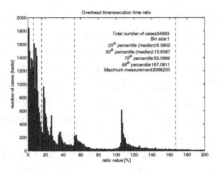

Figure 2. Overhead/execution time ratio

tasks, for which the overhead time may be relatively long in comparison with the execution time, we may expect considerable high fluctuations of the task execution which cannot be fully predicted in advance. As we showed in [14], by applying a sophisticated full-ahead scheduling approach to fully balanced workflows, we can achieve the execution time 20% shorter than in case of a simple "myopic" just in-time scheduling. In ASKALON, this theoretical value could be attainable for workflows consisting of relatively long tasks, which are characterized by highly predictable execution time and relatively short overheads. Since most of the tasks had rather short execution time, which makes the less predictable overheads more significant, and since some other factors like external load, file transfer overhead and task failure may also affect long-range predictions, the benefits coming from a full-ahead scheduling could become debatable. A light-weight just in-time scheduling strategy, which is better than a simple "myopic" algorithm, could be a valuable supplement to the full-ahead scheduling currently used in ASKALON.

3. Related Work

The problem of dynamic workflow scheduling has already been tackled many times in different ways. Some authors proposed full-graph scheduling applied in a dynamic way, by applying rescheduling. The approach proposed in [3] introduces workflow partitioning, which consists in dividing a workflow into a sequence of subworkflows. By introducing implicit barriers between arbitrarily created subworkflows, the approach may in some cases provide inefficient results. In ASKALON [4], an advanced model of scientific workflows is proposed, which includes loops, parallel loops, and conditional branches. The workflows are scheduled using HEFT, and a rescheduling is triggered when some assumptions considering the workflow structure fail. This execution model is extended in [17], where HEFT is applied dynamically during a workflow execution whenever the state of the Grid changes (the modified algorithm is called AHEFT). However, this approach is only adapted for simple DAGs. One of the algorithms proposed in [8] is also a dynamically applied full-graph scheduling algorithm, used for simple parameter sweep applications. The disadvantage of full-graph scheduling approaches is that they have a computational complexity of at least $\Theta(n \cdot r)$ (where n and r are the number of tasks and resources, respectively), which may introduce a significant scheduling overhead if applied many times during a single workflow execution.

A hybrid static-dynamic scheduling approach is proposed in [12]. Workflows (master-slave applications) are scheduled either in a static way at the beginning of execution, or in a dynamic way, during the execution. The static and the dynamic scheduling are referred to as *placement* and *replacement*, and are implemented using the algorithms called time-balancing and Guided Self-Scheduling (GSS), respectively. The resources are classified according to their load variance. Most of the jobs assigned to the resources with a low variance are scheduled using the static placement, while the resources with a high variance are assigned mostly by the dynamic replacement. The predictions for the execution time, the data transfer time and the resource availability are done by the Network Weather Service [16].

Many dynamic workflow scheduling approaches are based on task prioritization. The second algorithm proposed in [8] gives higher priority to the tasks whose children's ancestors have already been finished. This approach has been designed and examined for parameter sweep applications, and its usefulness for a broader class of workflows has not been proved. The work presented in [9] shows a survey of several dynamic list scheduling algorithms, and introduces a novel algorithm called Fast Critical Path (FCP). The tasks in the queue are sorted according to their positions on the critical path (the further from the end of the workflow, the higher priority the task has). The priority queue has a fixed size, and an additional unsorted queue is used to store the tasks which do not fit in the priority queue. The approach was proposed for homogeneous environment, and no consideration about a reliable performance prediction model has been made. The research proposed in [7] describes a model of multiple workflow applications competing independently for distributed resources. It optimizes the scheduling decisions using an extension of another priority-based scheduling algorithm called DLS (Dynamic Level Scheduling). Since there is no central execution engine which has control over the Grid resources, the dynamic scheduling processes performed for different workflows are synchronized by analyzing the lengths of the local queues.

Data transfer time was considered in several publications together with task execution time as an optimization goal in Grid workflow scheduling. The approach proposed in [2] is based on an initial partitioning of a workflow into a sequence of subworkflows (*levels*), where all tasks within a level do not depend on each other. The scheduling is done in a static way at the beginning of execution, based on advance reservation of the resources. The approach also assumes that exact predictions for data transfer and task execution time are known in advance, in order to partition the workflow and to make a proper scheduling. A dynamic scheduling approach has been proposed in [10]. The scheduling is performed for independent jobs with data requirements, and task and data scheduling are decoupled and performed by independent schedulers called External Schedulers (ES) and Data Schedulers (DS). External Schedulers perform schedule tasks and delegate them to Local Schedulers (LS), and Data Schedulers decide upon possible data replications.

Unlike the aforementioned works, we propose a dynamic workflow scheduling approach based on highly-adaptive performance predictions and combined task execution and data transfer optimization. By making the scheduling just in-time, we always consider the actual status of the Grid. And by applying a critical path task prioritization technique, the total workflow execution time is used as the main optimization goal. We do not make any special assumptions, neither concerning stability of the environment, nor the precision of predictions.

4.   Proposed Architecture

In the current architecture of ASKALON, the enactment engine, the scheduler, and the performance predictor are loosely coupled and communicate with each other sparsely. A full-graph scheduling is applied, and rescheduling is used as a way to make the execution more dynamic and adaptable to the variable Grid environment. The architecture of the light-weight workflow engine proposed in this paper is more tightly coupled, and the scheduling decisions are made more dynamically, by postponing them as long as it still does not bring any significant performance deterioration. The performance predictions are based on the user experience, the dynamically generated feedback, and the historical executions.

The proposed architecture is depicted in Fig. 3(a). It consists of 3 main components: the *executor*, the *scheduler* and the *performance predictor*. The executor is the main component responsible for processing and execution of workflows submitted by the user. It executes workflow tasks based on the decisions made by the scheduler, and also generates the feedback for the performance predictor, which can be used to support the current or the future executions of workflows. The scheduler schedules workflows by mapping the tasks to available resources. The performance predictor supports the scheduler by providing it with predictions about the task execution time and the data transfer time. The predictions are made based on the user experience defined in the submitted workflow, as well as the feedback coming from the current execution and the historical workflow executions.

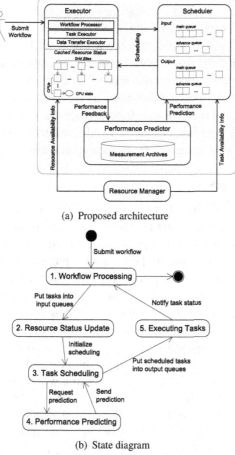

(a) Proposed architecture

(b) State diagram

Figure 3.   Proposed workflow engine

The state diagram describing the system is illustrated in Fig. 3(b). First, the user submits a workflow and the executor starts to process the workflow by selecting the tasks which are ready for execution (State 1). The executor then updates the cached resource status information acquired from the resource manager (State 2). The scheduler is invoked to schedule the tasks to the appropriate resources (State 3). To do this, the scheduler considers the task availability on different resources, and communicates with the performance predictor (State 4) to get the performance guidance supporting the scheduling decisions. The scheduler tries to find the optimal mapping between the tasks and the available resources. As soon as some tasks are mapped, the execution starts (State 5) and the system enters the idle state. The tasks which are not scheduled because of the lack of available resources remain in the input queues of the scheduler. Multiple workflow tasks which do not depend on each other may be executed at the same time. The system leaves the idle state once the status of task execution or of the Grid environment changes. If a task is completed successfully, the execution feedback is sent to the performance predictor and the workflow is processed again to find the tasks which are ready for execution (State 1). Then, a next scheduling cycle is invoked or the whole workflow execution is finished. If a task execution fails, then the executor analyzes the workflow (State 1) and decides whether to reschedule the task or to terminate the workflow execution with an error message. If the status of the Grid changes (some resources disappear or appear), then the executor updates the cached resource status information (State 2) and invokes the scheduler (State 3) to schedule more tasks onto the newly available resources, or to reschedule the failed tasks.

5. Challenges

The goal in developing a light-weight workflow engine of ASKALON is to take advantage of all the strong points of the just in-time scheduling approach, and to avoid its weaknesses. The performance prediction in the proposed model is highly dynamic, based on the performance measurements made in the current workflow execution. This allows for a satisfactory good estimation of the expected task execution time, the data transfer time, and the environmental overhead. In order to make the predictions possible even if the current measurements are not ready yet, we introduce the two additional prediction sources: *user experiences* and *historical measurements*. According to our experience, the user is very often able to make quite precise estimations concerning the relative execution times of individual tasks in a workflow. For instance in the Invmod workflow [13], the tasks of all types (but one) have the execution time on a resource equal to either t or $2t$ (where t may differ, depending on the input data). The user can define such relative execution time in AGWL workflows through *AGWL properties* [5]. The historical measurements come from the past executions of the same workflow. These measurements may include absolute values (e.g., "$t = 300s$") as well as relative values ("$t(A) = 2.1 \cdot t(B)$"). To make predictions for a given workflow, we will use only the performance data generated during the execution of workflows with the same input data as the given one. To this end, we compare the values on the corresponding AGWL input ports of the workflows. If an input port is not numerical (e.g., it transmits files), then we compare special numerical *AGWL properties* assigned by the user to those ports.

At least two major problem may arise when applying a just in-time scheduling. The first problem lies in the fact a just in-time decision which is optimal for a part of a workflow may be unefficient from the point of view of the workflow *makespan* (total execution time). This case has been studied in [14]. The second problem is related to the in-advance data transfer optimization: postponing the scheduling decisions until the last moment prevents the workflow engine from transferring a data file f from a task A (the producer of f) to a task B

(the consumer of f), as long as it is not decided where the task B is scheduled (i.e., an implicit barrier is introduced). This may have a major impact on the execution time, as all of the workflow executed by us have large parallel tasks producing data to be sent to a single task.

To deal with the first problem, we prioritize the tasks in the input queue of the scheduler (see Fig. 3(a)). Similarly to the HEFT algorithm used in ASKALON and to some other approaches [9, 7], we use the distance to the end of the workflow as the prioritization criterion. The tasks with the higher distance values are executed first, as the longer the distance is, the higher is the impact of the task on the workflow makespan. The distance $dist\ (W, \tau)$ of a task $\tau \in W$ to the end of workflow W is the maximal length of a path consisting of tasks $\tau' \in W$ and data transfers $dt \in W$, which leads from the task τ to the end of the workflow:

$$dist(W, \tau) = max_{p=path(\tau, \tau_{end}(W))}(\sum_{\tau' \in p} time(\tau') + \sum_{dt \in p} time(dt))$$

An estimated value of $dist(W, \tau)$ can be effectively computed based on the performance predictions and the workflow structure analysis. If the workflow contains loops and conditions, the estimation of $dist(W, \tau)$ may in some cases become undeterministic (we may not know in advance how many iterations will be executed and how the conditions will be evaluted). However, our experience with workflow executions in ASKALON shows that parallel iterations usually have balanced execution times, and the major part of the imbalance results from the heterogeneity of the environment and from task failures.

To address the second of the aforementioned problems, we introduce a second input queue of the scheduler, called *advance queue* (see Fig. 3(a)). All tasks in the *advance queue* are *immediate successors* of the tasks in the main input queue (i.e., they consume the data produced by the tasks in the main queue). The scheduler makes *advance scheduling* of such tasks, if it decides that an advance scheduling decision would bring a significant profit (for instance, if it consumes data produced by at least 10 other tasks).

The executor and the scheduler communicate with each other via two input queues and two output queues. The executor sends tasks to the main input queue and receives the scheduling decisions from the main output queue. The advance queues are used to support the advance scheduling. Description of the tasks in the input queues contains the following information:

- *Task ID* - unique task identifier,

- *Activity type* - needed for resource matching and performance prediction,

- *Workflow ID* - needed for performance prediction,

- *Distance to the end of workflow* - needed for task prioritization,

Site name	#CPUs	CPU type
karwendel	8	DC AMD Opteron, 2.4 GHz
altix1	8	Itanium 2, 1.4 GHz
schafberg	8	Itanium 2, 1.4 GHz
c703-pc2201	8	Pentium 4, 2.8 GHz
c703-pc450	8	Pentium 4, 1.8 GHz
hydra	8	AMD Athlon, 1.67 GHz

Table 1.   The Austrian Grid testbed

- *Immediate predecessors* - needed for advance scheduling,

- *Task retry info* - needed for proper rescheduling.

In certain situations, the proposed scheduling model can be extended by some additional optimization techniques. For instance, the scheduler may preempt some low-priority tasks to submit some higher-priority tasks, when it decides that it would bring a benefit in terms of the workflow makespan. This feature would only make sense if the workflow engine has control over the queue on the local resource manager. In case when the number of available resources is higher than the number of the tasks which can be run in parallel, the scheduler may use multiple resources to replicate the execution of a single task, in order to increase the probability of a successful and effective execution.

6.   Experimental results

At the moment, we have implemented the executor and the performance predictor based on relative execution time and historical execution time, which allows us to test partially the functionality of the proposed approach. In the experiments shown in this section, we will compare this approach (referred to as *proposed approach*) with a similar approach not supporting any predictions (*no-prediction approach*), and with a *full-ahead* scheduling approach using the implemented performance predictor. The Grid workflow application used in the experiments is MeteoAG [11], whose structure is illustrated in Fig. 4.

The comparison of the approaches with respect to the execution time and the parallel speedup measured for different Grid configurations is illustrated in Fig. 5. In the experiments, we ran the `parallelForEach` construct with two parallel loop iterations, each of which had two `parallelFor` constructs with 48 parallel loop iterations. A subset of the computational resources which have been used for the experiments is summarized in Table 1.

As illustrated in Fig. 5, the proposed approach provides a better performance in comparison to the no-prediction approach. This advantage was achieved through the performance predictions supporting the scheduling decisions. For the maximal Grid size (6 sites), the workflow execution time was much longer in the no-prediction approach (358 seconds) than in the proposed approach (271

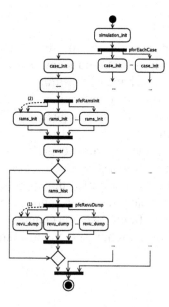

Figure 4.   MeteoAG workflow

seconds), as some large tasks were scheduled onto a slow Grid site *hydra*. The proposed scheduling approach was also better than the full-ahead approach, especially when the workflow was executed on 4 Grid sites and on 6 Grid sites. This is because in the full-ahead scheduling approach, the scheduling decision is made before the workflow execution starts, and there is no dynamic rescheduling to adapt the changes of the external load of Grid sites.

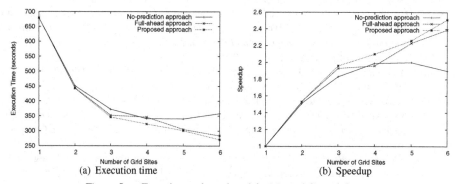

(a) Execution time   (b) Speedup

Figure 5.   Experimental results of the MeteoAG workflow

7. Conclusions

We presented our experience with workflow execution on the Grid using the ASKALON Grid environment, and showed the reasons why the current full-ahead scheduling approach may be insufficient for many of the workflows executed by us. We proposed a new workflow engine based on a just in-time scheduling approach using automatically generated feedback and tasks prioritization, which is significantly different from the approaches introduced so far in the related work. In the experiments performed in a real Grid environment, a first version of the new workflow engine, consisting of the executor and the performance predictor, outperformed the approach based on the old full-ahead scheduling, and a simple just in-time approach not based on performance predictions. In the nearest future, we are planning to implement the whole architecture proposed in the current work, and to examine its performance in a real Grid environment.

Acknowledgements

This work is partially funded by the European Union through the IST-034601 edutain@grid and FP6-004265 CoreGRID projects.

References

[1] The Austrian Grid Project. http://www.austriangrid.at.

[2] A. H. Alhusaini, V. K. Prasanna, and C. S. Raghavendra. A Unified Resource Scheduling Framework for Heterogeneous Computing Environments. In *Heterogeneous Computing Workshop*, pages 156–165, 1999.

[3] E. Deelman, J. Blythe, Y. Gil, C. Kesselman, G. Mehta, S. Patil, M.-H. Su, K. Vahi, and M. Livny. Pegasus: Mapping Scientific Workflows onto the Grid. In *European Across Grids Conference*, pages 11–20, 2004.

[4] T. Fahringer, R. Prodan, R. Duan, F. Nerieri, S. Podlipnig, J. Qin, M. Siddiqui, H.-L. Truong, A. Villazon, and M. Wieczorek. ASKALON: A Grid Application Development and Computing Environment. In *6th International Workshop on Grid Computing (Grid 2005)*, Seattle, USA, November 2005. IEEE Computer Society Press.

[5] T. Fahringer, J. Qin, and S. Hainzer. Specification of Grid Workflow Applications with AGWL: An Abstract Grid Workflow Language. In *Proceedings of IEEE International Symposium on Cluster Computing and the Grid 2005 (CCGrid 2005)*, Cardiff, UK, May 9-12, 2005. IEEE Computer Society Press.

[6] M. R. Garey and D. S. Johnson. *Computers and Intractability: A Guide to the Theory of NP-Completeness*. W. H. Freeman And Company, New York, 1979.

[7] M. Iverson and F. Ozguner. Dynamic, Competitive Scheduling of Multiple DAGs in a Distributed Heterogeneous Environment. In *HCW '98: Proceedings of the Seventh Heterogeneous Computing Workshop*, page 70, Washington, DC, USA, 1998. IEEE Computer Society.

[8] T. Ma and R. Buyya. Critical-Path and Priority based Algorithms for Scheduling Workflows with Parameter Sweep Tasks on Global Grids. In *Proceedings of the 17th International Symposium on Computer Architecture and High Performance Computing (SBAC-PAD 2005)*, Rio de Janeiro, Brazil, Oct. 24-27 2005. IEEE Computer Society Press.

[9] A. Radulescu and A. J. C. van Gemund. On the complexity of list scheduling algorithms for distributed-memory systems. In *Proceeding of the ICS 1999*, pages 68–75, 1999.

[10] K. Ranganathan and I. Foster. Decoupling Computation and Data Scheduling in Distributed Data-Intensive Applications.

[11] F. Schüller and J. Qin. Towards a Workflow Model for Meteorological Simulations on the AustrianGrid. In *1st Austrian Grid Symposium*, Schloss Hagenberg, Austria, December 01-02, 2005. OCG Verlag.

[12] N. T. Spring and R. Wolski. Application Level Scheduling of Gene Sequence Comparison on Metacomputers. In *International Conference on Supercomputing*, pages 141–148, 1998.

[13] D. Theiner and M. Wieczorek. Reduction of Calibration Time of Distributed Hydrological Models by Use of Grid Computing and Nonlinear Optimisation Algorithms. In *7th International Conference on Hydroinformatics (HIC 2006)*, Nice, France, Sep. 2006.

[14] M. Wieczorek, R. Prodan, and T. Fahringer. Scheduling of Scientific Workflows in the ASKALON Grid Environment. *ACM SIGMOD Record*, 35(3), 2005. http://dps.uibk.ac.at/ marek/publications/acm-sigmod-2005.pdf.

[15] M. Wieczorek, M. Siddiqui, A. Villazon, R. Prodan, and T. Fahringer. Applying Advance Reservation to Increase Predictability of Workflow Execution on the Grid. *e-science*, 0:82, 2006.

[16] R. Wolski, N. T. Spring, and J. Hayes. The network weather service: a distributed resource performance forecasting service for metacomputing. *Future Generation Computer Systems*, 15(5–6):757–768, 1999.

[17] Z. Yu and W. Shi. An Adaptive Rescheduling Strategy for Grid Workflow Applications. In *Proceedings of the 21st IPDPS 2007*, Mar 26-30 2007. IEEE Computer Society Press.

SUPPORTING WORKFLOW-LEVEL PARAMETER STUDY APPLICATIONS BY THE P-GRADE GRID PORTAL*

Peter Kacsuk and Zoltan Farkas and Gergely Sipos and Gabor Hermann
MTA SZTAKI, 1111 Kende utca 13
Budapest, Hungary
{kacsuk,zfarkas,sipos,gabor.hermann}@sztaki.hu

Tamas Kiss
University of Westminster
Cavendish School of Informatics
115 New Cavendish Street London W1W 6UW
T.Kiss@westminster.ac.uk

Abstract   Workflow applications are frequently used in many production Grids. There is a natural need to run the same workflow with many different parameter sets. P-GRADE portal has been providing a high-level, graphical workflow development and execution environment for various Grids (EGEE, UK NGS, GIN VO, OSG, TeraGrid, etc.) built on second and third generation Grid technologies (GT2, LCG-2, GT4, gLite). Feedback from the user communities of the portal showed that parameter study support is highly needed and hence the recent release (2.5) of the portal supports the workflow-level parameter study applications. The current paper describes the semantics and implementation principles of managing and executing workflows as parameter studies. Special emphasis is on the generation of the parameter input files, concurrent management of large number of files and jobs as well as collecting the large number of results generated at the PS execution time.

Keywords: Portal, Parameter Study, Workflow, Execution

---

*This research work is carried out under the FP6 Network of Excellence CoreGRID funded by the European Commission (Contract IST-2002-004265) and under the SEE-GRID-2 project funded by the European Commission (Contract number: 031775).

1. Introduction

One of the most promising utilizations of Grid resources comes to life with parameter study (or "parameter sweep") applications where the same application should be executed with a large set of input parameters. Such parameter study applications are easy to run in the Grid since executions started with different parameters are completely independent. Indeed, there are several projects [1],[2] that demonstrated that parameter study applications are easily manageable in the Grid. However, most of these projects tackled only single job based applications. The real challenge comes when complex applications consisting of large number of jobs connected into a workflow should be executed with many different parameter sets. There have been only two projects that tried to combine parameter studies with workflow-level support in the Grid. ILab [3], [4] enables the user to create a special parameter study oriented workflow. With the help of a sophisticated GUI, the user can explicitly define statically how to distribute and replicate the parameter files in the Grid and how many independent jobs are to be launched for each segment of the data files. The SEGL [5] approach puts much more emphasis on exploring the dynamic nature of the Grid. They also provide a GUI to define the workflows and to hide the low level details of the underlying Grid. The SEGL workflow provides tools for several levels of parameterization, repeated processing, handling conclusions and branches during the processing as well as synchronization of parallel branches and processes. The problem with this GUI is that it might be too sophisticated, requiring very large skill from the application developer.

Although our approach to support workflow-level parameter study applications in the Grid has many similarities with these two projects, there are significant differences, too. Our main goals are as follows:

1. Keep both the workflow GUI and the parameter study support concept as simple as possible. This enables the fast learning and easy usage.

2. Enable run any existing workflow with different parameter sets without modifying the structure of the workflow.

3. Provide an easy-to-use way of generating the various input parameter files needed for the PS execution.

4. Manage the execution of the workflows on as many Grid resources as possible. Enable the collection of Grid resources from several Grids.

5. Enable the access of the workflow-oriented GUI and the available Grids via a Grid portal without installing any software on the user's machine.

6. Provide an easy-to-use way of collecting and processing the large number of result files generated during the PS execution.

The starting point for our project was the previous version of P-GRADE Grid portal[6]that provides a workflow-oriented GUI as well as workflow-level interoperability between various Grids even if they are built on different Grid technologies. This means that the same portal can be connected to several different Grids and the portal manages the workflow execution among these Grids according to the users' requirement [7]. The portal even enables the parallel exploitation of the connected Grids, i.e., different jobs of the same workflow can simultaneously be executed on Grid resources taken from different Grids. Such a multi-Grid workflow execution mechanism is a unique feature of the P-GRADE portal that is now widely used for many different Grids (e.g. SEE-GRID, VOCE, HunGrid, GILDA, UK NGS, TeraGrid, GIN VO of OGF, etc.).

Experiences of the previous version of the portal revealed that many applications require not only the single execution of a workflow rather they seek for parameter study support to execute an existing workflow with many different parameter sets. Therefore, our motivation was to extend the existing single workflow support of the portal towards a generic workflow-level parameter study execution support. Such support should enable the automatic starting, execution, monitoring and visualization of all the workflows belonging to the same parameter study. Of course the same way as in the case of the single workflow management environment the users should neither know any details of the underlying Grids nor insist on any particular programming language. Even legacy codes should be used as services in the workflows if the portal is integrated with the GEMLCA legacy code architecture service[8].

In order to reach the six main goals mentioned above we have developed the so-called "black-box" algorithm to manage workflow-level parameter studies across multiple Grids. This algorithm requires only the modification of those input ports that are used to feed the various input parameters for the workflow. In order to generate input parameters we extended the portal with "Generator" job types. Finally, in order to facilitate the collection and processing of result files we introduced the concept of "Collector" job types. The paper describes the semantics of the black-box algorithm, the Generator and the Collector.

In Section 2 the paper explains the "black-box" execution semantics and its portal support both at the user interface and the portal workflow manager level. Section 3 introduces the concept of Generator and Collector jobs as well as their execution mechanism.

2.   The "black-box" execution semantics of workflow-level parameter study execution

The "black-box" execution semantics means that we consider a workflow as a black box that should be executed with many different parameter sets. These parameter sets are placed on the so-called PS input ports of the workflow. An input port is called PS input port if a set of parameter files can be received on that port. If a workflow has one such PS input port, it should be executed as many times as many elements are in the parameter file set of that port. If there are several PS input ports, the workflow should be executed according to the cross-product of these input sets as shown in Figure 1. From now on we say that a workflow (WF) which has got at least one PS input port is called a PS workflow (PS-WF).

In order to manage the execution of workflows according to the "black-box" execution semantics the workflow manager of the portal was extended in the following way. Let $M = N_1 x N_2 x \ldots x N_m$, where m is the number of PS input ports and N_i denotes the number of input files on the i-th PS input port. At run-time the portal PS-WF manager generates M executable workflows (e-WFs) from the original PS-WF. Every e-WF is labeled by m labels: $1 - n_1, 2 - n_2, \ldots m - n_m$, where the internal structure of $label_i$ is: $i - n_i$, where i identifies the i-th input PS port and n_i represents the ordering number of the input file taken from the i-th PS port in the identified execution instance: $0 \leq n_i < N_i$.

This labeling scheme identifies for the PS-WF manager which input file to take from the different PS input ports in the case of different execution instances (e-WFs). It also helps in identifying the output files generated at the output ports. Every output file is labeled with the label of the e-WF that generated it. Notice that output files can be local and remote. Remote output files are always permanent and once they are produced by an e-WF they can be immediately read by the user. This enables the user to study the partial results even if an e-WF is not completed. Local output files can be permanent or volatile. Permanent means that the user would like to get access to this output file only when the whole e-WF execution has been completed. These partial results are collected and stored by the portal meanwhile the e-WF runs. When the e-WF is completed these files are zipped (together with the standard output and error logs) and placed by the portal to a Grid storage resource that was defined by the user. These local permanent files should be typically small files and collecting and storing them by the portal the number of access to Grid storage resources can be significantly reduced resulting in the reduction of the overall execution time. Finally, local volatile files represent temporary partial results. As they are consumed by the connected job(s) they can be removed from the portal. This is important from the point of view of reducing the load of the portal storage resources. Developing and running PS-WF applications according to the "black-box" execution semantics require three main steps. The first step is the development of the WF application that the user would like to run as a PS-WF application. The development process of a WF application has been described in previous publications[6]as well as in the User's Manual [9] of the portal release 2.4.1 and hence we do not describe it in this paper.

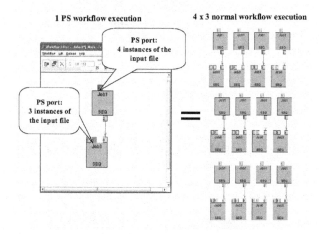

Figure 1.   Concept of "black-box" execution semantics

The second step is the transformation of the WF into a PS-WF. Finally, the third step includes the submission of the PS-WF application to the Grid and monitoring the execution of the PS-WF application. Consequently, the PS-WF user interface has two major parts:

1. Definition of PS-WF graphs
2. Monitoring the PS-WF graph execution

2.1   PS-WF graph definition

In order to turn a WF application into a PS-WF application the graphical Workflow Editor (WE) of the portal was slightly extended. The user can open the existing WF by the WE and can turn any of the existing input port into a PS input port.

In order to illustrate the process we use the Ax_EQUAL_B workflow application depicted in Figure 2. The figure shows a simple example workflow that is used for solving the $Ax = B$ equation where A is a matrix, B and X are vectors. The application consists of 5 jobs (all of them having sequential executable code). The first job called as "Separator" accepts the A and B matrices as input parameters on its input port, separates them and then copies A to jobs "Invert_A" and "A_mul_X", and copies B to "Multip_B" and "Subtr-B". The job "Invert_A" creates the invert matrix of A that is multiplied by B in job "Multip_B". The output of "Multip_B" is the searched X vector. The next two jobs are used to check the quality of the result. If we want to execute this workflow as a PS application the task is to modify this WF in order to solve the equation for a set of A and B parameters. Figure 3 shows how to turn the input port of

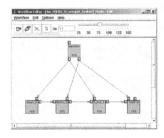

Figure 2. Workflow for Computing the $Ax = B$ equation

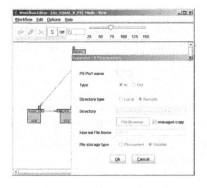

Figure 3. Definition of a PS input port

the Separator job into a PS port. Notice the difference between the input port and PS input port definition. In case of a normal input port a file is associated with the port. This file can be either local (originating from the user's machine and part of the input sandbox) or remote (placed in a storage resource of the Grid). In case of a PS port (Figure 3) a directory is associated with the port. This directory always should be placed in a storage resource of the Grid. The user should place the series of input files into this directory that must not contain any other file. After defining the PS input ports the user should identify the Grid and its storage resource where the local permanent files should be stored at the end of each e-WF execution. As a summary we can say that turning an existing WF into a PS-WF is an extremely easy task. Simply turn some of the input ports to PS input ports and define the target Grid storage resource for the local permanent files. This was exactly our aim: to simplify for the user the process of utilizing existing workflows and run them as parameter studies.

2.2   Monitoring the PS-WF graph execution

Even monitoring a single job is important for the user not mentioning when he runs thousands of jobs as part of a PS-WF execution. The challenge here is how to visualize the execution status of thousands of e-WFs and jobs in an easily understandable and manageable way. The ordinary WFs of a user are listed by the portal under the Workflow Manager window. Here the user can submit the WF, attach the WF to the Workflow Editor to see the graphical view of the WF, and delete the WF. Moreover, the "Details" button enables the user to see the details of the WF, i.e., to see the component jobs and their assignment to Grid resources. The PS-WFs are listed in the Workflow Manager window in the same way as the WFs. The only difference is that the PS-WFs have a "PS Details" button to show their internal details.

Once the user submits the PS-WF, the portal workflow manager (WM) creates all the e-WFs that are defined by the cross-product of the PS input ports' file sets. Then WM submits simultaneously as many e-WFs as many are permitted by the portal administrator. After the PS-WF submission the user can see the statistics of the e-WFs: how many were initiated, submitted, finished and how many went on Rescue or Error. Figure 4 shows the situation where the "Ax_EQUAL_B_PS" PS-WF was submitted with 6 input parameter sets. As a result 6 e-WFs were generated by the portal. 2 of them already finished, 3 submitted and one still in init state, i.e. waiting for submission. The figure also shows that any submitted e-WF can be viewed in detail by using the "Details" button. Clicking there the detailed view of the e-WF shows the component jobs of the e-WF, their Grid resource assignment and their status. Notice that any e-WF can be aborted at any time. It kills the selected e-WF but the other e-WFs can continue their activity. Figure 5 also reveals that those e-WFs that are finished cannot be viewed in the PS Workflow Details window. Their results (including every stdout and stderr files) are already stored in the defined Grid storage resource so the user can check those files there.

3.   Generators and Collectors

As seen in Section 2 turning an existing WF into a PS-WF is extremely easy from the user's point of view. However, generating the input parameter files and processing the result files still would be a tedious and time consuming job for the user if the portal was not able to support even these activities. Recognizing the importance of these activities in managing PS-WF applications, we introduced two new job types in the PS-WF concept of the portal.

Generator (denoted as GEN in the PS-WF): Its task is to generate the necessary input parameter files and place them in the selected storage elements in the same form as the PS-WF concept requires it. The executable code of a Generator should be written by the user and it will be executed as the executable of an

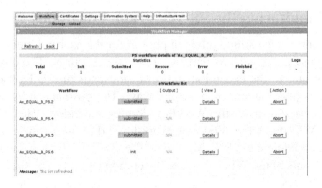

Figure 4. Detailed monitoring view of a PS-WF's execution

ordinary job at any grid site. The only difference is that the output port of the Generator should be defined and handled as a PS output port. The PS output port of a Generator should be always connected to the PS input port of a PS-WF job. The Generator job has a special version called as Automatic Generator (denoted as A-GEN in the PS-WF). The executable code of A_GEN is provided by the portal and runs on the portal server. The user must give only those parameters based on which A-GEN can generate the input parameter files. For example, A_GEN can generate integer input parameters in the range from a certain lower limit to a certain upper limit and the task of the user is only to give the value of the lower limit, upper limit and the increment. Details of the A-GEN support can be found in the portal User's Manual.

Collector (denoted as COLL in the PS-WF): Its task is to collect and process the output files created at PS execution time at any output port of the PS-WF provided that this output port generates remote output files (i.e. files that are stored in grid storage elements). The executable code of a Collector should be written by the user and it will be executed as the executable of an ordinary job at any grid site. The only difference is that the input port of the Collector should be defined and handled as a special input port. Figure 5 shows how the Generator and Collector jobs can be connected to a PS-WF. Notice that several Generators and Collectors can be connected to the same PS-WF. We call the new workflow as the Extended PS-WF (E-PS-WF) that consists of three main parts:

1. Generator part: containing the Generator jobs
2. PS-WF part: containing the original PS-WF
3. Collector part: containing the Collector jobs

The execution of the three parts is separated in time. First, the Generator part is executed. In this first phase each Generator job is executed once and they can be executed in parallel. When all Generator jobs are successfully finished,

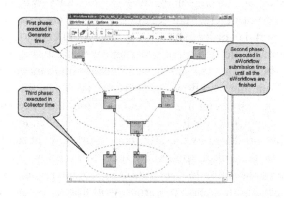

Figure 5.   Structure of an E-PS-WF

the portal starts the second phase in which the e-workflows generated from the PS-WF are executed (again in parallel as described in Section 2). When all the e-workflows are either finished or aborted the portal starts the third phase of E-PS-WF execution. In the third phase all Collector jobs are executed simultaneously. All these phases are monitored and visualized for the user in a similar way as shown in a Figure 4.

4.   Conclusions

The workflow concept of P-GRADE portal was very successful and popular among Grid users because its simplicity and expressiveness. Developing and monitoring Grid applications based on the workflow concept of the portal is extremely easy. Due to these advantages it was asked to set up for many different Grids (OGF GIN VO, EGRID, SwissGrid, Turkish Grid, BalticGrid, BioInfoGrid, CroGrid, Bulgarian Grid, Macedon Grid, etc.) meanwhile it runs as official portal of several Grids (SEE-GRID, HunGrid, VOCE) and serves other Grids as volunteer service (UK NGS, GILDA, etc.). The feedback from the users made it clear that they want a parameter study support at the workflow level but in a way that keeps the simplicity and expressiveness of the original workflow concept. Based on their request we have extended the portal with the workflow-level parameter study support. The new version of the portal has been prototyped and was publicly demonstrated at the EGEE conference in September 2006. The new version of the portal (version 2.5) that gives service quality full support for the workflow-level parameter study was released in February 2007 and now serves the following Grids: SEE-GRID, HunGrid, VOCE, OSG, GILDA.

As seen in Section 2 turning an existing WF into a PS-WF is extremely easy from the user's point of view but required a significant extension of the WF manager of the portal in order to handle the large number of jobs and workflows in parallel. Furthermore, the monitoring and visualization capabilities of the portal have also been extended and they enable the simultaneous surveillance of large number of running workflows and jobs. In order to facilitate the creation of the necessary input parameter file sets Generator jobs have been introduced into the portal. The new Collector jobs support the easy collection and processing of the output files produced by the different e-workflows at run time.

The black-box algorithm applied by the PS workflow manager gives an optimal solution concerning the utilization of storage resources but generates redundant job execution in case of certain workflows. We pursue research in order to avoid such redundant job execution. The current execution method of PS-WFs enables the static distribution of nodes between different Grids and different Grid resources if brokers are not available in the connected Grids. If brokers are available Grid resources can be assigned dynamically but the Grid assignment is still static. To provide a fully dynamic allocation of Grids and Grid resources a meta-broker should be developed and connected to the portal and to the Grids. The development of such a broker is subject of further research in the framework of the EU CoreGrid project[10].

References

[1] Casanova, H., Obertelli, G., Berman, F. and Wolski, R., The AppLeS Parameter Sweep Template: User-Level Middleware for the Grid, Proceedings of the Super Computing (SC 2002) Conference, Dallas / USA, 2002.

[2] Abramson, D., Giddy, J., and Kotler, L., High Performance Parametric Modeling with Nimrod/G: Killer Application for the Global Grid?, IPDPS'2000, Mexico, IEEE CS Press, USA, 2000.

[3] Yarrow, M., McCann, K. M., Tejnil, E., and deVivo, A., Production-Level Distributed Parametric Study Capabilities for the Grid, Grid Computing - GRID 2001 Workshop Proceedings, Denver, CO, November 2001.

[4] McCann, K. M., Yarrow, M., deVivo, A. and Mehrotra P., ScyFlow: An Environment for the Visual Specification and Execution of Scientific Workflows, GGF10 Workshop on Workflow in Grid Systems, Berlin, 2004.

[5] N. Currle-Linde, F. Boes, P. Lindner, J. Pleiss and M.M. Resch, A Management System for Complex Parameter Studies and Experiments in Grid Computing, in: Proc. of the 16th IASTED Intl. Conf. on PDCS (ed.: T. Gonzales), Acta Press, 2004.

[6] P. Kacsuk and G. Sipos, Multi-Grid, Multi-User Workflows in the P-GRADE Grid Portal, Journal of Grid Computing, Vol. 3, No. 3-4, pp. 221-238, 2005.

[7] P. Kacsuk, T. Kiss and G. Sipos, Solving the Grid Interoperability Problem by P-GRADE Portal at Workflow Level, Proc. of the Grid-Enabling Legacy Applications and Supporting End User Workshop, in conjunction with HPDC'06, Paris, pp. 3-7, 2005.

[8] T. Delaitre, et al., GEMLCA: Running Legacy Code Applications as Grid Services, Journal of Grid Computing, Vol. 3, No. 1-2, pp. 75-90, 2005

[9] http://www.lpds.sztaki.hu/pgportal/v23/manual/users_manual/
UsersManualReleaseV2.html

[10] A. Kertesz and P. Kacsuk, Grid Meta-Broker Architecture: Towards an Interoperable Grid
Resource Brokering Service, CoreGRID Workshop on Grid Middleware in Conjunction
with EuroPar'06, Dresden, 2006.

APPLYING PATTERNS FOR PORTING COMPLEX WORKFLOWS ONTO THE GRID*

Alex Villazón, Malik Junaid, Mumtaz Siddiqui, and Thomas Fahringer
Institute of Computer Science, University of Innsbruck
Technikerstraße 21A/2, A-6020 Innsbruck, Austria
{avt|malik|mumtaz|tf}dps.uibk.ac.at

Abstract   The Grid is becoming a mature infrastructure for running complex scientific applications, not limited to one single domain. Recently, an increasing interest to port applications to the Grid (legacy or not) has emerged in different scientific communities, and several higher level portals and tools have been developed. Unfortunately, very little attention has been given to the manner in which an application should be re-designed or modified to be executed on the Grid. Based on our experience, we propose a set of patterns for porting applications onto the grid, which collect typical problems or design decisions to be done during the "gridification" of applications. We present some results obtained by the application of these patterns to real-word applications that were ported onto the Grid.

Keywords: Grid, Workflow, Pattern, Attraction Pattern, Pipe-line pattern, gLite, Ganga, Wien2k, Askalon, Pattern-oriented, Activity, Porting, Gridification, Pull model, Push model, Sandbox, Storage Element

*This work is partially funded by the EU through the FP6-031688 EGEE II and FP6-004265 CoreGRID projects.

1. Introduction

The Grid infrastructure is evolving rapidly and becoming mature. Several Grid middlewares such as Globus [8], gLite [6], and Unicore [7] have been deployed at a very large scale worldwide. In addition, increasing number of scientific communities have shown their interest to use the Grid for their applications. To help this porting, tools and higher level Grid portals and environments of great help are proposed such as P-grade [12] and the ASKALON [5]. But there is a lack of guidelines to help a developer to design the application for porting it onto the Grid. In addition, Grid environments have their own features which imposes deep modification on the original application, so that it can be successfully executed. This effort is repeatedly needed for porting the same application to another infrastructure.

As pattern-oriented software [3] are based on object-oriented paradigm, scientific application programmer cannot easily apply them directly to their code, which is mostly based on conventional legacy procedural approach. Some other design patterns for parallel programming have been proposed [10], but they mostly concern the implementation of application code and ignore complex data dependencies, as is the case when running applications on the Grid.

We propose to apply patterns at another level, i.e. not to modify the application code itself, but to apply them during the adaptation of the application to be run on the Grid. In this context, we can identify a new kind of (Grid) application developers, who has the responsibility of redesigning the application for the Grid. This includes, structural analysis of the original application (often represented as a workflow), identification of components suitable for Grid based execution, selection of code distribution schema to handle control and data dependencies, and the implementation of code for the Grid (including scripts to wrap legacy code and to handle data management). This new kind of developer is not an expert on the application to be ported, but has strong Grid skills, and therefore can apply some patterns for the gridification.

In this paper we propose patterns to port and execute workflow applications onto the Grid. We show how these patterns are applied to real world applications ported on Grid environments based on Globus and gLite middlewares. We present experiment results to demonstrate and compare various approaches.

The rest of the paper is organized as follows: Section 2 discusses about execution models followed by the Section 3 which describes data management models followed by the Section 4 that describes execution patterns for porting workflows onto the Grid. In Section 5 we discuss our findings. Related work is described in Section 6. Finally we conclude the paper in Section 7.

2.   Execution models

Since there are several possible ways of executing applications on the Grid, an important step is to identify the execution model being used for the porting. Even though the basic form of Grid activity is a job submission, the execution model can vary, depending on how this activity is extended.

Notice that we differentiate between an *application activity* which is the executable of the original application to be ported, and a *Grid activity*, which is the activity that is executed on the Grid. A Grid activity can be mapped one-to-one to an application activity, but in general it is a completely new activity, which can have additional code to wrap the application activity and perform other tasks, e.g. environment setting, data management, and execution control.

In general, the execution is controlled by a process that triggers the jobs and coordinates the execution of the different activities. This *execution enactor* often works together with a scheduler process which finds the adequate Grid resources. In this model, the execution of several jobs in parallel is triggered and controlled by the enactor, which is as a direct application of the master/slave or star pattern.

The star pattern can be extended, so that a single Grid activity can also control the execution of several other parallel executables. This model aims at delegating part of the control of the execution. Such a model can be seen as a distributed enactor. This model can be applied only if there is no data dependency between the sub activities controlled by the sub enactor.

Following the notion of delegation, rather than submitting a job containing the actual executable, an "execution agent" could be submitted. The execution agent will be somehow a mini execution enactor, but only to use local resources, in contrast of the delegated star that submits jobs on other Grid sites. The actual jobs descriptions are put on a intermediate repository. The execution agents pull the jobs for the actual execution. This allows execution optimization, because one job is not bound to the execution of a single activity. This model however is not well suited for applications with activities having high execution time and complex data dependencies, because the execution agent does not have a global vision of the structure of the application.

Figure 1 shows the three different execution models related to the central star pattern, delegated star pattern, and delegated agent execution.

3.   Data management models

There are several data management models possible, depending on the size of the files, locality of the data, and also related to the execution models. If we consider that an activity that runs on the Grid is co-located with the execution enactor, there are two ways to move the data to the node where the activity is executed. This depends on the size of the data: If the data is small (typically

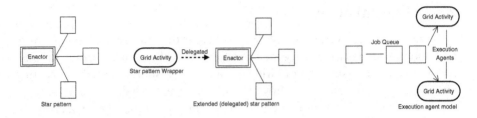

Figure 1.   Different execution models on the Grid.

few MBytes), the data can be transferred together with the Grid activity using staging mechanism available in most of the Grid middleware (e.g. in Globus through the GASS service or the *sandbox* mechanism used in gLite).

The second case addresses much bigger data (hundreds of MBytes or GBytes) and that is in the same location of the execution enactor or close to the user. In this case, it is necessary to perform a data transfer explicitly to the Grid node, where the activity will be executed. Here we can distinguish *push* or *pull* model.

The **pull model** is applied by performing the data transfer before the job execution. This implies prior knowledge of the execution site. Such a model is well adapted to Grid systems, where the Grid application developer can have control on the scheduling and resource brokerage (i.e. the developer can select where to run the application). With this model, the Grid activity related to the execution of the task, and the data transfers are logically decoupled. The Grid activity only knows that the data will be available beforehand.

The **push model** is applied by integrating the file transfer directly in the Grid activity. The data is required to be available on a location from where the Grid activity can access it. Therefore, an additional intermediate data transfer is necessary (on the client side) to transfer the required data from its current location, to a given data storage location. The Grid activity then pulls the data directly to the node before the execution starts. This model couples the file transfer and the activity. Due to the intermediate data transfer (which follows push model), this approach requires to coordinate the execution of the data transfers and the job submission, so that when the job is executed, the data is available. In this case, the final data location needs to be known before job submission. For retrieval of output data similar approaches as were used for input data can be applied. Figure 2 shows the three mentioned data transfer models.

4.   Applying patterns for porting application

Let's consider a very simple application based on a simple sequence of activities, where the control-flow is equal to data-flow. The most natural design

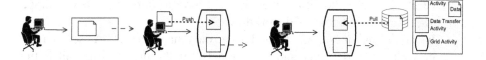

Figure 2.   Different data management models on the Grid.

patterns to apply will be the *pipe-line* pattern, as defined in the context of patterns for parallel programming [10]. However, job execution on the Grid, has a new parameter to be considered: the *Grid overhead* which comprises different elements such as job submission, queuing time, security, file staging, data transfer, among others (see [11] for a detailed discussion on Grid workflow overhead). Thus, applying the pipe-line pattern could lead to performance loss (i.e. the application run on the Grid, could be slower than the application run on a single computer sequentially), if we ignore this new parameter.

In addition, if we apply the pattern by making a one-to-one mapping between an *application activity*, and a *Grid activity*, without considering application related information, it may happen that the execution of the application activity takes only some seconds. In such a case, submitting a job on the Grid to execute it, will be a clear bottleneck.

There are two reasons to this common error made during the porting. The first one, is that often the Grid application developer asks for a description of the original application to the developer or scientist. The resulting description (often made using textual or ad-hoc graphical representation) only shows the main application components and data dependencies, without including any information about the approximate execution time of the different executables described in the workflow. The second one, is that the Grid application developer creates a Grid workflow by mapping each application executable to a Grid job. To overcome this problem, we propose the following basic pattern that we call the *attraction pattern*.

4.1   The Attraction pattern

Let's once again consider our simple sequential workflow, as described by the application developer. This time we ask him to include performance information (i.e. approximate execution time of the executable depending on the input values). Performance related information, is something known by the scientist based on his experience, and that the Grid developer must consider it in order to adapt the application to the Grid.

The attraction pattern follows the idea of planet attraction, i.e. bigger planets attract smaller ones. Here we consider the work (i.e. the approximated execution time/transactions) to represent the diameter of a planet (i.e. the activity). Thus, new Grid activities will be the combination of several application activities. For this, the Grid developer will have to implement new wrapper scripts, resulting in a reshaped workflow.

One additional question is related to the data management. As seen earlier, we have different data management models. If the data to transmit is big, we consider the data management activities as new planets which have to be merged to form new Grid activities (using push or pull approach). In case of small amount of data, we consider them as satellites, i.e. data management activities "follow" the Grid activity. This is the case represented by the file staging mechanism.

Lets now see an example of the application of the attraction pattern, when we have the information about execution time and file transfer.

Figure 3(a) shows the original workflow given by the application developer. Here we consider that the information about the execution time and size of data produced by the activities represent two different applications, If no pattern is applied, each activity in the workflow is simply mapped to a Grid activity, which will introduce performance loss. In this particular example, several of the application activities may only run for seconds and others for minutes or hours.

By applying the attraction pattern, we can see that the new Grid activities differ depending on the additional information about data and performance and the application of the different execution and data management models.

Figure 3(b) (left) shows how the Grid activities are designed using the additional information (*Case 1*). In such a case, activity *B* is attracted by activity *A*, resulting in a new Grid activity *G1-1*. Because of the size of the input data for activity *A*, it is necessary to apply the pull model, where the data needs to be stored on an external storage. The activity *A* inside *G1-1* should perform the pull of the data for execution. Since *A* and *B* run on the same location, there is no need to transfer any data. Notice also that the output data form activity *A* (file *Y*) is of small size, and therefore can be transferred to the new Grid activity *G1-2* (which wraps activity *C*), directly through staging mechanism.

Figure 3(b) (right) shows the application of the attraction pattern, this time using the additional information (*Case 2*). Now we can see that Grid activity *G2-2* is the merging of activities *B* and *C*. The input file to Grid activity *G2-2* is done using staging mechanism only.

We can see that even if the structure of the application remains very similar, the actual implementation of the Grid activities is optimized for the execution of the application based on the execution time and data information. This will have an impact on the execution performance on the Grid, compared to the naive approach based on one-to-one mapping of activities to Grid activities, as will be shown in the next section.

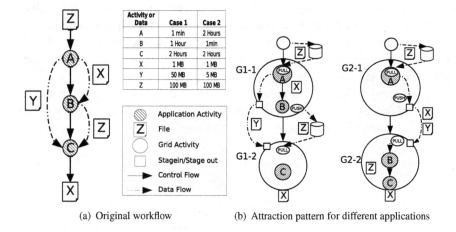

(a) Original workflow   (b) Attraction pattern for different applications

Figure 3.

5. Experiments

Our experiments are based on porting a real application called Wien2k [2], which has a complex workflow including loops, computing intensive activities as well as computing non-intensive and complex data dependencies.

The idea was to start a complete new porting of the application to gLite [6] middleware and to compare the effort to the prior porting of the same application to the Austrian Grid using ASKALON system [5]. This porting was to be done only based on the description provided by the application developer. The team that worked on ASKALON didn't communicate any details or know-how about the first porting to the other one. After the successful porting, we figured out that the same design decisions, mistakes and re-design were done by both teams, and application of the patterns presented here would have been of great help.

Figure 4(a) shows the original application description provided by the Wien2k developers. After analysis, a new workflow description was made which is more suitable for execution on the Grid (see 4(b)). This workflow was then used to implement the Grid activities. Figure 4(c) shows the one-to-one mapping of the workflow to Grid activities (naive workflow) and also the resulting workflow when applying the attraction pattern.

We conducted experiments using a simulated Grid environment and a real gLite based Grid testbed. In the first case, the activities were executed on independent locations in the cluster and data was transferred to a central repository before and after an activity executes.

We implemented the Grid application using Ganga [1], which is a programming environment for Grids based on python. The Grid activities were done using shell scripts and using commands to perform data management such as sandbox or using an external storage element. Figure 5(a) shows a comparison of the execution on the local system, the local backend, and on a real Grid testbed. One can notice the important Grid overhead, even if all the nodes used for the experiments were reserved for the execution.

When applying the naive approach, we measured the data management overhead based on staging, i.e. we measured the overhead introduced by the sandbox mechanism applied independently of the file sizes.

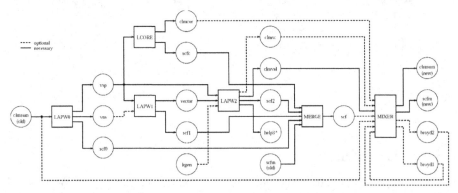

(a) Original application workflow provided by application developers

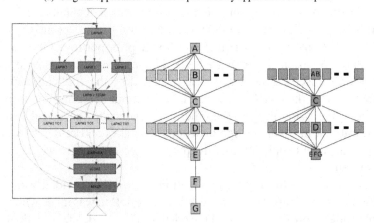

(b) Translated Workflow for Grid

(c) Naive Grid workflow vs Attraction Pattern based Workflow

Figure 4.

Finally, we applied the attraction pattern to the workflow using the information about the approximated execution time of the activities and size of the data. This information was provided by the Wien2k developers. We have run this new workflow on the gLite testbed under the same conditions as for the naive workflow. The execution time of the full workflow execution of both approaches is shown in Figure 5(b). In this figure, we only report the execution time of the full workflow without the Grid overhead for the sake of simplicity. We can see up to 50% of performance gain, which is due to the optimization made to the structure of the workflow when applying the pattern, and also to the selection of the most adapted data transfer model. This experiment depicts that applying such a pattern for application porting to the Grid can improve performance by design. The Grid activities that we implemented can be later on ported to more sophisticated Grid environments such as ASKALON or P-Grade. These systems will then be able to optimize even more the execution of the workflow by applying techniques as described in [4], making our approach a good complement to improve the performance of applications on the Grid.

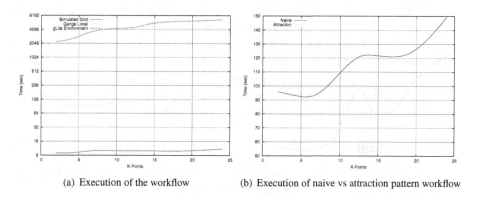

(a) Execution of the workflow   (b) Execution of naive vs attraction pattern workflow

Figure 5. Peformance comparison

6. Related work

Some efforts have been done to identify workflow patterns that addresses data and computational aspects of a workflow. An initiative to provide a conceptual basis of workflow patterns is described in [15, 14, 16]. A classification framework for exception handling in process-aware information systems based on patterns is described in [13]. A collection of patterns for parallel programming are described in [10]. All these patterns can be helpful for implementing Grid application, but focus more in the implementation or redesigning of applications to take into account parallelism or distribution. In our approach, we consider a different type of developer, which is the Grid application developer. And the pattern that we propose, takes into account execution and data management models that are specific to Grid computing.

The work in [9] proposes three design patterns to implement Grid Services: Grid Abstract Factory, Template and Interface patterns. This work focus on implementation of Grid services in the context of a Service Oriented Architecture, and not on the porting of existing applications on the Grid.

In [4] the workflow is partitioned to optimize the execution. The optimization is done at the execution enactor level and assumes a fixed structure of the workflow. In addition, it assumes the scheduling of the activities in order to make the partition. In our case, we make the workflow partition based on the knowledge of the activity execution time of the application user or developer and already obtain performance gain by design. As mentioned before, both approaches are not opposite, but complementary.

7. Conclusion

We explored the use of patterns to simplify porting of applications on the Grid. We showed that based on experience and considering execution and data management models, it was possible to improve the performance of a Grid application. We proposed the attraction pattern, which takes into account not only the structure of the application to be ported, but also approximate execution time and data size. This is a valuable information that only the application developer or scientist can give to the Grid application developer. We show how the application of the pattern can improve the execution of a real world application on the Grid. This is a first step to a set of patterns that could be very useful for porting more complex applications on the Grid.

Acknowledgment

We would like to thank Johannes Schweifer, Reinhard Bischof, Wolfgang Jais, and Martin Rabanser for their valuable help.

References

[1] Ganga. http://cern.ch/ganga.

[2] P. Blaha, K. Schwarz, G. Madsen, D. Kvasnicka, and J. Luitz. *WIEN2k: An Augmented Plane Wave plus Local Orbitals Program for Calculating Crystal Properties*. Institute of Physical and Theoretical Chemistry, Vienna University of Technology, Vienna. ISBN 3-9501031-1-2, 2001.

[3] Frank Buschmann, Kevlin Henney, and Douglas C. Schmidt. *Pattern-Oriented Software Architecture: On Patterns and Pattern Languages*. Wiley and Sons, 2007.

[4] Rubing Duan, Radu Prodan, and Thomas Fahringer. Run-time optimization for Grid workflow applications. In *International Conference on Grid Computing*. IEEE Computer Society Press, 2006.

[5] Thomas. Fahringer. ASKALON - A Programming Environment and Tool Set for Cluster and Grid Computing. http://dps.uibk.ac.at/askalon, Institute for Computer Science, University of Innsbruck.

[6] Enabling Grid for E-science (EGEE). Lightweight middleware for grid computing. http://cern.ch/glite.

[7] Unicore Forum. Unicore. http://www.unicore.org/.

[8] Globus. The globus alliance. http://www.globus.org/toolkit.

[9] E. Katsiri, J. Cohen, J. Darlington, and S. Drossopoulou. Design patterns for grid services. In *2nd IC SCCE*, Athens, Greece, 2006. x.

[10] Berna L. Massingill, Timothy G. Mattson, and Beverly A. Sanders. Reengineering for parallelism: An entry point for plpp (pattern language for parallel programming) for legacy applications. In *Twelfth Pattern Languages of Programs Workshop (PLoP 2005)*. bnet, 2005.

[11] Francesco Nerieri, Radu Prodan, Thomas Fahringer, and Hong Linh Truong. Overhead analysis of Grid workflow applications. In *International Conference on Grid Computing*. IEEE Computer Society Press, 2006.

[12] P-Grade. Parallel grid runtime and application developement environment. http://www.lpds.sztaki.hu/pgrade/.

[13] N. Russell, W.M.P. van der Aalst, and A.H.M. ter Hofstede. Exception handling patterns in process-aware information systems. Technical report, 2006.

[14] Site. Workflow data patterns. http://www.bpm.fit.qut.edu.au/projects/babel/dp/.

[15] Site. Workflow patterns. http://www.workflowpatterns.com.

[16] Site. Workflow resource patterns. http://www.bpm.fit.qut.edu.au/projects/babel/rp/.

VIII

DATA MANAGEMENT

REAL TIME CLASSIFICATION MECHANISM FOR THE CAUSES OF DATA LOSS AND ITS INTEGRATION INTO A HIGH PERFORMANCE DATA TRANSFER SYSTEM FOR GRID COMPUTING

Phillip M. Dickens
Department of Computer Science
University of Maine
Orono, Maine 04469
dickens@umcs.maine.edu

Abstract   The importance of high-performance communication to the success of Grid applications makes it critical to develop communication protocols that can take full advantage of the underlying bandwidth when system conditions permit, can back-off in response to observed (or predicted) contention within the network, and can accurately distinguish between these two situations. Achieving this goal requires the development of classification mechanisms that are both accurate and efficient enough to execute in real time. In this paper, we discuss one such classifier that is based on the analysis of the patterns of packet loss and the application of Bayesian statistics. We describe two different analysis techniques that we apply to such patterns, one based on complexity theory and one based on a simple measure of the distance between successive packet losses. In addition, we discuss the integration of the classification mechanism into the control structures of an existing high-performance data transfer system for computational Grids. We present empirical results showing that the classifier is extremely accurate, efficient enough to execute in real time, and that utilizing the information it provides can have a tremendous impact on the performance of a large-scale data transfer.

Keywords: Communication protocols, high-performance networks, Classification Mechanisms, Grid Computing

1. Introduction

Computational Grids create powerful distributed computing systems by connecting geographically distributed computational/storage facilities via high-performance networks. Such systems can aggregate tremendous computational power on a single large-scale problem, enabling scientific discovery in areas that were heretofore impossible to explore. Critical to the success of such large-scale Grid applications is a high-performance networking infrastructure that can efficiently move extreme-scale data sets between nodes on the Grid. However, even though advances in networking technologies have significantly increased the bandwidth available to Grid applications, actually obtaining a large percentage of such bandwidth has turned out to be a difficult issue.

One problem is that TCP, the transport protocol of choice for most wide-area data transfers, was not designed for and does not perform well in the high-bandwidth, high-delay networks typical of computational Grids. This has led to significant research activity aimed at modifying TCP itself to make it compatible with this new network environment (e.g., Highspeed TCP [15]), as well as systems that monitor the end-to-end network to diagnose and fix performance problems (e.g., [2, 22]. An alternative strategy has been the development of application-level protocols that can largely circumvent the performance issues of TCP. This includes, for example, UDP- based protocols (e.g., FOBS [10], UDT [16]), and approaches that spawn multiple TCP streams for a single data flow (e.g., GridFTP [4]).

UDP-based protocols can be attractive for two reasons: First, some applications require a smooth transfer rate that can be difficult to obtain with TCP. Second, such protocols are well-suited for high-bandwidth, high-delay network environment and are able to obtain a significant percentage of the underlying bandwidth. However, because UDP-based protocols execute at the application level, the protocol developer must provide a mechanism to detect and respond fairly to competing traffic flows. Also, application-level protocols can lose data packets for any number of reasons unrelated to network congestion. This second issue can result in very poor performance if the control mechanisms interpret such loss as growing network contention and, in response, trigger very aggressive congestion control actions.

This research is developing a classification mechanism that can be Used by UDP-based protocols to distinguish between data loss caused by network contention from loss caused by factors outside of the network domain. In particular, we focus on distinguishing between network contention and contention for CPU resources. This distinction is important because contention for CPU cycles can be a major contributor to packet loss in UDP-based protocols. This happens, for example, when the receiver's socket-buffer becomes full, additional data bound for the receiver arrives at the host, and the receiver is switched out and thus unavailable to pull such packets off of the network. The receiver could be switched out for any number of reasons including preemption by a higher priority system process, interrupt processing, paging activity, and multi-tasking. This last point is particularly important in a Grid environment where resource availability, including the CPU cycles allocated to a particular application, can fluctuate significantly during the execution of a long-running application.

To illustrate the importance of this issue, consider a data transfer with a sending rate of one gigabit per second and a packet size of 1024 bytes. Given these parameters, a packet will arrive at the receiving host around every 7.9 micro-seconds, which is approximately the amount of time required to perform a context switch on the TeraGrid systems [3] used in this research (as measured by Lmbench [21]). Thus the receiver does not need to be switched-out long before packets can begin to get dropped. We have observed, for example, tens to hundreds of packets being dropped when the operating system creates three to four new processes.

This paper discusses the development of a classification mechanism for the causes of data loss that is both very accurate and highly efficient. Also, we show how it is integrated into the control structures of an existing UDP-based data transfer system, and provide experimental results showing that the use of the classifier can result in significant performance gains. The classification mechanism is based on the analysis of what we term packet-loss signatures, which show the distribution (or pattern) of those packets that successfully traversed the end-to-end transmission path and those that did not. These signatures are essentially large selective-acknowledgment packets that are collected by the receiver and delivered to the sender upon request. We chose the name "packet-loss signatures" based on previous studies showing that different causes of data loss have different "signatures" [12]. In this paper, we briefly describe how the signatures are analyzed and used by the classifier, and direct the interested reader to this same paper for a detailed discussion of the approach.

The major contribution of this paper is showing how a classification system can be developed, integrated into the control mechanisms of a data transfer system, and used to increase performance. This paper should be of interest to a large segment of the Grid community given the interest in and importance of exploring new approaches by which data transfers can be made more intelligent and efficient.

The rest of the paper is organized as follows. In Section 2, we discuss related work. In Section 3, we describe FOBS, the data transfer system in which the classification mechanism is implemented. We provide an overview of the classification algorithms in Section 4. In Section 5, we discuss the experimental design and provide the experimental results in Section 6. We provide our conclusions in Section 7.

2.   Related Work

The issue of distinguishing between causes of data loss has received significant attention within the context of TCP for hybrid wired/wireless networks (e.g., [5, 8]). The idea is to distinguish between losses caused by network congestion and losses caused by errors in the wireless link, and to trigger TCP's aggressive congestion control mechanisms only in the case of congestion-induced losses. This ability to classify the root cause of data loss, and to respond accordingly, has been shown to improve the performance of TCP in this network environment [5, 20]. These classification schemes are based largely on simple statistics on observed round- trip times, observed throughput, or the inter-arrival time between ACK packets [7, 20]. Debate remains, however, as to how well techniques based on such simple statistics can classify loss [20]. Another approach being pursued is the use of Hidden Markov Models where the states are characterized by the mean and standard deviation of the distribution of round-trip times [20].

Our research has similar goals, although we are developing a finer-grained classification system to distinguish between network contention and contention for CPU resources. Another major difference is that the analysis of packet-loss signatures appears to be a more robust classifier than (for example) statistics on round-trip times, and could be substituted for such statistics within the mathematical frameworks established in these related works.

Also related are efforts such as Web100 [22] and Pathdiag [1], that provide sophisticated monitoring systems and tools with which performance issues in TCP networks can be diagnosed and fixed. The goal of these systems is to provide ordinary users, i.e., those without significant networking expertise, with high-performance networking in a completely transparent manner. A major difference between our work and these related projects is the timescale at which each operates. In particular, these projects are iterative in nature, with possible consultation with network administrators between iterations. Our classification mechanism performs on a much smaller timescale, where it very quickly computes the probability that the cause of data loss was within the network or outside of the network. However, it is unable to diagnose performance problems such as inadequate buffer sizes, under-configured network paths, or problems with the software stack as these related works can provide. Thus while the goal of providing high-performance networking are shared, the problems being addressed are quite different. In fact, such work is orthogonal to our efforts in that any improvements to the networking infrastructure such projects can provide would also benefit the performance of our data transfer system.

Research into other application-level alternatives to TCP is also related (e.g., [17]). However, projects such as this do not attempt to determine the root cause(s) of packet loss that is a major focus of this research.

3.   Data Transfer System

The test-bed for this research is FOBS[1]: a high-performance data transfer system for computational Grids [10]. FOBS is a UDP-based data transfer system that provides reliability through a selective-acknowledgment and re-transmission mechanism. It is precisely the information contained within the selective-acknowledgment packets that is collected and analyzed by the classification mechanism. FOBS can be executed as a window-based protocol where all packets within the current transmission window are put onto the network at a constant sending rate. It can also be used as a rate-based system, where a constant sending rate is used until a congestion event occurs, at which point a new sending rate is determined based on the long-term loss rate.

FOBS is multi-threaded to take advantage of nodes with multiple processors or processors with multiple cores. In such cases, the classification mechanism can execute as a separate thread that runs concurrently with the ongoing transfer. In fact, we have observed that when the data sender is executing on a dedicated node with dual-processors, there is no additional cost incurred by executing the classifier (that is, the data transfer rate is unchanged when it is executed).

3.1   Congestion Control

An important design goal for FOBS is that it competes fairly with other network flows. Toward this end, FOBS uses a modified version of the TCP Friendly Rate Control (TFRC) protocol [18] for its congestion control. TFRC is equation-based, where the sending rate is computed as a function of the steady-state loss rate. The primary difference is that FOBS replaces the TFRC response function with that derived for Highspeed TCP [15], a more aggressive version of TCP for high- performance network environments with very low loss rates. The use of this more aggressive congestion control mechanism is completely appropriate given that FOBS is designed for the well-provisioned, high-bandwidth, high-delay networks associated with computational Grids, and is not intended for the Internet1 environment.

We do not discuss the derivation of the HighSpeed TCP response function here, and direct the interested reader to[15] for a complete analysis. For our purposes, it is sufficient to note that a parameter termed Low_Window is defined, which sets the lower bound on the congestion window at which the HighSpeed TCP response function will be used. That is, if the current congestion window is greater than Low_Window, then the HighSpeed response function will be used to determine the size of the next congestion window in the event of packet loss. This response function is defined as:

---

[1] Fast Object-Based Data Transfer System

$$w = 0.12/p^{0.835} \tag{1}$$

Otherwise, the standard TCP response function will be used [2]:

$$w = 1.2/\sqrt{p} \tag{2}$$

where w is the size of the next congestion window and p is the loss rate.

3.1.1   Integration of Classifier into FOBS.   While the algorithms used by the classification mechanism are somewhat complex, the way the information is used by the controller is relatively simple. When a congestion event occurs, the classifier is queried to determine the cause of such loss. The classifier then assigns a probability to the event that the data loss was caused by contention for CPU resources (and thus one minus this probability that the cause of loss was network related). If the probability exceeds a certain threshold that the cause of data loss was CPU related (currently set at 95and the loss rate is not modified. Otherwise, the cumulative loss rate is updated appropriately, and Equation (1) or (2) is invoked to determine the new sending rate (depending upon the size of the current congestion window).

4.   Classification Mechanism

Having discussed how the results of the classification mechanism are used in FOBS, we briefly discuss how these probabilities are computed. The interested reader is directed to [12–13] for a complete discussion of the statistical analysis.

4.1   Classification Metrics

The classification mechanism is based on the application of Bayesian statistics, which centers on how the value of certain metrics can be used to identify a cause of packet loss. Assume there are two causes of data loss: network contention and CPU contention. The idea is to find a metric that has very different statistical properties under the two causes of data loss, the greater the difference the more accurate the classification.

Our research has identified two excellent metrics upon which the classification mechanism is based, both of which are derived from the packet-loss signatures. The first metric is the complexity of the packet-loss signatures that is derived using techniques from symbolic dynamics. In symbolic dynamics [19], the packet-loss signature is viewed as a sequence of symbols drawn from a finite discrete set, which in our case is two symbols: 1 and 0. One diagnostic that quantifies the amount of structure in the sequence is complexity. There are

---

[2] As noted by the authors, this equation assumes a loss rate that is less than where the effects of TCP retransmit timeouts can be largely ignored.

numerous ways to quantify complexity. In this discussion, we have chosen the approach of d'Alessandro and Politi [9] which has been applied with success to quantify the complexity and predictability of time series of hourly precipitation data [14]. The approach of d'Alessandro and Politi is to view the stream of 1s and 0s as a language and focus on subsequences (or words) of length n in the limit of increasing values of n (i.e., increasing word length). First-order complexity, denoted by C^1, is a measure of the richness of the language's vocabulary and represents the asymptotic growth rate of the number of admissible words of fixed length n occurring within the string as n becomes large. The number of admissible words of length n, denoted by $Na(n)$, is simply a count of the number of distinct words of length n found in the given sequence. The first-order complexity (C^1) is defined as

$$C^1 = \lim_{n \to \infty} (\log 2\, Na(n))/n \qquad (3)$$

The first-order complexity metric characterizes the level of randomness or periodicity in a string of symbols. A string consisting of only one symbol will have one admissible word for each value of n, and will thus have a value of $C^1 = 0$. A purely random string will, in the limit, have a value of $C^1 = 1$. A string that is comprised of a periodic sequence, or one comprising only a few periodic sequences, will tend to have low values of C^1. We have developed simple empirical models that relate complexity measures to the different causes of data loss as a function of the loss rate, and it is these models that are used by the classification mechanism.

While the calculation of complexity measures is simple and efficient, the size of the words that can be examined in real time (without negatively affecting performance) is somewhat limited. In the experiments reported here, the maximum word size was set to $n = 17$, which was sufficient for discerning the basic structure of the signatures (i.e., either random or periodic) when the loss rate was greater than approximately 0.0004. However, for significantly lower loss rates, the dropped packets (and the corresponding 0s in the packet-loss signatures) were too far apart to be detected with a word size of 17. While increasing the word size can help, it cannot be increased enough to detect the randomness in the string at very low loss rates. Thus, complexity measures are unable to serve as a classification metric at very low loss rates.

To address this issue, we developed another metric based on the distance between two consecutive dropped packets. The idea is that the fundamental structure of the packet- loss signatures will not be significantly different at very low loss rates, and thus data loss caused by CPU contention will still be largely contiguous in the signature, and loss caused by NIC contention will still be random. To develop this metric, we define "success" as two consecutive packet drops (i.e., two consecutive 0s in the signature). We then performed a large number of experiments to learn the proportion of successes for each cause of data loss at very low loss rates. These proportions were then used as parameters to a beta distribution (that provides the probability of a given proportion of successes), in hopes that the statistical properties of the distribution would be very different under different causes of packet loss. The beta distribution takes two parameters, a and b, and has the following density function, where p is the proportion of successes.

$$p^{a-1}(1-p)^{b-1} \qquad (4)$$

Figure 1 shows the considerable difference in the statistical properties of the complexity metric under both causes of data loss. Figure 1 further shows the empirical data models derived in association with complexity measures. This figure demonstrates quite clearly the power of this metric in distinguishing between causes of data loss. Due to space constraints, we do not show the differences of the statistical properties for the beta distribution.

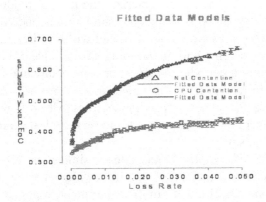

Figure 1. This figure shows the mean complexity measures at each data bin, and 95% confidence intervals around the mean, for each cause of data loss. Also, it shows how the data lay along the fitted data model.

5. Experimental Design

All experiments were conducted on the TeraGrid [3]: a high-performance computational Grid that connects various supercomputing facilities via networks operating at 40 gigabits per second. The two facilities used in these experiments were the San Diego Supercomputing Center (SDSC), and the National Center for Supercomputing Applications (NCSA, located at the University of Illinois, Urbana). The host platform at each facility was an IA-64 Linux cluster where each compute node consisted of dual 1.5 GHz Intel Itanium 2 processors. The operating system at both facilities was Linux 2.4.21 SMP. Each compute node had a gigabit Ethernet connection to the TeraGrid network.

We were interested in whether or not the classification mechanism could improve performance in the case where data loss was caused by contention for CPU resources. To test this, we executed one set of transfers where the results of the classification system were used by the controller, and another set where they were not used (and thus all data loss was assumed to be network related). We implemented a background process on the data receiver which periodically caused data to be dropped. The number of packets lost per congestion event was based largely on operating system behavior (e.g., process scheduling), and was thus somewhat out of our control. However, the long-term loss rate in all experiments was on the order of 0.0002. We performed three long data transfers (of about 3 hours each), under each condition (i.e., results of classifier used/not used). The results of interest were the percentage of successful classifications and the throughput achieved in each instance. The classifier used the beta distribution to compute the required probabilities when the loss rate was <= 0.0004. Otherwise, the complexity measures were used.

We used the technique of direct-execution simulation [11] to determine the throughput achieved in each situation. In this approach, the behavior of the network connection, the behavior of the system in the presence of contention for CPU resources, and the packet-loss signatures generated by such contention, were all obtained by actually executing the data transfer. That is, there was an ongoing data transfer between NCSA and SDSC and a physical background process that created contention for CPU resources. The resulting packet-loss signatures were generated by such contention, and these signatures were analyzed by the classification mechanism in real time (i.e., as the transfer was progressing). Thus all of these aspects of the problem were real.

However, the results of the classification were provided to the simulator, which then determined the new (virtual) sending rate and new (virtual) loss rate by applying the congestion control mechanism described in Section (3.1). The simulator then computed the number of (virtual) seconds that had elapsed since its last invocation, and, based on this and the previous (virtual) sending rate, determined the amount of data that would have been transferred during that time. It is the throughput calculated by the simulation that is presented in the experimental results discussed in the following section.

We chose to use this approach because the physical network connection between the nodes on the TeraGrid was limited by the one gigabit link between the compute nodes and the backbone network. We wanted to study the impact of the classification mechanism with essentially the same parameters as those used to define the HighSpeed TCP response function, which assumed a 10 gigabit per second connection.

6.   Experimental Results

Total trials	Percentage of inconclusive classifications	Percentage of incorrect classifications	$P(CPU \vert CPU)$	Av. TP with Classifier	Av.TP without Classifier
265	5.6 %	0.7%	94%	8697 mps	168 mps

The results of these experiments are shown in the table above. Column 1 shows that there were 265 congestion events in all six trials combined. Column 2 shows the percentage of the congestion events for which the classification was inconclusive (returning a probability of 50classifications generally occurred at very low loss rates (i.e., less than 0.0001). Column 3 shows the percentage of incorrect diagnoses (0.7 the classifier diagnosed the loss as being network related when it was in fact CPU related. This again occurred at very loss rates. Column 4 shows the percentage of times that the classifier diagnosed the loss as being CPU related when this was in fact the cause (94 second when the results of the classifier were being utilized (column 6), and when they were not (column 7).

As can be seen, the diagnostic abilities of the classification mechanism were quite good, correctly diagnosing the cause of data loss 94unsuccessful, it returned an inconclusive rather than incorrect diagnosis in a vast majority of cases (15 out of 17). These results also demonstrate that having a real- time classification mechanism can significantly improve performance when the cause of data loss is contention for CPU resources (in fact, by orders of magnitude). These are all very encouraging results.

7.   Conclusions

In this paper, we have presented a highly accurate classification mechanism that can distinguish between data loss caused by contention for CPU resources from that caused by network contention at loss rates as low as 0.0001. We have also shown that the classifier can be quite easily integrated into the control structure of FOBS, an existing high-performance data transfer system for computational Grids. We further discussed that the classifier is efficient enough to execute in real time, incurring no reduction in the transfer rate when the data sender is executing on a dedicated dual- processor node. Otherwise, we have observed a performance penalty of approximately 12 price to pay when the cause of data loss is largely CPU related.

One question that this research does not answer is how often data will be lost due to contention for CPU resources. Given the highly dynamic nature of a Grid environment, it is reasonable to think that contention for CPU resources can become problematic during the execution of a long-running application. In such circumstances, the technology descried here could be quite useful. However, if data loss were always caused by network contention, then this technology would not be particularly helpful. Extensive monitoring of long-running Grid applications may help to shed light on this question.

References

[1] Enabling High Performance Data Transfers.
http://www.psc.edu/networking/projects/tcptune

[2] Net100: Development of Network Aware Operating Systems.
http://www.csm.ornl.gov/ dunigan/net100/

[3] The Teragrid Project. http://www.teragrid.org

[4] Allcock, W., et.al. Secure, Efficient Data Transport and Replica Management for High-Performance Data-Intensive Computing. In the Proceedings of the IEEE Mass Storage Conference, (2001).

[5] Balakrishnan, S., Padmanabhan, V., Seshan, S. and Katz, R. A Comparison of Mechanisms for Improving TCP Performance Over Wireless Links. IEEE/ACM Transactions of Networking, 5 (6). 756-769.

[6] Balakrishnan, S., Seshan, S., Amir, E. and Katz, R. Improving TCP/IP performance over wireless networks. In the Proceedings of the ACM MOBICON, (1995). November 1995.

[7] Barman, D. and Matta, I. Effectiveness of Loss Labeling in Improving TCP Performance in Wired/Wireless Networks. In the Proceedings of the ICNP 2002: The 10th IEEE International Conference on Network Protocols, (Paris, France, 2002). November 2002.

[8] Biaz, S. and Vaidya, N. Discriminating Congestion Losses From Wireless Losses using Inter-Arrival Times at the Receiver. In the Proceedings of the IEEE Symposium ASSET '99, (Richardson, TX, 1999). March 1999.

[9] D'Alessandro, G. and Politi, A. Hierarchical Approach to Complexity with Applications to Dynamical Systems. Physical Review Letters, 64 (14). 1609-1612.April 1990.

[10] Dickens, P. FOBS: A Lightweight Communication Protocol for Grid Computing. In the Proceedings of the Europar 2003, (2003).

[11] Dickens, P., Heidelberger, P. and Nicol, D. Parallelized Direct Execution Simulation of Message-Passing Parallel Programs. IEEE Transactions on Parallel and Distributed Systems, 7(10). 1090-1105.October 1996.

[12] Dickens, P., Larsen, J. and Nicol, D. Diagnostics for Causes of Packet Loss in a High Performance Data Transfer System. In the Proceedings of the 2004 IPDPS Conference: The 18th INternational Parallel and Distributed Processing Symposium, (Santa Fe, New Mexico, 2004).

[13] Dickens, P. and Peden, J. Towards a Bayesian Statistical Model for the Classification of Causes of Data Loss. In the Proceedings of the International Conference on High Performance Computing and Communications, LNCS 3726.

[14] Elsner, J. and Tsonis, A. Complexity and Predictability of Hourly Precipitation. Journal of the Atmospheric Scinces, 50(3). 400-405.

[15] Floyd, S. Modifying TCP's Congestion Control for High Speeds.
http://www.aciri.org/floyd

[16] Gu, Y., Hong, X. and Grossman, R.L. Experiences in Design and Implementation of a High Performance Transport Protocol. In the Proceedings of the SC 2004, (Pittsburgh, PA). November 6 - 12.

[17] Hacker, T., Noble, B. and Athey, B. Improving Throughput and Maintaining Fairness using Parallel TCP. In the Proceedings of the IEEE INFOCOM '04, (2004).

[18] Handley, M., Floyd, S., Padhye, J. and Widmer, J. [RFC 3448] TCP Friendly Rate Control (TFRC): Protocol Specification.

[19] Hao, B.-L. Elementary Symbolic Dynamics and Chaos in Dissipative Systems World Scientific, 1988.

[20] Liu, J., Matta, I. and Crovella, M., End-To-End Inference of Loss Nature in a Hybrid Wired/Wireless Environment. In the Proceedings of the Modeling and Optimization in Mobile, Ad Hoc, and Wireless Networks (WiOpt '03), (Sophia-Antipolis, France, 2003).

[21] LMbench. http://www.bitmover.com/lmbench/

[22] Mathis, M., Heffner, J. and Reddy, R. Web100: Extended TCP instrumentation for research, education and diagnosis. ACM Computer Communications Review, 33 (3).July 2003.

DEPENDABLE GRID SERVICES: A CASE STUDY WITH OGSA-DAI

Javier Alonso and Jordi Torres
Technical University of Catalonia
Barcelona Supercomputing Center,
Barcelona,Spain
alonso@ac.upc.edu
torres@ac.upc.edu

Luis Moura Silva and Paulo Silva
University of Coimbra
CISUC, Portugal
luis@dei.uc.pt

Abstract   Grid middleware usually makes use of several software modules that due to their complexity and development approach may have some latent bugs and leaks. These bugs can cause visible performance failures and undesired service crashes. To cope with this sort of transient failures we present a proactive software rejuvenation approach that exploits the use of virtualization middleware. To prove the effectiveness of our mechanism we decided to apply it to OGSA-DAI, a sound example of a middleware that has been widely used in several Grid-related projects. OGSA-DAI makes use of Tomcat/Axis as the SOAP container and Axis v1.2.1 suffers from memory leaks. When it is not configured properly these leaks will result in a crash of the OGSA-DAI server. In this paper, we explain the application of our rejuvenation scheme in this particular example and we show that it is easy to get a software-based approach to improve the availability of a Grid Service even when one of the underlying layers suffers from clear symptoms of software aging. Our ultimate goal is to give a contribution for the techniques and concepts that can be used to achieve dependable Grid services.

Keywords: Dependability, High-Availability, Software Rejuvenation, OGSA-DAI, Grid

1.   Introduction

Grid computing understands the usage of large scale and heterogeneous resources in geographically dispersed sites. The target applications for Grid are
usually long-running. In those systems the overall MTBF (Mean-time-between-
failures) can be even lower than the total execution of a single application. It
is thus mandatory that Grid middleware should have some effective support for
fault-tolerance and mechanisms for high-availability, otherwise Grids cannot
be used.

Most of the failures that happen in nowadays systems are just transient failures that happen from time to time and can be potentially solved by some automatic action of fault-tolerance. One scenario that is also expectable in complex
software systems, such as any Grid middleware, is the occurrence of software
aging. Aging is usually observed as a progressive degradation through time,
which can lead to system crashes or undesirable hang ups. This phenomena is
particularly troublesome in long-running applications, which can be found in
Grid environments. It has also been observed in telecommunication systems
[1], web-servers [2], enterprise clusters [3], OLTP systems [4] and spacecraft
systems [5].

The most natural procedure to combat software aging is the technique of
software rejuvenation [6]. Two basic approaches for rejuvenation have been
proposed in the literature: time-based and proactive rejuvenation. Time-based
rejuvenation techniques are widely used today in some real production systems,
such as web-servers [7]. Proactive rejuvenation techniques have been studied
in [3–4][8–9] and it is widely understood that this technique of rejuvenation
provides better results than the previous one, resulting in higher availability
and lower costs. In our previous work [17], we have presented a self-recovery
technique that makes use of virtualization. The main goal of the mechanism
is to avoid the occurrence of software aging by applying clean planned restarts
and replicated execution of application-services in different virtual machines
that will be running on top of the same physical server.

The main reasons for using virtualization middleware [10–12] in our solution
is to offer the chance for server consolidation and to support the compatibility at
the level of binary code: no re-compilation or dynamic re-linking is necessary to
port legacy application from physical machines to virtualized machines (VMs).

In this paper, we want to show how useful is our mechanism if we want
to apply it to Grid Services. To achieve this goal we present a case-study
using a very well-known grid middleware: OGSA-DAI. We present the default
performance behavior and the improvement using our self-recovery mechanism.

The rest of the paper is organized as follows: Section 2 presents an overview
about our case-study (OGSA-DAI). Section 3 presents some performance results taken in two different infrastructures. Section 4 describes our virtualized

clustering approach to obtain dependable Grid Services. Section 5 presents some new results with the application of our technique into OGSA-DAI and the measured impact. Finally, Section 6 presents the conclusions of this paper.

2. An Overview about our case-study: OGSA-DAI

One of the most popular Grid middleware packages is OGSA-DAI [13], a package that allows the remote access to data-resources (files, relational and XML databases) through a standard front-end based on Web services specification. The software includes a collection of components for querying, transforming and delivering data in different ways, and a simple toolkit for developing client applications. In a short sentence, OGSA-DAI provides a way for users to Grid-enable their data resources.

The front-end of OGSA-DAI is a set of Web-services that in the case of WSI require a SOAP container to handle the incoming requests and translate them to the internal OGSA-DAI engine. This SOAP container is Tomcat/Axis 1.2.1. The detailed description of the OGSA-DAI internal is out-of-scope of this paper. At the moment OGSA-DAI middleware is used in several important Grid projects [14], including: AstroGrid, BIoDA, Biogrid, BioSim-Grid, Bridges, caGrid, COBrA-CT, Data Mining Grid, D-Grid, eDiaMoND, ePCRN, ESSE, FirstDIG, GEDDM, GeneGrid, GEODE, GEON, GridMiner, InteliGrid, INWA, ISPIDER, IU-RGRbench, LEAD, MCS, myGrid, N2Grid, OntoGrid, ODD-Genes, OGSA-WebDB, Provenance, SIMDAT, Secure Data Grid, SPIDR, UNIDART and VOTES. This list is clear representative of the importance of OGSA-DAI and the relevance of this particular benchmarking study.

3. Performance Study

In this section we present some performance figures of OGSA-DAI (version WSI 2.2) taken with different configurations and workloads to have a better view of its performance.

3.1 Experiments in Grid5000

In [16], the authors present a benchmarking study of OGSA-DAI. That study has been made with the use of QUAKE [9], a dependability benchmarking tool that was developed to evaluate the performability and dependability figures of Grid and Web-Services. That study was conducted on Grid5000, an experimental platform dedicated to computer science for the study of grid algorithms, and partially founded by the French incentive action "ACI Grid". Grid5000 consists of 14 clusters located in 9 French cities with 40 to 450 processors each, with a total of 1928 processors. Most of the tests were executed on Grid Explorer which is a major component of the Grid5000.

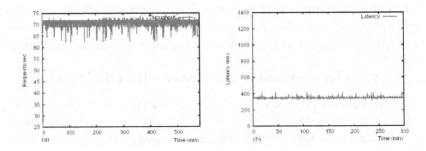

Figure 1.   Results with OGSA-DAI (WSI) application scope

One of the experiments was executed with the default configuration of OGSA-DAI. It was conducted with 25 nodes, each one executing 100,000 requests. All nodes were dual-processors AMD Opterons running at 2.0GHz with 2GB of RAM, and each computer has a 80 GB IDE hard drive and a GigaEthernet network interface card. The server was running with a Debian Linux Operating system, with a kernel 2.6.13-5, including java 1.5.0, Tomcat 5.0.28, Axis 1.2.1 and OGSA-DAI WSI 2.2.

The results are presented in Figure 1. This experiment shows that the default configuration of OGSA-DAI presents a quite stable level of performance. In that configuration the OGSA-DAI Web-services are instantiated with application scope. This means the service is instantiated only once and is shared by every request of every different client. This is not the usual way of deploying Web-Services unless the service is completely stateless or provides global data that should be shared by all the clients. It is more common to instantiate the services as session scope. This way it is possible to avoid sharing between different users and it is possible to correlate different requests from the same user. However, if we configure OGSA-DAI with session scope it is very prone to the occurrence of software aging: not because there is any bug on OGSA-DAI, but because it makes use of Apache/Axis (v1.2) that is known to be an unreliable SOAP router due to the existence of internal memory leaks.

The results with session scope are presented in Figure 2. This result was taken with a burst workload and we can observe a very unstable level of performance leading to frequent suffered hangs up and crashes of the OGSA-DAI server. Right to be truth, this only happens when the web-services are configured with scope session. In application scope the internal leaks of Axis are not triggered and the problem is not spotted in the performance figures of OGSA-DAI.

3.2   Experiments with a Local Cluster

In this sub-section we present some similar results that were collected in a small cluster in the University of Coimbra. In these experiments we used

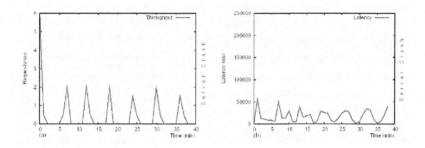

Figure 2.   Results with OGSA-DAI (WSI) session scope

a cluster of 5 machines: 3 running the client benchmark application, one for the Database Server (Tania) and another server for the grid-services front-end (Katrina). All the machines were interconnected with a 100 Mbps Ethernet switch. The detailed description of the machines is presented in Table 1.

In Figure 3 we present the latency of the OGSA-DAI server when applying different constant workloads of 1 request every 10, 20 and 30 seconds every client. In Figure 4 is presented the latency with a burst workload. It can be seen that in both cases the latency is completely unstable. Figure 5 presents the throughput that is measured when applying a burst mode.

	Katrina	Tania	Clients Machines
CPU	Dual AMD64 Opteron (2000MHz)	Dual Core AMD64 Opteron 165 (1800MHz)	Intel Celeron (1000MHz)
Memory	4GB	2GB	512MB
Hard Disk	160GB (SATA2)	160GB (SATA2)	
Swap Space	8GB	4GB	1024MB
Operating System	Linux 2.6.16.21-0.25-smp	Linux 2.6.16.21-0.25-smp	Linux 2.6.15-p3- net-boot
Java JDK	1.5.0_06, 64-bit Server VM	1.5.0_06-b05 Standard Edition	
Tomcat JVM heap size	1024MB		
Other Software	Apache Tomcat 5.0.28, Axis 1.2.1 and OGSA-DAI WSI 2.2	MySQL 5.0.18	

Table 1.   Detailed Machines Description

Figure 6 presents the memory usage of the Tomcat JVM. It can be seen that the server starts to make a fast use of memory that is not made free by the Java garbage collector. When the server starts to run in the memory limits it starts to lose requests, as presented in Figure 7. If we want to use OGSA-DAI in some real applications that would require a configuration of session scope in the web-services front-end then this behavior is totally unacceptable.

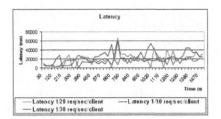

Figure 3. Latency with constant workloads

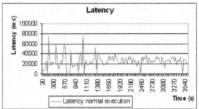
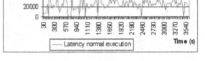

Figure 4. Latency with Burst workload

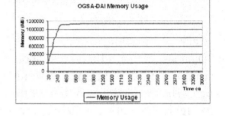

Figure 5. Throughput performance

Figure 6. OGSA-DAI Memory consumption

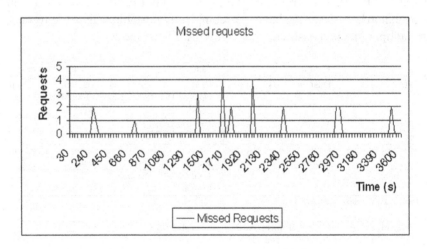

Figure 7. OGSA-DAI Requests missed during 1 hour with burst workload

OGSA-DAI WSI 2.2 is using of an unreliable SOAP router: Axis v1.2. Since this SOAP module suffers from severe memory leaks it can clearly undermine the reliability level of any Grid deployment based on OGSA-DAI.

The best solution is definitely to re-engineer the OGSA-DAI WSI implementation by making a new version or by using Axis v2, a more reliable implementation of SOAP from the Apache group. For the time-being we decided to select the current WSI version of OGSA-DAI as a case-study. We applied our rejuvenation mechanism to this Grid middleware and we observed if it would work effectively without changing any piece of the grid software. Next section we presented a summary description of our mechanism.

4.   A Rejuvenation Scheme by using Virtualized Clustering

Our approach has been designed to use over any server or service. It is just necessary to install a virtualization layer and install some software modules. We have adopted XEN [15] virtualized middleware in our experiments, but we may have used any virtualization middleware. On top of our virtualization layer we create 3 virtual-machines: one VM to run a software load-balancer (VM-LB); one VM to run the main OGSA-DAI server; and a third VM where we create a hot-standby replica of the OGSA-DAI server. The VM-LB also runs some other software modules that will be responsible for the detection of software aging or other potential anomalies. When something anomalous is detected this module will trigger a rejuvenation action. In this action we do not restart the main server right away: we start the standby server, all the new requests and sessions are sent by the LB to this second server. The session-state is migrated from the primary to the secondary server and we wait for all the on-going requests to be finished in the primary server. When we are able to do this we can restart the main server without losing any in-flight request or session state. We call this a "clean" restart. During that restart process no in-flight request is lost, since we have a window of execution where we have both servers running in active mode. When all the requests are finished in the main server, then the server is restarted, as shown in Figure 8.

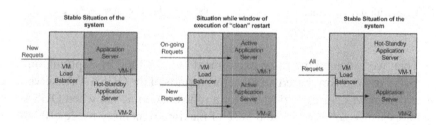

Figure 8.   Virtualized Clustering for Server Rejuvenation process

For lack of space, we refer the interested reader about the details of this rejuvenation mechanism to [17]. The most we can say is that the deployment of this framework is straightforward and does not require any change to the applications or the middleware containers. They are also neutral to the virtualization layer. Our scheme was applied to some other benchmarks in [17] and in the next section we present the results collected with OGSA-DAI.

5. Experimental results

To demonstrate the effectiveness of our rejuvenation mechanism we decided to make a deployment of OGSA-DAI using our virtualized clustering scheme followed by the installation of some software modules that provide the support for anomaly and aging detection and the triggering of rejuvenation actions. Since the problem of OGSA-DAI WSI 2.2 was spotted due to the memory leaks of Axis1.2 we decided to configure our framework to trigger some planned restarts depending on some thresholds of the memory usage. The memory use is collected every 10 seconds and when the available memory falls down that defined threshold our mechanism applies a clean and planned restart that, as a matter of fact, does not produce any downtime to the OGSA-DAI service.

In Figure 9 and Figure 10 we present the latency and throughput figures. First, we executed an experiment for one hour with 3 clients using a burst distribution workload. In this case we used the normal version of OGSA-DAI, with session scope.

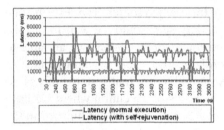

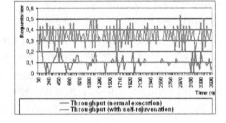

Figure 9. Latency (normal execution) vs Latency (with self-rejuvenation)

Figure 10. Throughput(normal execution) vs Throughput (with self-rejuvenation)

Then we executed the same experiment but this time by applying our self-recovery mechanisms based on proactive restarts of the OGSA-DAI server. Our mechanism was configured to trigger a rejuvenation action when OGSA-DAI memory usage achieved around 50% of maximum memory usage (1024MB).

In Figure 11 we present the graph with the memory usage from one of servers. The graph clearly shows the moments in time when a rejuvenation action is triggered. In Table 2 we present more detailed numbers. We can observe that our approach achieve a very acceptable performance without any disruption of the service. Our approach was able to achieve a better throughput and latency than the default OGSA-DAI without missing any request. This proves the effectiveness of our scheme: we have been able to increase the availability and the performance of a Grid-Service that suffers from internal memory leaks in the SOAP layer. Our scheme brings a contribution for dependability.

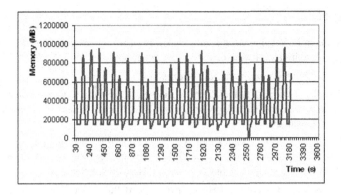

Figure 11. Memory Usage Performance using Self Recovery mechanism

	Avg. Latency	Avg. Throughput	Avg. Memory Usage	Miss Requests
OGSA-DAI (normal version)	29013,2 ms	0,105 req/s	1100784,4 Bytes	25
OGSA-DAI (with self-rejuvenation	9049,5 ms	0,345 req/s	313384,0 Bytes	0

Table 2. Detailed results from 1 hour of execution

6. Conclusions

In this paper, we have presented the application of a self-healing mechanism that was developed by us in a case-study of a Grid-Service: OGSA-DAI. The normal version of this middleware suffers from some aging problems due to the use of Axis v1.2. The resulting performance is really unstable and we have been able to spot some undesired hang-ups when applying a burst distribution. We decided to apply our rejuvenation mechanism based on the thresholds alerts in the memory usage and we have been able to increase the availability and performance of OGSA-DAI without incurring in any additional investment of hardware: it is only necessary to install a virtualization layer and a set of software modules that provide support for self-recovery actions. The results presented in this paper clearly show the potential of our approach to achieve a dependable grid service.

Acknowledgments

This research work is supported by the FP6 Network of Excellence Core-GRID funded by the European Commission (Contract IST-2002-004265) and the Ministry of Science and Technology of Spain and the European Union (FEDER funds) under contract TIN2004-07739-C02-01.

References

[1] A.Avritzer, E.Weyuker. *Monitoring Smoothly Degrading Systems for Increased Dependability*. Empirical Software Eng. Journal, Vol 2, No 1, pp. 59-77, 1997

[2] Apache.[Online] *http://httpd.apache.org/docs/*

[3] V.Castelli, R.Harper, P.Heidelberg, S.Hunter, K.Trivedi, K.Vaidyanathan, W.Zeggert. *Proactive Management of Software Aging*. IBM Journal Research & Development, Vol. 45, No. 2, Mar. 2001

[4] K.Cassidy, K.Gross, A.Malekpour. *Advanced Pattern Recognition for Detection of Complex Software Aging Phenomena in Online Transaction Processing Servers*. Proc. of the 2002 Int. Conf. on Dependable Systems and Networks, DSN-2002

[5] A.Tai, S.Chau, L.Alkalaj, H.Hecht. it On-board Preventive Maintenance: Analysis of Effectiveness an Optimal Duty Period. Proc. 3rd Workshop on Object-Oriented Real-Time Dependable Systems, 1997

[6] Y.Huang, C.Kintala, N.Kolettis, N. Fulton. *Software Rejuvenation: Analysis, Module and Applications*. Proc. of Fault-Tolerant Computing Symposium, FTCS-25, June 1995

[7] K.Vaidyanathan, K.Trivedi. *A Comprehensive Model for Software Rejuvenation*. IEEE Trans. on Dependable and Secure Computing, Vol, 2, No 2,April- 2005

[8] K.Kaidyanathan, K.Gross. *Proactive Detection of Software Anomalies through MSET*. Workshop on Predictive Software Models (PSM 2004), Sept. 2004

[9] L.Silva, H.Madeira and J.G.Silva. *Software Aging and Rejuvenation in a SOAP-based Server*. IEEE-NCA: Network Computing and Applications, Cambridge USA, July 2006

[10] M. Rosenblum and T. Garfinkel. *Virtual Machine Monitors: Current Technology and Future Trends*. IEEE Internet Computing, May 2005, Vol. 38, No. 5.

[11] R. Figueiredo, P. Dinda, J. Fortes. *Resource Virtualization Renaissance*. IEEE Computer, 38(5), pp. 28-69, May 2005

[12] Renato J. Figueiredo , Peter A. Dinda , José A. B. Fortes. *A Case For Grid Computing On Virtual Machines*. Proceedings of the 23rd International Conference on Distributed Computing Systems, p.550, May 19-22, 2003

[13] OGSA-DAI.[Online] *http://www.ogsadai.org.uk/*

[14] Projects that use OGSA-DAI.[Online] *http://www.ogsadai.org.uk/about/projects.php*

[15] XEN Source.[Online] *http://www.xensource.com/*.

[16] W. Hoarau, S. Tixeuil, N. Rodrigues, D. Sousa, and L. Silva. *Benchmarking the OGSA-DAI Middleware* CoreGRID Technical Report Number TR-0060. October 5, 2006.

[17] Luis Silva, Javier Alonso, Paulo Silva, Jordi Torres and Artur Andrzejak. *Using Virtualization to Improve Software Rejuvenation* Proceedings of the 6th IEEE International Symposium on Network Computing and Applications (IEEE NCA07). 12-14 July, 2007. Cambridge, MA USA.

Author Index